9 396556420

D0548032

THE
UNITED TRINITY

THE
UNITED TRINITY
THE REMARKABLE STORY OF BEST, LAW AND CHARLTON

DAVID MEEK

**SIMON &
SCHUSTER**

London · New York · Sydney · Toronto · New Delhi

A CBS COMPANY

First published in Great Britain by Simon & Schuster UK Ltd, 2013
A CBS COMPANY

Copyright © 2013 Manchester United Football Club Ltd

This book is copyright under The Berne Convention.
No reproduction without permission.
All rights reserved.

The right of David Meek to be identified as the author of this work
has been asserted by him in accordance with sections 77 and
78 of the Copyright, Designs and Patents Act, 1988.

1 3 5 7 9 10 8 6 4 2

Simon & Schuster UK Ltd
1st Floor
222 Gray's Inn Road
London WC1X 8HB

www.simonandschuster.co.uk

Simon & Schuster Australia, Sydney
Simon & Schuster India, New Delhi

A CIP catalogue record for this book is
available from the British Library.

ISBN 978-1-47112-955-1

Typeset in UK by M Rules
Printed and bound by CPI Group (UK) Ltd, Croydon, CR0 4YY

Contents

Foreword
by Sir Alex Ferguson

It is 50 years since Sir Bobby Charlton, Denis Law and George Best were giving football a new dimension by playing together in the same team, a trio of dynamic players who took Manchester United to a new level. I am glad their achievements are being extolled in this new book, *The United Trinity*.

The club itself has already paid tribute to this trio of famous players with the bronze statue of them standing on their plinth and gazing towards their mentor Sir Matt Busby and the Old Trafford stadium that became the theatre of dreams for those who like excellence in their football. All three were voted European Footballers of the Year, a unique happening, the like of which I doubt we will see again. They set a benchmark for managers like me to follow, and anything I achieved in my time at the helm at Old Trafford came with the help of the inspiration they provided and the standards they set.

Here we have their daring deeds recalled in print from a man who was there at the time, and in fact has been there for over half a century now, reporting and writing about the achievements of the club I was proud to manage until my retirement at the end of the 2012-13 season. Now I am a director and ambassador for Manchester United, and I have every confidence in David Meek's ability to bring to life the thrilling story of a period in the club's history that was such an important stepping-stone to our more recent successes.

I grew up with Denis Law my special hero. I thought he epitomised what we Scots like to think of as typical of our people: bold, adventurous and, in the case of Denis, a footballer with the heart of a lion, prepared if challenged to fight his own shadow. He was so exciting to watch, electric in his reactions and with that amazing ability to seemingly hang in the air, ready to power in one of his trademark headers.

Although he had a totally different character, I also felt a special affinity for Sir Bobby Charlton. It doesn't need me to spell out his qualities as a player, his long-serving achievements speak for themselves, but my particular admiration is for Bobby as a person. He never wavered in giving me his total support in my time as manager, stretching from my appointment and through all the ups and downs that a manager inevitably encounters with a club like Manchester United, always so much in the public eye. I admire the way he has become one of the statesmen in our game, prepared to put as much into representing what is best for football as he did as a player.

George Best I didn't know as well as Bobby and Denis, but I certainly knew all about his great gifts as a footballer. His career ended sadly, but don't let that obscure his great achievements. George not only had a genius talent, he also had a courage that said: 'Kick me and I'll roast you with my football.' He would simply come back at them with his mercurial ability that wouldn't allow anyone to bully him, and he had a strength that in his peak years rarely saw him miss games through injury. He was brave and sturdy as well as delicate with his work on the ball.

Don't be confused, either, by the talk that he quit the game early. Yes, he was only 27 when he walked out on Manchester United, but by that time he had made close on 500 appearances and scored almost 200 goals, hardly the record of a fly-by-night! He also went on to a substantial career in America and he was able to leave a mark on people's lives, arriving at a liberated time that made him something new in football: a celebrated superstar. I can picture him now, flying down the wing and riding tackles from seriously tough defenders who were around in his era.

George Best, Denis Law and Sir Bobby Charlton added up to a marvellous trinity of great players who did Manchester United proud and deserve all the accolades David Meek has gathered for this book.

1

The United Trinity

The Sixties were a golden era for Manchester United, and indeed for English football generally. In those days we didn't appreciate how fortunate we were to have three European Footballers of the Year playing in the same team, as Sir Bobby Charlton, Denis Law and George Best – the so-called United trinity – came together at Old Trafford.

I almost said holy trinity, and for those fans for whom football is a religion, it's perhaps not too wide of the mark, because this talented trio of footballers were worshipped for their dazzling gifts that graced Manchester United during the Swinging Sixties. Everything was on the move – music, dancing, fashion – and football embraced the new scene because youth was at the forefront of changing attitudes to entertainment and social life. In that era, players like Charlton, Law and Best raised the game to new heights, while even the neighbours at Maine Road could boast their own terrific trinity of Colin Bell, Francis Lee and Mike Summerbee.

But it was United setting the pace back then. Today the gilded trio stand side by side, cast in bronze, on a pedestal outside Old Trafford, gazing at what Charlton once called the theatre of dreams and facing a similarly imposing statue, also sculpted by Philip Jackson, of Sir Matt Busby, the founding father of what is now arguably the most famous football club on the planet. It was of course Sir Matt who brought together the trinity, two of them products of his own scouting and coaching system and one of them secured expensively in the transfer market. Looking up at them now in their metal glory, it is easy to conjure up thoughts of the three musketeers – *all for one and one for all.* Certainly when they were in action together they were team players, and all three were dedicated to the club. Yet they brought contrasting skills to the game, and off the field they were diverse personalities. They certainly weren't pals, though this did not stop them responding to the leadership of Busby.

United have known periods of more sustained success; indeed recent times brought us the peerless management of Sir Alex Ferguson, who, during his 26½ years at the helm before handing over to David Moyes for the start of the 2013-14 season, provided Old Trafford with an unparalleled number of trophies. Having said that, Sir Alex would probably be the first to acknowledge that his work was built on a foundation, history and tradition first established by his fellow Scot, Matt Busby, in the years after the Second World War, with the launch of the Busby Babes. It was Sir Matt who first revitalised the team and introduced his philosophy of recruiting young players to bring them up in the way he wanted with the emphasis on expressing themselves. It's a policy that has stood the passage of time, and was vital to the recovery after the

Munich air crash that wiped out virtually the entire team and coaching staff on their way back home from a European Cup tie against Red Star in Belgrade in February 1958. To survive as a club was a football miracle, but to recover from the tragedy to become the first English team to be crowned champions of Europe, just ten years after the devastation of Munich, was an achievement of heroic proportions.

I was privileged to watch the drama unfold as the reporter assigned to follow Manchester United home and away for my local newspaper, the *Manchester Evening News*. My journalistic place at the heart of the club's media as the main Manchester correspondent for 37 years started at Munich, when I was switched from writing about politics to the sports desk to replace Tom Jackson, one of the eight journalists killed in the crash. That was when I met the first of the trinity, Sir Bobby Charlton, a player who many felt had gone out to Belgrade as a boy only to emerge from hospital and the horror of the crash as a man. As Sir Matt once told me: 'When things looked their blackest after the Munich accident – and there were times when I felt great despair – I was enormously cheered to think that Bobby Charlton was there. His presence was a great source of inspiration to keep working for the restoration of Manchester United.'

Jimmy Murphy, assistant manager and Sir Matt's inspirational lieutenant, had missed the Belgrade trip because he was on international duty as the manager of Wales. While Sir Matt lay in hospital at death's door, it was Murphy who shouldered the monumental task of keeping the club going. Many thought it was the end of United as a football club but Murphy, following Busby's whispered plea from his hospital bed, 'kept the flag flying' until the manager was restored to health.

It was a chaotic period, with youngsters promoted before their time to play alongside Charlton and other survivors like Harry Gregg and Bill Foulkes, but Busby also had to compromise his principle of producing his own players and turn to the transfer market to bolster his depleted resources.

That was how Denis Law arrived at the club, signed for a then record fee of £115,000 from Torino in July 1962 to become the second of the awesome trinity at Old Trafford. It was hardly a straightforward capture. As Sir Matt said at the time: 'Denis Law was the most expensive signing I ever made, but on achievement he turned out to be the cheapest. The Italians dragged me and my chairman all over Europe before we were able to complete the signing, and at one time I was so angry at the way we were being treated that I almost pulled out of the deal.

'I'm extremely glad that I didn't. Once we had got Denis to Old Trafford, I knew that we had the most exciting player in the game. He was the quickest thinking player I ever saw, seconds quicker than anyone else. He had the most tremendous acceleration, and could leap to enormous heights to head the ball with almost unbelievable accuracy, and often with the power of a shot.

'He had the courage to take on the biggest and most ferocious opponents, and his passing was impeccable. He was one of the most unselfish players I have ever seen. If he was not in the best position to score, he would give the ball to someone who was.

'When a chance was on for him, even only a half-chance, or in some cases no chance at all for anyone but him, whether he had his back to goal, was sideways on, or the ball was on the deck or up at shoulder height, he would have it in the net with such power and acrobatic ability that colleagues and opponents alike could only stand and gasp. No other player scored as many "miracle" goals as Denis Law.'

Along with other shrewd signings, United were now good enough to beat Leicester City at Wembley to win the FA Cup in 1963, just five years after the Munich tragedy and an important stepping stone on the way to the ultimate glory of beating Benfica in the final of the European Cup on a sunny May day in 1968.

By that time the third part of the trinity had forced his way into the team, with George Best shooting through the junior and reserve teams to make his league debut, aged 17 years and four months, against West Bromwich Albion on 14 September 1963.

It was the start of something really big, with the trinity soon adding lustre to what was already a good side. At home, we knew their worth, and our excitement was confirmed when the wider football world recognised the special ones with three European Footballer of the Year awards* arriving at Old Trafford in the space of four seasons. First up was Denis Law, the Lawman, whose global fame had been boosted by his time playing in Italy and for Scotland, and he was voted European Footballer of the Year in 1964. Two years later, Charlton's dazzling displays for England at the 1966 World Cup clinched the award for him. In fact, Charlton was very much in the frame every season around that time, finishing runner-up for the next two years. Then George Best floated on to the honours board on the back of his magic and achievements in Europe in 1968.

* The European Footballer of the Year award had been the brainchild of Gabriel Hanot, chief writer of *France Football* magazine, who in 1956 asked his colleagues to vote for the best player in Europe. Stanley Matthews was the inaugural winner, followed the next year by Billy Wright. English footballers figured prominently in the early years, players like Johnny Haynes and Jimmy Greaves finishing in third place, but no club swept the board so emphatically as the United trinity and still hasn't.

From reaching the quarter-finals of the European Cup in 1966 – where a virtuoso performance by Best against Benfica saw the young Irishman come home from Portugal tagged as 'El Beatle', football's answer to the music revolution – to winning the trophy two years later at Wembley, many considered it United's destiny to be European club champions. Not least Sir Bobby Charlton, who had travelled the entire journey.

2

Through the Mist

Bobby Charlton was the first of the trinity to arrive at Old Trafford after chief scout Joe Armstrong had been sent to check out reports of a promising 15-year-old in the north-east. Armstrong went to watch East Northumberland Boys at Jarrow and came dashing back to say: 'I had to peer through a mist, but what I saw was enough. This boy is going to be a world beater.' It might have been a foggy day but Joe was clear about the boy's potential.

When Bobby began to score goals for the England Schoolboys team, scouts from all over the country came with offers to sign him, such was his youthful prowess. At one stage, there were said to be as many as 18 clubs interested and dropping in at his home, but he remembered an early first promise to Joe Armstrong, a charming old fashioned kind of guy who always came across as your favourite uncle. Bobby instinctively felt he could trust him, as did his parents, and despite more attractive offers from elsewhere, he joined Manchester United in 1953 at the age of 15.

It was always on the cards that Bobby would become a soccer player, given that his mother, Cissie, came from the famous Milburn soccer family in the north-east of England. Three of her brothers, Jack, Jim and George, played for Leeds United, while a fourth brother, Stan, played for Leicester City. Cissie's cousin was the legendary Newcastle United centre-forward, 'Wor' Jackie Milburn, while grandfather 'Tanner' Milburn kept goal for his local team.

So it was hardly surprising that first Bobby's brother, Jack, grew up to play for Leeds United and England, then Bobby himself soon attracted attention as a schoolboy and went on to enjoy an even more famous career. Born in Northumberland on 11 October 1937, the son of a miner in the coal pit village of Ashington, Bobby went to the local junior school. He first caught the eye of United fans playing in three successive FA Youth Cup winning teams. A regular reserve team player who scored freely, Bobby was in fact doing so well that he couldn't understand why he wasn't getting a chance in the first team. Eventually the call came, and he made his league debut against Charlton Athletic at Old Trafford on 6 October 1956. First, though, he had to gamble, as he explains: 'Mr Busby asked me if I was OK. Actually, I had a sprained ankle but I wasn't going to admit to it, so I crossed my fingers and said yes.' His gamble paid off and he scored twice in a 4-2 win, though that wasn't enough to see him stay in the team. He was dropped for the following match at Sunderland one week later to make way for the return of the injured Tommy Taylor. Competition was severe, and it was tough to break into a team christened the Busby Babes, the gifted group of young men who took English football and Europe by storm.

I hadn't been in Manchester very long, after spending a year in Australia on a British Memorial Fund scholarship in journalism, when Bobby Charlton made his bow, but I had already realised something special was stirring around Old Trafford. I was leader writer for the *Manchester Evening News*, busy studying politics and covering by-elections such as Ludovic Kennedy's bid to become MP for Rochdale. Meetings in dusty school rooms couldn't compare with duties at Old Trafford and Maine Road, but at least Ludovic was invariably accompanied by his film star wife, Moira Shearer, who in my eyes at least did for politics what George Best would later do for football!

My soccer reporting experience had been limited to the modest endeavours of York City for the *Yorkshire Post*, but friends persuaded me to go with them to watch Manchester United, and that was when I realised that Matt Busby had launched a visionary concept on an unsuspecting football world. Back from the war in 1945, he had this idea of recruiting boys straight from school and teaching them while they were still of an impressionable age to learn to play the game the way he wanted, with the emphasis on artistry, creative attack and freedom of expression. Busby saw football as something that should be exciting, and while he accepted that the foundation of the team must be a solid defence, he certainly didn't limit his players to rigid tactics or defensive plans.

United had always believed in encouraging youngsters and under Walter Crickmer, their long-serving secretary, who had also acted as manager during the war, they had set up the MUJAC, the Manchester United Junior Athletic Club, and had also used the local works team at Goslings as a nursery for bringing on promising boys. Louis Rocca, MUJAC chief scout and a key backroom Mr Fixit for United for many years, knew his way round the scouting system and in those important post-war years United made some canny appointments, with Bob Bishop and Bob Harper in Belfast and Billy Behan in Dublin.

Back home, United had lured Joe Armstrong from Manchester City and his job with Post Office telephones to become club chief scout. When it came to persuading anxious parents to let their footballing sons come to Old Trafford, especially when it involved crossing the Irish Sea from good Roman Catholic families, Armstrong was the proverbial charmer. Like both Busby and Murphy, he was a Catholic but sincere and principled with it. Busby had good men right through his coaching staff: people like Bert Whalley, gifted and high-minded, Tom Curry the kindly trainer, the dependable assistant trainer Bill Inglis, and good-living part-timers like Jack Pauline who ran the junior teams.

The FA Youth Cup was launched in 1952 and straightaway appealed to United's accent on developing their own youngsters. (Ironically, it was the year United won the league championship, and it signalled the beginning of the end of the old guard.) Not only did United win the inaugural youth competition, they won it for five successive seasons. Jimmy Murphy used to say that big oak trees all start as little acorns and that's how he regarded their young footballers. Only Wolves at that time had really cottoned on to the importance of a club developing their own players. It's commonplace now, but Busby, along with Major Frank Buckley and Stan Cullis at Molineux, were the first managers to plan so far ahead with real conviction.

United's youth team ran up some cricket scores against lesser teams in those early days, and they enjoyed an emphatic win in their first final when they beat Wolves 7-1 in the home first leg before playing safe and drawing 2-2 at Molineux. The following year, somewhat inevitably, they met their big rivals in the final again, emerging with a 4-4 draw at Old Trafford before a 1-0 win in the second leg. With the finals drawing crowds of over 20,000, the discerning fans knew that they were watching the stars of tomorrow, and that is exactly how it worked out when Matt Busby realised that his team of one-time soldiers, featuring some great players like Charlie Mitten, Jack Rowley, Stan Pearson, John Aston and Allenby Chilton, were getting a bit long in the tooth.

Nevertheless, the football world still gasped when the manager, eager perhaps to blood the youngsters he had groomed, began to break up the old sweats. It must have been difficult for the medal-winning and much admired players who had given Busby his first trophies to accept their fate. Indeed, it *was* tough, as John Aston Snr admitted when he told me: 'It was very disappointing for the players who had brought the championship to Old Trafford for the first time in over forty years, to have to give way to new men. But at the same time, we were not blind to the fact that the boss had also been busy creating a tremendously successful youth team that had won the FA Youth Cup five times off the reel.

'Matt Busby had also been at the club long enough to have established himself as a very far-seeing and shrewd manager. He had won the respect of all of us, which meant that it was easier for him to put over these new ideas. We just accepted the changes because when he said it was for the good of the club, we knew it was.'

The 1952 championship cheers had hardly died down before Busby started to introduce what would become his Busby Babes. One of the first youngsters to break in was wing-half Jeff Whitefoot, the youngest ever to play in the league team – younger even than Duncan Edwards – at 16 years and 105 days. So, too, did the young office boy, Les Olive, a goalkeeper but later destined to play a much more important role in the club's affairs as secretary. It was a period that was also notable for a relatively rare but nonetheless vital splash in the transfer market, with Busby paying the unusual fee of £29,999 to Barnsley for the dashing Tommy Taylor, with a view to continuing the high scoring rate of his original side.

It was a time of change and experiment that was reflected in the club's First Division finishing position of eighth, with Arsenal the champions, but Busby knew what he was doing and the following season, 1953-54, saw players like Edwards, Taylor and Whitefoot, along with Dennis Viollet, Jackie Blanchflower and Bill Foulkes, become regulars and the team did better, finishing fourth behind champions Wolves. The pivotal moment had come in late October after United had taken a team of youngsters to Kilmarnock for a friendly. As Busby explained: 'I walked the golf course thinking that this was the time to go the whole way. From the very start, I had envisaged making my own players, having a kind of nursery so that they could be trained in the kind of pattern I was trying to create for Manchester United.'

His new team was still in a transitional stage, but young players were coming through all the time to provide even fiercer competition for places. Billy Whelan, the talented inside-forward from the Republic of Ireland, was another youngster beginning to make a mark in the first team, while new boy David Pegg found that he was in competition for the left-wing spot with Albert Scanlon, another speedster. Mark Jones was also in contention with Blanchflower for the centre-half position.

Season 1954-55 saw them finish fifth, though only five points behind Chelsea, the new champions. It was tight at the top. United were performing well but they still had to make the final leap, and it came the following year with yet another talented kid in their ranks, the Salford wing-half Eddie Colman, as they roared their way to the 1956 league championship.

Only Roger Byrne and Johnny Berry remained from the team that had taken the title four years before. They made a slow start to the season. In fact they won only three of their opening eight matches, but they went up a gear in the New Year and lost only once between the start of January and the end of the season to take the title. The significance was that they were champions with an average age of only 22, and they won it by a mile with 60 points, 11 points ahead of runners-up Blackpool. Matt Busby said: 'I never doubted their spirit or ability to pull through. I have never known a spell so tense and hard, but this young team has done me proud. I am proud indeed of all my young players, right down from the First Division side to the colts.

'Two or three years ago, at the annual meeting of the club's shareholders, I said that United had youthful potential worth tens of thousands of pounds. I'm proud the boys have proved me right.'

So Busby had put his masterplan into action. He had swept away the old boys, most of whom had seen service like him during the war and who had won him the FA Cup in 1948 and the league in 1952; stalwarts like Jack Rowley, Charlie Mitten, Johnny Carey, Jack Crompton and Stan Pearson. They had to go though, so that he could set the Busby Babes free to fly at the top level, with players coming through like Duncan Edwards, Eddie Colman, Wilf McGuinness, David Pegg and Albert Scanlon. In the wings, of course, was the original member of the trinity, the teenage Bobby Charlton, who hadn't even made his first-team debut at this stage.

Not only had United run away with the league in 1956 but that year marked the club's first experience of European competition, and it was in Europe that the Busby Babes caught the imagination. The fact that they were competing in Europe at all was ground-breaking stuff. The previous year Chelsea had turned down an invitation from UEFA to enter the championship of champions as English title winners under pressure from the insular Football League, who didn't like this challenge to their own domestic competition.

It took a man of vision like Matt Busby to grasp the enormous potential of Europe, both financially and in terms of quality, and he persuaded United chairman Harold Hardman that it was something they should do. Busby took the view that he had pitted his club against the best England could produce and come out on top; now he wanted this chance to go up a notch and discover how his boys could measure up against the best of Europe. It was an enticing prospect, and, in my opinion, this step into the unknown was hugely important in propelling Manchester United to a level that these days sees them a global force.

The Red support certainly took to it, especially when their team started winning. In their very first home tie in the European Cup in September 1956, played at Manchester City's Maine Road ground because Old Trafford didn't have floodlights, United delivered a sensational 10-0 victory against Anderlecht. It was the first game I had been to in Manchester and my enthusiasm was fired. I was not on my own. The 43,635 attendance zoomed to 75,598 for the next round, and then, after knocking out Borussia Dortmund, came an epic United performance following a first leg 5-3 defeat against Athletic Bilbao in Spain.

The Bilbao manager said no team had ever scored three goals against them but United did exactly that at Old Trafford to reach the semi-finals, where Real Madrid proved too experienced and strong for them. United, though, had lit a flame for English football. Internationally, England had been at a low ebb. The Hungarians had beaten us 6-3 at Wembley and repeated the humiliation with a 7-1 win in Budapest six months later. These defeats followed the embarrassment of the 1950 World Cup when we had failed to get beyond the opening group after losing to the United States. Now suddenly, the nation had a club side that looked capable of not only challenging the best in Europe but also supplying enough players to restore the England team to its former glory.

For a start, there was Duncan Edwards. After captaining the England Schoolboys team and the Under-23 side, he was regarded as the natural successor to Billy Wright at senior level. He had become the youngest post-war England international when he was given his first cap in April 1955, at the age of 18 years and six months, a debut marked by England beating Scotland 7-2 at Wembley.

Walter Winterbottom, the England manager, had no doubts about the player's international worth: 'Duncan was a great footballer and he had the promise of being the greatest of his day. He played with tremendous joy and his spirit stimulated the whole England team. It was in the character and spirit of Duncan Edwards that I saw a true revival of British football.'

The former Blackpool and England captain Jimmy Armfield, now a brilliant and highly respected radio pundit, played with Edwards for England, as well as for national service teams in the army. He told me: 'With Duncan Edwards, Roger Byrne and Tommy Taylor in the team, I believe England would have reached the final of the 1958 World Cup, and probably won it. Playing in the same team [as Duncan], I can still see this powerful figure stalking the dressing room, and at the time I would think: "I'm glad he's playing for us."'

The shooting of Edwards was eye-catching. The Germans were so impressed when he played in England's 3-1 win over them at Wembley in December 1954 that when United landed in West Berlin a few months later for the start of a pre-season tour, German fans were calling for 'Boom Boom'.

When Edwards played for England, it posed a problem for

United coach Jimmy Murphy when he wore his Welsh manager's hat. Before one particular England–Wales match, Murphy was running through the opposition detailing their strengths and weaknesses. He referred to every England player bar Edwards, which left Reg Davies, the Welsh and Newcastle inside-forward, feeling a little neglected because he was in direct opposition to the United and England wing-half.

'What about Edwards?' queried Davies.

Murphy replied: 'There's nothing I could say which would help us. Just keep out of his way, son!'

As Murphy poignantly recalled in his book *United, Matt and Me*: 'If I shut my eyes, I can see him now. Those pants hitched up, the wild leaps of boyish enthusiasm as he came running out of the tunnel, the tremendous power of his tackle – always fair but fearsome – and the immense power on the ball.' Jimmy also used to tell me that when he heard Muhammad Ali proclaim in the papers and on television and radio that he was the greatest, he had to smile because the greatest of them all, in his view, was an English footballer named Duncan Edwards.

He said: 'From the first time I saw him as a boy of fourteen, he looked like and played with the assurance of a man, with legs like tree trunks, a deep and powerful chest and an unforgettable zest for the game. He played wing-half, centre-half, centre-forward and inside-forward with the consummate ease of a great player. He was never bothered where he played. He was quite simply a soccer colossus.'

Bobby Charlton told me once that on one of his early trips to Manchester, he was met at the railway station by Murphy who spoke non-stop about Duncan's merits all the way to Old Trafford, so much so that Bobby was thinking: 'Why do they want me when they already have such a world-beater!?'

Colossus though Edwards undoubtedly was, United were certainly not a one-man team under Matt Busby. They had a blend and balance that was quite bewitching, with a fierce competition for places. Busby had an attack oozing goals, led by the powerful centre-forward Tommy Taylor. At inside-forward, he had the likes of Billy Whelan, Dennis Viollet and John Doherty. He had a dazzling array of wingers in David Pegg, Albert Scanlon, Johnny Berry and Kenny Morgans. He had the beguiling Eddie 'Snakehips' Colman to balance the power of Edwards in the half-back line. While at the back, he could choose between the finesse of Jackie Blanchflower or the rugged Mark Jones for centre-half. Busby had what Sir Alex Ferguson these days would describe as great options.

So this was the daunting situation that faced Bobby Charlton as he readied himself for the tough challenge of trying to break into a new Manchester United team. He was scoring important goals quite freely in the youth teams, but it was the manner of them that was catching the imagination of the fans and mesmerising me, for one. It was not something he acquired as he grew more confident – his rocket shooting was there right from the start. He clearly had a natural aptitude for hitting the ball hard, even as a schoolboy, but I believe it was his mentor, coach Jimmy Murphy, who was key to him scoring his blockbusters so readily.

Murphy kept hammering into Charlton the value of him utilising his most natural asset. He taught him to hit through the top of the ball, to keep it low and always be aware of where the goal is. He used to tell him that the fans would forgive him if he shot and missed, but that they wouldn't if he had a chance to shoot and didn't. He said not to worry if he didn't really know where the ball was going when he shot, because the goalkeeper wouldn't know either, so you were in with a good chance of beating him. It was a philosophy that served Charlton well throughout his career for both club and country and was in evidence right from the start. He blasted his way through games for the youth teams, but unlike many players who move up a level, he didn't try to feel his way by playing cautiously. He would go for it, just as he did when he finally got into the league team to join the Busby Babes and make his senior debut at Charlton Athletic on 6 October 1956, aged 18.

Johnny Berry equalised an early goal by the Addicks and then Charlton scored twice in five minutes. His first came when he got the ball on his right foot, turned inside and simply battered it in the general direction of goal. Following Murphy's law, the ball flew into the back of the net for what the player describes as the sweetest of moments. He says the second goal came when the ball cried out to be volleyed, which of course he duly did, to make an impressive bow in senior football with the kind of express shooting that would be repeated many times over throughout his playing career.

At first, he played only when there was an injury to Taylor, Viollet or Whelan in the forward line. Gradually, though, his appearances became more regular, and towards the end of the 1956-57 championship season he had settled into the side on a fairly regular basis to make a total of 14 appearances. His eye for goal was remarkable, and though surrounded by more experienced players, he made his presence felt to score 10 goals as the Busby Babes won their second successive championship, finishing eight points in front of Spurs.

Charlton also won a place in the FA Cup team for the later stages of the 1956-57 season, scoring in the semi-final win against Birmingham City and then playing in the final against Aston Villa, when they seemed set to achieve a league and cup double until goalkeeper Ray Wood had his cheekbone smashed by Villa forward Peter McParland, and ten-man United lost 2-1.

Still only 18, Charlton also made his debut in the European Cup that season with a prominent display for such a young player in the 2-2 semi-final second leg against Real Madrid. It was a vintage era and it needed a special talent to break into a side which seemed to score goals for fun, and indeed had rattled in 103 on their way to winning the league. It meant Charlton still had to fight for a permanent place and it didn't really come until midway through the following season of 1957-58. When he got in, though, he really made his mark, such as a hat-trick in a 7-2 home win over Bolton on 18 January, and scoring both goals in an FA Cup fourth round tie, won 2-0 at Old Trafford against Ipswich the following week.

He also took Europe in an effortless stride that season when, in the first leg of the quarter-final against Red Star Belgrade at Old Trafford, he scored in a 2-1 win to book a trip for the second leg in Belgrade. He scored twice in the 3-3 draw that secured United a place in the semi-finals.

Charlton grew up surrounded by the precocious Busby Babes and this elite university of football shaped his future. Like the rest of the young men flying home from Belgrade for the Saturday match against Wolves, the football world lay at his feet.

3

Dark Days

Bobby Charlton was about to suffer a tragedy that took the lives of so many and wrecked the careers of others at Manchester United Football Club. He was, in fact, one of the lucky ones, physically, but emotionally he had to dig very deep to come through and play his full part in the United trinity.

Charlton was only 20 at the time and the newest of the new boys who had just come into the United team that flew to Yugoslavia for the second leg of their European Cup quarter-final against Red Star Belgrade in February 1958. It was Charlton, among the host of young stars jockeying for first-team places, who caught the eye of Jackie Blanchflower, on his last trip as a player.

Blanchflower didn't even play in Belgrade because he had lost his place after going off to play for Northern Ireland in a World Cup qualifying game against Scotland. He once set the scene for me in an interview about Charlton a few years before he died, when he told me: 'The quarter-final against Red Star illustrated the power of a club just getting into its European stride. It was such a young team, but learning ever so fast.

'We had won the first leg in Manchester two-one. One goal was not a big advantage to take away, but the mood of the players was one of confidence. The boys had just beaten Arsenal five-four in the league at Highbury and we always felt we could go up a gear if necessary.

'I remember it was a pea-souper on the day we were flying [to Belgrade] and I thought we would never get off, but the fog cleared. Because it was Bobby's first European trip he had been kidded about the shortage of food in Eastern Europe. He packed his suitcase with biscuits and sweets. He might have been just a kid, but there was nothing of the novice once the game had begun on a freezing cold day.

'We made a great start, with Tommy Taylor forcing an early error for Dennis Viollet to score after only a couple of minutes. I recall [their midfielder] Sekularac as a danger, a busy little man who also chopped people. He got Kenny Morgans on the thigh, but Bobby was the star of the show. He scored with the kind of rocket which was to become his speciality and he also nicked in another to give us a three-goal lead and a five-one advantage on aggregate.

'It looked as good as over, except of course Red Star were a great team as well and they got back into it with a goal from Kostic, a penalty and a free-kick from just outside the box. The match ended three-all but we were through five-four on aggregate and celebrating a semi-final appearance for the second year running. It was the last match for so many ...'

The football world lay at the feet of Busby's bravehearts as they readied themselves for the journey home from Belgrade. They had resisted a terrific onslaught from Red Star to come out with their aggregate win and they also had high hopes of retaining their championship. No sooner had they quietly celebrated their progress in Europe with a few drinks after the match, than thoughts were turning to their challenge in the league and that Saturday's match against title rivals Wolves.

They had everything to play for, everything to live for, as their Elizabethan charter aircraft headed for home on 6 February via a refuelling stop at Munich. The plane landed at Munich airport in a snowstorm and the players hurried quickly into the terminal building for tea and coffee. The refuelling did not take long though, and they were soon back on board ready for take-off and the flight home. The airfield was covered in snow. At 14.19 hours, Captain Ken Rayment, the co-pilot, with Captain James Thain, the pilot, sitting alongside him, requested permission to taxi out for take-off. At 14.30 hours, radio officer Bill Rodgers told the control tower that 609 Zulu Uniform was rolling and a dramatic sequence of events had begun.

Some 40 seconds later the plane pulled up. The pilots had noticed that the engines were giving out an uneven note. Power surging was not uncommon with Elizabethans and apparently the pilots were not unduly worried. They requested permission for a second attempt. Another charge down the runway began but again Captain Thain abandoned the take-off after thundering half its length. This time, he was not satisfied with the pressure reading from the port engine.

The aircraft returned to the terminal building and the passengers disembarked to the lounge while the pilots conferred with the station engineer, William Black. The question of an overnight stop cropped up, but no one really wanted that kind of inconvenience and everyone trooped out for a third attempt. Alf Clarke, the

Manchester Evening Chronicle reporter, was nearly left behind because he had been on the phone to his office with the story of the delay. He dashed out just in time and at 14.56 hours the plane taxied out to the runway. At 15.03 hours, 609 Zulu Uniform started a third attempt to take-off.

This time, there was no pulling up.

The plane left the runway, crashed through a fence and hit an isolated house, setting it on fire, but the inhabitants, Anna Winkler and her children, miraculously escaped unhurt. Then came an impact with a hut and a truck carrying fuel that exploded as the rear section of the fuselage was torn off and was caught up in the fire.

Journalists travelling with football teams invariably sit at the back of the plane to leave the main section free for the players. Those at the back on this occasion had little chance. Frank Taylor, of the *News Chronicle,* was the one sportswriter who was sitting further to the front, and though he was seriously injured, his freak decision undoubtedly saved his life. Fate worked the other way for David Pegg, who had been sitting towards the front in a card school, until suddenly announcing before the third attempt to take-off that he was going to the rear end because he felt it was safer there. David died but the card school he left – Bill Foulkes, Kenny Morgans and Albert Scanlon – all survived.

Meanwhile the plane careered on, spinning wildly and throwing out several of the passengers through the gaping hole where it had been ripped in two. Others were trapped inside. Matt Busby was one of those flung out on to the snow.

Goalkeeper Harry Gregg was one of the first to stumble from the wreckage, and then, as he stood bewildered, he was ordered to run clear by Captain Thain who feared an explosion. But the United goalkeeper had heard the cry of a baby and plunged straight back in to bring out 22-month-old Vesna Lukic, daughter of the Yugoslavian air attaché in London, who had been travelling with her mother courtesy of a lift on United's charter plane. The people involved all talk about Captain Thain going back to the flight deck for the portable fire extinguisher to put out a blaze in one of the engines, promising to return for his friend and co-pilot, Ken Rayment, whose feet were trapped and who had received what proved to be a fatal blow on the head from a tree that had smashed through the cockpit. Peter Howard and Ted Ellyard, two photographers on board the flight, were also heroes who risked the plane going up in flames to free Ray Wood and Albert Scanlon who had been trapped in the tangled mess inside. Then they pulled Frank Taylor clear.

With great presence of mind, Gregg used his tie as a tourniquet to put round Jackie Blanchflower's badly bleeding arm. Kenny Morgans, trapped under a wheel, was freed by Howard and radio officer Bill Rodgers, who, along with Gregg, Ellyard and the stewardesses, Margaret Bellis and Rosemary Cheverton, ignored the dangers to help their fellow passengers.

The survivors were rushed to the Rechts der Isar Hospital in Munich and into the care of a highly organised and expert medical team headed by Professor Georg Maurer, the chief surgeon, who had planned for just such an emergency. The professor knew all about major disasters from his previous life as a doctor under fire in the war and had been awarded the Iron Cross for his work on the beaches of Dunkirk. Critically injured survivors like Matt Busby and Frank Taylor subsequently paid tribute to the skill and care of the doctors and nurses. As Taylor put it: 'Professor Maurer and his angels of mercy set to work.'

Frank Swift, former Manchester City goalkeeper turned media man, died almost as soon as they got him to hospital. Captain

Rayment was in a coma from his fearful head injury and never came out of it before he died. The football world held its breath while Duncan Edwards fought bravely, kept alive on a kidney machine flown specially to Munich.

Matt Busby lay terribly ill in hospital. He had been flung out of the plane and Bill Foulkes recalls seeing him sitting up. 'I remember kneeling down by the boss, and he kept saying: "It's my side, it's my side." I wrapped him in my jacket and sat holding his hand. Then suddenly Bobby Charlton woke up, as if he had just been enjoying a nap, and without a word walked over to us, took off his jacket, and put it underneath the boss, who was lying in the slush.'

Supporters gathered outside Old Trafford, waiting for news or perhaps simply hoping for some miracle. Walter Crickmer, who had been with the club from 1919 and secretary from 1926, died in the crash and the next in line was a young man, Les Olive, who had joined as office boy and a player for the colts team. Immediately he had to take on the role of secretary, which he later became officially until his retirement in 1988 and subsequent election to the board of directors. Tremendous responsibility was thrust on to young shoulders but he rose to the occasion to help steer the club through the most exacting period of its history.

Assistant manager Jimmy Murphy turned for help to Jack Crompton, United's goalkeeper in the 1948 FA Cup final who had joined Luton as trainer in 1956, and they invited him to return to help in the emergency, an invitation he readily accepted to become a key figure at Old Trafford again for many years.

In the background was also a chairman, Harold Hardman, of immense quality who had quickly grasped the perspective of the tragedy to make clear that Manchester United had no intention of surrendering to the calamity that had overtaken them. The Saturday match against Wolves was called off, but they were back in business to play their postponed FA Cup fifth round tie against Sheffield Wednesday on 19 February which they won 3-0, and three days later on the Saturday they faced Nottingham Forest at Old Trafford. It was a match they drew 1-1, but the real significance was the message from the chairman printed on the front page of the *United Review* programme. Under a headline 'UNITED WILL GO ON', Harold Hardman wrote: 'On 6 February 1958 an aircraft returning from Belgrade crashed at Munich Airport. Of the twenty-one passengers who died, twelve were players and officials of the Manchester United Football Club. Many others still lie injured.

'It is the sad duty of we who serve United to offer the bereaved our heartfelt sympathy and condolences. Here is a tragedy which will sadden us for years to come, but in this we are not alone. An unprecedented blow to British football has touched the hearts of millions and we express our deep gratitude to the many who have sent messages of sympathy and floral tributes. Wherever football is played United is mourned, but we rejoice that many of our party have been spared and wish them a speedy and complete recovery.

'Words are inadequate to describe our thanks and appreciation of the truly magnificent work of the surgeons and nurses of the Rechts der Isar Hospital at Munich. But for their superb skill and deep compassion our casualties must have been greater. To Professor Georg Maurer, chief surgeon, we offer our eternal gratitude.

'Although we mourn our dead and grieve for our wounded, we believe that great days are not done for us. The sympathy and encouragement of the football world and particularly of our supporters will fortify and inspire us. The road back may be long and hard, but with the memory of those who died at Munich, of their stirring achievements and wonderful sportsmanship ever with us, Manchester United will rise again.'

United had paid a heavy price in pursuit of their European

dream, but from the heart-searching and the agonising sprang a commitment and determination to ensure that, like the phoenix they wore as a badge on their Cup final shirts three months after the tragedy, they would recover to play football once more.

Their resilience and courage was well reflected in the immediate reaction of their goalkeeper who had bravely gone back into the wreckage of the crash to help trapped team-mates and other passengers. Harry Gregg had been the final piece in Matt Busby's jigsaw, his last signing before Munich to complement his 'Babes'. He represented Northern Ireland at school and youth levels, and played for Linfield and Coleraine before joining Doncaster Rovers where he spent five years until recruited by United in December, 1957, for £23,500, to take over from Ray Wood. In all, he played for United for 10 years and won 24 caps for Ireland, excelling in the 1958 World Cup in Sweden. Stoke City launched him into management and later he returned to Old Trafford as Dave Sexton's goalkeeping coach before going back to Ireland to live on the coast in County Londonderry.

Harry Gregg marked the 40th anniversary of the Munich air crash by casting his mind back to put into words for the first time and explain to me the anguish that is still very much part of his life: 'We landed at Munich for a refuelling stop. It was snowing slightly and there were footprints in the snow as we made our way into the terminal. We got back on and there was nothing untoward as we set off down the runway.

'I watched the telescopic leg of the wheel on my side extend as we went towards lift-off. I watched the wheel lock and unlock with the plane swerving about a little bit. Then the aircraft stopped and someone came on to say we would be going back to make another attempt. I just supposed it was a technical hitch.

'We set off again, going a little bit further this time. It was like a speedboat at sea with a bow wave as the snow got deeper. We pulled up again and it was quite unnerving. This time they said we would be going back into the terminal and the party would disembark.

'In less than five minutes we were called back on and we boarded again. I watched the steward belting himself in and I thought it was perhaps more serious than I had realised. So I made a point of getting well down in my seat, undid my collar and tie, and put my feet on the chair in front.

'We started to roll until someone said we were one short. It was Alf Clarke from the *Evening Chronicle* who had stayed behind to phone a story about the delay. He came on board and we set off once again. I was reading a book that wasn't too kind to the way I had been brought up, so I put it down. I thought if I get killed reading a book like that, I'd go to hell, which was the way of life in those days.

'I kept watching the wheels and I thought we were away this time, because we were going past places I had not seen before. I couldn't see the fence because you can't see ahead from inside a plane. I thought we had lifted until all of a sudden there was this horrendous noise. It felt as if everything was upside down, one minute daylight the next darkness, with the awful sound of tearing, ripping, smoke and flames.

'The first thump I got was on the back of the head, then on the front of my head. I felt something going up my nose and I just didn't know what was going on. I had not long joined Manchester United, I was married and had one child, and in my simple mind I thought I had done well for the first time in my life and that I wouldn't see my wife, little girl and parents again. I also worried that I couldn't speak German; why I thought that I have no idea. Everything seemed to be in slow motion.

'All of a sudden it stopped. There was nothing but darkness and I thought it must be hell because of the blackness. I just lay there for a while and felt the blood running down my face. I was afraid to reach up for fear of what I would find.

'Then I realised I couldn't be dead. There was some burning and sparks from wires. Above me to the right was a hole and daylight. I started to crawl towards it, and in the darkness went over one or two people. I looked out of the hole and directly below me was lying Bert Whalley, the team coach, wearing an air force blue suit. His eyes were wide open and he hadn't a mark on him.

'I made the hole bigger and dropped down beside Bert. In the distance, I could see five people running through the snow and shouting, "Run, run, it's going to explode!" I just stood there. I think the fear factor had gone, I really don't know, but from around what was left of the cockpit came the pilot, Captain Thain, and he also shouted, "Run, you stupid bastard, it's going to explode!", and ran back the way he had come.

'Just then, I heard a child crying and I shouted there are people still alive in here. I crawled back in terrified of what I was going to find. I found the child under a pile of rubbish and crawled out. The radio operator came back and I gave him the child. I went back in and found the mother. She was in a shocking state and I had to literally kick her through the hole to send her on her way.

'I found Ray Wood and was sure he was dead. I couldn't get him out. I saw Albert Scanlon and he looked even worse. I tried to drag him out but he was trapped by the feet and I had to put him down.

'I got out and went round the back of the aircraft where I found Bobby Charlton and Dennis Viollet hanging half in and half out of the stump of the plane. I dragged them clear by the waistbands of their trousers and left them about fifteen yards away.

'I got round the other side and at that point realised how bad it was, with the rest of the plane sticking out of what I later learned was a fuel store and it was on fire. Between that, and the part of the plane I had come out of, was the boss. He was sitting up on his elbows with his hands across his chest and moaning a terrible "aargh".

'He had a bad cut behind his ear and one of his feet was bent back the wrong way, but he didn't look too bad compared with what I had seen. I thought I could leave him. I put something behind him to support his back and said, "You're OK, boss."

'I went another twenty yards and found Jackie Blanchflower. The snow was melting around him because of the heat and the burning part of the aircraft. He was crying out that he had broken his back and was paralysed. I looked and saw Roger Byrne lying across him and I don't think Jackie had realised that it was Roger's body that was holding him down.

'Roger didn't have a mark on him. He was a handsome fellow, handsome in life and handsome in death. I kept talking to "Blanchy". His right arm was almost severed and I took my tie off to tie round his arm. I pulled so hard I broke it. I looked up and one of the stewardesses was standing there. I asked her to get something to tie his arm with, but the poor girl was in shock, so I just used what was left of my tie.

'I stayed with him until a fellow in a tweed coat turned up with a medical bag and carrying a syringe. There were explosions going on and one made him jump so much he ended up on his backside but still holding the syringe up in the air.

'People came from across the fields, ordinary people, not rescue people. I didn't see any of those at all. Eventually a Volkswagen arrived which was a coal van. Jackie was put into it, also Johnny Berry who I didn't even recognise as a player until I saw the badge on his blazer. Myself, Billy Foulkes and Dennis Viollet were also put in and we were driven to the hospital.

'I remember breaking down and crying when we got there and I saw Bobby Charlton, Peter Howard, Ted Ellyard and a Yugoslav. I was just relieved that there were more of us alive. Some of us were asked to identify people they were working on. Ray Wood was lying on the floor as they attended to his eye.

'They gave us a bowl of soup and the Yugoslav collapsed. He just slid down the wall. He had been walking around with a broken leg that suddenly gave way. They started to give us injections. Bobby fainted and so he was kept in hospital. Billy Foulkes, Ted, Peter and I were taken to a hotel where the people looked after us wonderfully.

'Jimmy Murphy turned up the following day with Jean Busby, Sandy Busby, Duncan's father, Gladstone, Jimmy Payne, Duncan's best friend, Jackie's dad and the wives like Jean Blanchflower. Jean Busby at that time was remarkable. She took care of everyone and encouraged the other wives, while all the time her own husband was upstairs fighting for his life. She was strong, very, very strong.

'I had to go back to the hospital the next day. I could hardly get out of bed because of my back. They gave me injections to the point where I said that's enough because the injections were worse than the bad back.

'Jimmy Murphy asked Bill and I to stay for a few days so that those lying in hospital wouldn't realise the full extent of the accident.

'Eventually Professor Maurer took Jimmy, Bill and myself round the wards and would stop at the foot of each bed to tell us their chances of survival. The boss: fifty-fifty because he was a strong man, Jackie Blanchflower OK, Duncan fifty-fifty, but when he got to little Johnny Berry he whispered, "No, no, I am not God." Johnny survived of course but died in subsequent years.

'Duncan Edwards woke up when we went into his room and he asked us: "What time is kick-off?" Quick as a flash, Jimmy Murphy told him: "Three o' clock, son." Duncan responded: "Get stuck in."'

Bobby Charlton, who suffered only minor injuries from the crash, recalls in his autobiography, *My Manchester United Years*, visiting both Matt Busby and Duncan Edwards in their oxygen tents. Edwards was in obvious pain when he saw him, but Charlton said: 'When he [Duncan] saw me, he threw back his head and said: "I've been waiting for you. Where the bloody hell have you been?" I whispered my encouragement, feeling my eyes smart while wondering all over again how it could be that this young giant of the game was so stricken while I could prepare to walk down the stairs before packing for home.'

As for Busby, Jackie Blanchflower says: 'A lot of people wondered where Matt Busby got the strength from to return to football and start all over again. I went to see him shortly after he got back to England. He had aged terribly and he told me that the hardest part for him after the crash was the way Johnny Berry kept coming to his room to say: "Tommy Taylor's some friend of mine, he hasn't even been to see me." Johnny didn't know that Tommy was one of the players killed and Matt said he just didn't know what to say to him.

'Matt told me: "Son, they couldn't give me an anaesthetic to set my broken foot because of my chest injuries, so they set it a bone at a time, one every day. It was cruel, but it didn't hurt me like Johnny Berry coming into my room every day to say Tommy Taylor was a poor friend."

33

'It was awful for Jimmy [Murphy] after the crash, too. He had so much to do. I remember in Munich walking up the stairs to my room and I was one flight from the top when I heard this terrible crying. At first I couldn't figure it out but as I got nearer I could just make out Jimmy sitting in the dark, on the empty staircase, crying his eyes out. I just quietly walked away.

'Matt and Jimmy were oil and water as people, but they were a wonderful partnership. I believe the greatness of Manchester United was founded on their strength and friendship, but after Munich it was the strength of Matt's wife, Jean, which enabled him to carry on.

'Bill [Foulkes] and I came home and I remember about ten days afterwards all the newspapers in my house kept disappearing. I couldn't figure what was going on, until I realised they were being hidden from me. Big Duncan had died. I found that hard. It hit me terribly ...

'The rest of the season was an anti-climax. I threw myself totally into my football. I could get out there and fight and shout and get rid of the pent-up emotions that boiled within me. It was the only thing that kept me on the rails.

'But I will always remember standing on that snowswept airfield feeling helpless and alone. I will always feel a part of something great; the greatest club in the world. Maybe not always the best team – maybe they never were – but they were the most loved. They carried the passions of the people and when I still see the legions that follow them, I realise that it did not all end on that airfield all those years ago.'

In the aftermath of the tragedy, the bodies of the unlucky victims were flown home. Some of the coffins were put into the gymnasium at Old Trafford as what seemed to be a never-ending series of funerals, every one attended by Jimmy Murphy, took place. Of the 43 people on board the aircraft, 23 died either in the crash or soon afterwards as a result of their injuries*.

Jackie Blanchflower believes that the quality of the talent at Old Trafford, and the depth of it at that time, was frightening and that but for the accident, Manchester United would have gone on to dominate English and European football like Real Madrid did for many years and Benfica after them. He believes that if all those players who were killed and injured had been spared, the course of football history would have been very different. Blanchflower himself was grievously injured with a fractured pelvis and a badly mangled arm. He wasn't even able to attempt to play again and it took him some years to come to terms with the harsh hand fate had dealt him.

Jimmy Murphy faced up to the most daunting task of his career. Lying grievously injured in his hospital bed in Munich, Matt Busby had whispered to his second in command: 'Keep the flag flying, Jimmy ... keep things going until I get back.' The team had been destroyed, the management and coaching structure had been virtually wiped out and Busby, the architect of the club's achievements and ambitions, lay at death's door fighting for his life in an oxygen tent and twice given the last rites.

United's assistant manager had missed the trip to Belgrade because of his part-time post as manager of the Welsh national

---

* Those who died as a result of the Munich air crash: Roger Byrne, Geoff Bent, Eddie Colman, Mark Jones, David Pegg, Tommy Taylor, Liam (Billy) Whelan, Duncan Edwards (died 21 February), Walter Crickmer (Secretary), Tom Curry (Trainer), Bert Whalley (Coach). Alf Clarke (*Evening Chronicle*), Don Davies (*Guardian*), George Follows (*Daily Herald*), Tom Jackson (*Manchester Evening News*), Archie Ledbrooke (*Daily Mirror*), Henry Rose (*Daily Express*), Frank Swift (*News of the World*), Eric Thompson (*Daily Mail*), Captain KG Rayment (co-pilot), Mr W T Cable (steward), Mr B P Miklos (travel agent), Willie Satinoff (United supporter).

team. He had stayed at home to steer Wales through to a World Cup group qualifying win against Israel in Cardiff. News of the crash was given to him by Alma George, the manager's secretary, on his arrival back at Old Trafford. He was greeted with the terrifying message as he hurried to his office: 'The United plane has crashed at Munich.'

Murphy recounts his reaction in his book *Matt, United and Me* with the words: 'My feet stopped. So did my heart. The fingers of the clock on the wall pointed to four o'clock ... but time now meant nothing. The numbing horror of that moment will live with me till I die. I dashed into my office and picked up the phone.'

The weight of the burden handed to Murphy that day must have seemed intolerable. For here was a man overwhelmed with anguish for personal friends, and many of his beloved players either killed, dying or suffering injuries that would end their careers. Simply to absorb such an experience was asking a great deal, but to be charged also with restoring order out of such tragic chaos and keep Manchester United playing football was a frightful challenge. The hurdles ahead were enormous, because not only was there the league programme to complete but United were still in the FA Cup, and thanks to their 3-3 draw against Red Star in Belgrade just hours before the crash, they were through to the semi-finals of the European Cup with a daunting draw pitting them against AC Milan on the horizon.

The fact that United battled on to finish a respectable ninth in the First Division, reached Wembley to play Bolton in the FA Cup final and gave the Italians two fair games in the European Cup, including a 2-1 victory in the first leg at Old Trafford, says it all for the management and ability to inspire of Jimmy Murphy.

Always a shy, retiring man as far as the public were concerned, he rose to the occasion to reveal a strength of character and wisdom that had been somewhat hidden by his role as number two to the much more outgoing and genial Matt Busby. But cometh the hour, cometh the man and the Welshman who had perhaps been rather taken for granted made sure that Manchester United not only survived but also did so with pride and a surprising success. Jimmy Murphy has probably never been given the acknowledgement he deserves for his superhuman contribution after Munich. Partly it was because it was something he never wanted for himself, and perhaps it was ever thus for a number two in all walks of life.

The grand European adventure had exacted a terrible price but Murphy had one staunch ally left at the club, a tough little old man too frail to have gone on the trip himself, but resilient and clear thinking. Harold Hardman, a solicitor by profession but steeped in football as a former amateur England international who had played for both United and Everton, had become a United director under James Gibson before being elected chairman. Hardman was determined that the club would survive and he told Murphy: 'You have got to keep it going, Jimmy. Manchester United is bigger than you, bigger than me, bigger than Matt Busby. It is bigger than anybody. The club must go on.'

They were noble words, but where was Murphy to start? Just who was there left capable of playing for Manchester United? Murphy hurried back to Manchester after Busby's whispered plea, heartbroken and empty. He did not know whether he would see Busby alive again. As the Rhinegold Express thundered out of Bavaria, Murphy says he sat numb while the wheels of the train drummed into his tired brain: 'Where do you find the players? Where do you find the players?'

With him were two of the survivors, goalkeeper Harry Gregg and defender Bill Foulkes. They had escaped the destruction with hardly a scratch, though nobody was sure they wouldn't suddenly collapse from delayed shock. Both men certainly showed signs of claustrophobia, insisting that the windows of the train were kept open, and they travelled from London to Manchester by taxi.

They went home to join their families to leave Murphy to wrestle with the problem of trying to raise a team good enough to represent Manchester United. The crash happened on a Thursday. The league fixture on the Saturday was quickly postponed while their FA Cup fifth round tie against Sheffield Wednesday due the following Saturday was delayed until the Wednesday. It was a welcome breathing space but still cruelly short with under a fortnight to find a team.

It was a nightmare situation that posed difficult problems for those running the competitions. The basis for football, or any sport for that matter, is competition, but however sorry you felt for United in their predicament you couldn't suddenly start awarding them league points or gifting them a cup win. Rivals showed great sympathy, but only two clubs, Nottingham Forest and Liverpool, actually offered what they most needed ... replacement players. United quickly realised that they were on their own, and I'm sure many clubs in that position would simply have folded.

Harold Hardman and Jimmy Murphy showed an amazing courage and determination. Murphy described his task: 'To start with I was in a mental turmoil through sheer sorrow. I also felt completely on my own. Not only was Matt not there, but also my great friend, Bert Whalley our coach, had been killed and so had Tom Curry, the trainer.' Murphy was going to funerals and at the same time trying to sort out what to do. His first move was to call on Joe Armstrong, the chief scout and old faithful, to draw up a complete list of remaining players. When he looked down the list at those left, he must have been shocked, for it read like a team of schoolboys. There was plenty of promising talent, which might, and indeed did, show itself in two or three years time, but he needed people immediately.

Murphy refused to panic and just take anyone. He didn't want to complicate the future because he knew that eventually their own injured players would return to action. For a time, he contemplated trying to sign Ferenc Puskas, the 'Galloping Major' from Hungary who had starred against them for Real Madrid, but eventually decided against it because it seemed contrary to their efforts to bring through their own players. He decided that at the end of the day it had to be British players and British guts which would see them through.

Perhaps nowadays, with the English game almost taken over by foreign stars, it seems an old fashioned viewpoint but that's how it was in the Fifties, and who's to say he was wrong, because in fact he produced a team which, given the circumstances, pulled the club through in quite astonishing fashion.

He made just two immediate ventures into the transfer market. Ernie Taylor was unsettled at Blackpool and wanted to move back to his native north-east but with the help of a mutual friend and United enthusiast, Paddy McGrath, Taylor agreed to answer the SOS. He was 31, took only size four in boots, but had been a key man in Newcastle United's FA Cup final victory in 1951 and again after a transfer when he had schemed Blackpool to their Wembley triumph two years later in the 'Stanley Matthews final' against Bolton. Murphy paid £8,000 for him and then looked round for a harder man to help him in midfield. He remembered Stan Crowther playing against them for Aston Villa in the previous season's final at Wembley and doing equally well in that season's league fixture at Old Trafford. The hard-tackling Crowther cost £24,000, but importantly he was granted special permission to play for United in the FA Cup after appearing for Villa in a third round defeat against Stoke City. The deal was rushed through, but the dispensation for him to play against Sheffield Wednesday was not granted until the afternoon of the match.

The United team had Gregg in goal, and Foulkes in his normal right-back role. Ian Greaves, who had a little first-team experience, was a natural for left-back. Another reserve, Freddie Goodwin, who like Greaves went on to a career in senior management, was picked at wing-half with the newly signed Crowther on the other flank. Colin Webster, a Welsh international, and Taylor, went into the forward line but that was the extent of players with a modicum of experience – and there were still four more places to fill. Bobby Charlton, of course, was still recovering from his injuries and so was unavailable.

Murphy called up Ronnie Cope from the A-team to play centre-half and selected three other unknown teenagers for the remaining places. Mark Pearson, a small but sturdy player from the Sheffield area, was brought in at inside-forward; Alex Dawson, a brawny centre-forward, powerful in the air and a schoolboy team-mate of Denis Law, was to lead the attack; while a slightly built youngster with an Irish background from Manchester, Shay Brennan, nominally a full-back, was put on the left-wing to make up the numbers.

In fact Brennan, a dark-haired stripling, emerged the hero in that first match after Munich, scoring twice in a 3-0 win. Sheffield Wednesday faced a 60,000 human tide of emotion, as well as a patched-up football team. Bill Foulkes, promoted to captain in place of Roger Byrne, described the occasion: 'I felt very sorry for Sheffield Wednesday. They were never in the game with a chance, for I'm sure that everyone who took an interest in football, and even those who didn't, were willing us to win that night.'

There was certainly an extraordinary atmosphere, frightening in its intensity and with the poignancy of the occasion illustrated by the match programme that had been unable to print the line-up of the United team. Underneath the numbers were lines of dots and the crowd had to write in the names themselves when the team was announced over the loudspeakers. The makeshift team went on to become 'Murphy's Marvels' as they drew 2-2 at West Bromwich in the next round before Colin Webster scored for United in a 1-0 win in the replay. The semi-final against Fulham at Villa Park saw Bobby Charlton return to the team in favour of his pal, Brennan, and he scored both goals in a 2-2 draw. Murphy brought Brennan back for the replay at Highbury and this time left out Pearson to make room for Charlton in a thrilling high-scoring match. Alex Dawson scored a hat-trick, with other goals from Charlton and Brennan, in a 5-3 victory that took them to Wembley and an all-Lancashire final against near neighbours Bolton. Dennis Viollet was back in time for this one, and on paper the team looked its strongest since the crash, but it was as if the tide of emotion had exhausted itself and of course Bolton had their own agenda. A fortnight before Munich, United had beaten Bolton 7-2 in the league, but as their rugged England centre-forward, Nat Lofthouse, put it: 'All that mattered from our point of view was that Bolton should win the FA Cup.'

Matt Busby was at Wembley but only with the help of a walking stick, and he left it to Jimmy Murphy to lead out the team. Lofthouse scored twice in a 2-0 win, his second the result of charging Gregg in the middle of the back and knocking the ball and player into the back of the net, a foul even in those days, but in truth, United were never really in it. Even reaching Wembley had been a football miracle and the point had been well made that United had survived the greatest misfortune ever to befall an English football team.

41

Their amazing reaction to chilling adversity had been reinforced on the European front with a spirited display in the first leg of their semi-final against AC Milan that saw the Reds youngsters emerge with a 2-1 win. The Italians scored first when Bredesen intercepted a pass, allowing Schiaffino, the talented Uruguayan international centre-forward, to glide the ball round Gregg after 24 minutes. It was a lead Milan deserved, but five minutes before the interval Dennis Viollet put United back in the fight by snapping up a half-chance in the box from a mishit back pass. With Murphy no doubt winding up his players during the interval, United came out to launch themselves into the Italians with a blazing fury. Schiaffino was now sporting a big plaster over a cut eye, the result of a collision with Gregg, and his team began to waver. Goodwin and Taylor forced Buffoni to make great saves and Webster shot high as the Reds tore into the opposition. United grabbed their winner just 11 minutes from the end after Viollet had been brought down by Maldini. The centre-half flung himself to the ground in anguish as Danish referee Leo Helge awarded a penalty, and his team-mates protested violently. But all that meant nothing to little Ernie Taylor, who stayed cool amid the scenes of excitement, to smash his spot-kick into goal off the underside of the crossbar.

It was a slender lead and it proved far from enough as United crashed to a 4-0 defeat in the second leg. Little went right for them. To start with, the English FA, insensitive and unfeeling, insisted on Bobby Charlton going with them on a tour as part of their preparation for the World Cup. Then, for obvious reasons given the Munich crash, they had travelled overland by boat and train to Milan rather than by plane, not ideal preparation for an examination in the mighty San Siro stadium. Once there, they couldn't even gain entry to the ground as their coach was turned away from a succession of gates as not being at the 'right' entrance. They didn't reach their dressing rooms until 25 minutes before the kick-off in a ground filled by a volatile crowd. The players felt it was gamesmanship to upset them and they also had to deal with some surprising decisions from the German referee Albert Dusch, but Harry Gregg admitted: 'Milan were really a class above us.'

United withstood the pressure in the first half, but the fact that it took them until nearly half-time to win their first corner tells the story. Four minutes into the second half, Schiaffino lobbed over Gregg. Ronnie Cope saved on the line but conceded a penalty for handling which Liedholm converted. Schiaffino went on to score twice with the other goal coming from Danova. Young Kenny Morgans had recovered from his injuries in time to play in the semi-final but that didn't compensate for the absence of Bobby Charlton, playing meaningless friendly matches with England.

Bill Foulkes found the game in Milan an intimidating experience: 'The Italian crowd didn't show us much sympathy. As we walked out, we were bombarded with vegetables. I remember being hit by cabbages and the biggest bunch of carrots I have ever seen. It was very hostile, with all the flares and fireworks. Milan had a good team, too, with players like Schiaffino and Liedholm, and they crushed us in the second half.

'It was a sad end to a horrific season but inevitable when you think about it. Emotion and spirit had kept us going for a long time, but after a while it was not enough.

'I think we just ran out of emotional steam. I know that in the summer I was happy just to rest and count my good fortune that I was at least playing football, while so many of my friends and team-mates just hadn't made it.'

Jimmy Murphy had certainly earned the right to relax for a spell. He had indeed kept the flag flying, and Matt Busby was always quick to acknowledge the contribution of his assistant in a long and creative partnership that had turned a blitzed and bankrupt club into a dynamic force in football and then ensured its survival through the dark days of Munich.

Murphy was undoubtedly the inspiration of the Manchester United post-Munich, yet few would want to rank his makeshift marvels alongside the all-time great sides of Old Trafford. A writer who recognised immediately the greatness of Murphy and his importance during the dark days of Munich, and who did not hesitate to say so at the time, was Keith Dewhurst, who took the place of Alf Clarke when the *Evening Chronicle*'s United correspondent was among the journalists killed in the crash. Keith, in later years a playwright and novelist, paid tribute to the club's emergency manager in an illuminating piece he wrote for his Manchester evening paper on the eve of the FA Cup final against Bolton just a few weeks after the accident.

'Manchester United's Jimmy Murphy is a short, explosive character who hates crowds and publicity, and people who do not know him well think that he is hard and difficult to approach,' wrote Dewhurst. 'When they know him a little better, they think that he is a kind of spectacular joker. His team talks are epics of colourful language and wild gestures, far removed from the calm analysis of Matt Busby. His stock greeting of "Hello, my old pal" – equally effective for handling pressmen, players, genuine old pals, barmen, waiters and the people who pretend to be genuine old pals in the hope of scrounging tickets – has in fact become a joke among the team. Everyone is "old palling" everyone else.

'The players may smile at Jimmy's jokes and mannerisms, but they know that these mask one of the shrewdest soccer brains of all time. When you really know Jimmy Murphy, you know a man of deep feelings and sympathy which he does not choose to expose all the time for the world to knock around. You know a masterly talker and storyteller. You know perhaps the best football coach Britain has ever seen.

'Murphy has the managerial flair, too. His handling of the Manchester United team since Munich has been superb. He has had only a handful of players, and some of those are not really up to first-team standards. Yet look at the way he has used them. Look at the hunch that paid off when Shay Brennan hit two goals in the Sheffield Wednesday cup tie. Look at the dropping of Mark Pearson and the restoration of Brennan in the Highbury (semi-final) replay – another match-winning move. Look at the switching of Ken Morgans to the left-wing, a move which has at least solved a desperate problem, and may yet win the Cup.

'Look at Murphy, buffooning to keep the players' morale up, and yet all the time thinking, thinking. Staying up all night in London before the semi-final. Deciding on the Morgans switch when everyone thought he was asleep in the corner of the train compartment.

'I know what he will say to skipper Billy Foulkes before the Cup final. I can only say the same to Jimmy: "Best of luck, my old pal."'

Bobby Charlton had gone straight home to Ashington on his return from Munich, but he turned up to cheer on the patched-up team in the cup tie against Sheffield Wednesday, and quickly realised that his place was with his club, battling to avoid relegation and perhaps giving notice that United were still in business by reaching the Cup final.

By the time he was back, he had missed most of the funerals but that was probably a good thing because I am sure he would have found the emotional demands quite overpowering. For Charlton had been playing with the Busby Babes for long enough to consider them close friends. Eddie Colman had gone out of his way to make him feel at home in Manchester as a new arrival in the big city from Ashington. He was made to feel welcome at his home in Salford, just as Wilf McGuinness had palled up with him.

Charlton confesses that he was too much in awe of the skipper, Roger Byrne, to get to know him, but he was somehow drawn to the easy-going Duncan Edwards, admiring him hugely as a footballer and striking up a friendship. Edwards was equally taken by the emerging talent of Charlton and the modest way he settled into the dressing room as a young boy among young men. When they found themselves together in the army doing their national service, Edwards went out of his way to help his shy friend adjust to another challenging way of life. Charlton is not embarrassed to say in his book *My Manchester United Years*: 'He [Duncan] was fantastic and I loved him.'

The dressing room in professional football can be a hard place, as Charlton discovered when as a new boy he had gone into the first-team dressing room uninvited and had been bawled out by the captain, the no-nonsense Allenby Chilton. But just as he had been finding his feet alongside the Busby Babes, suddenly he had been projected into a quite different world, with players even younger and less sure of themselves than him needing help if the club were ever to prosper again. To his great credit, Charlton seemed to step up to the plate, ready to accept responsibility and become a leader. He reminded himself that he had made a decisive contribution to winning the championship of 1957, playing in 13 of the remaining 31 league games after his first-team debut to score 10 goals. He had come of age and reflected that he had played on the same pitch as stars like Alfredo di Stefano and Raymond Kopa in European combat. And after Munich, he said that he felt ready to help prove that there was still life left in Manchester United.

Wilf McGuinness, later to become manager of United, was a huge fan of Bobby Charlton. 'Bobby and I, we grew up together as young players. We were in fact pals and first met ironically at Maine Road, Manchester City's ground. That was because I was playing for Manchester Schoolboys while Bobby represented East Northumberland. We beat them three-nil by the way.

'Then we became team-mates in the England team when I was captain. Sometimes, if there was a match in the Manchester area, Bobby's mum and dad would stay with my parents in Blackley, North Manchester.

'Bobby was a reserved character with a strong Geordie accent, and I got to know him well. Bobby, Shay Brennan and myself, we used to knock around together, and in the summer we used to go to Butlins at Pwllheli and the Isle of Man. We grew up together and had some fun times at the dance halls like the Plaza, the Ritz and Sale Locarno. We were all single of course, and liked going to town. Bobby was quiet, but he had a good sense of humour with a sharp answer to the banter that came his way.

'As we got a bit older, the three of us started to think it would be good to open a café, like the ones we used to go to in Manchester for lunch after training. Then we graduated to thinking more ambitiously about a restaurant until we finally hit on the idea of opening a nightclub – and this was before George Best was on the scene. Anyway, that idea didn't last long because Sir Matt got wind of it – how, I don't know – and one day he was waiting at the players' entrance for us to arrive for training. I was first in and he said he wanted a word with me. I followed him to his office where he asked, what was all this he had been hearing about us and a nightclub? Suddenly, it didn't feel such a good idea, particularly when he said, forget it, because from what he said he had heard, we went into enough nightclubs without owning one!

'So it was back to training and trying to improve ourselves. Bobby would be the first to agree that Jimmy Murphy was a big help in his development, as indeed he was with us all. On a Sunday morning after a game, he would take us all aside, one at a time, and explain where we could improve. We have a lot to thank Jimmy for.'

'As Sir Matt's assistant, he used to specialise in the development of the younger players. He had infinite patience. He could see the potential of Bobby's innate gifts and as a result he used to spend hours with him. I remember him telling me once: "Bobby was a difficult pupil. He did so many things superbly and by instinct, but he kept spoiling it by hitting long balls to the right or left wing and then standing still. So many long passes were made when shorter ones would have been better."'

For all his later greatness, not everything came naturally. Indeed, Charlton believes he might not have made it to the top without the toughening up process of going through Murphy's mangle on the training pitch.

'When we played in practice matches he used to come up behind me and kick me. I used to think, what's going on here? I couldn't always understand what he was trying to do, but now of course I realise he was teaching me what to expect from the harsher side of professional football,' Charlton explained.

'Jimmy was so intense he used to frighten me. He was hell to work for but everything was done for a purpose, and I owe more to Jimmy Murphy than any other single person in football. I shall always be grateful to him, and the success of Manchester United over so many years is a testimony to his work.'

Wilf McGuinness agrees: 'Without him, a lot of us would never have made it as professional footballers. At times we almost hated him, because he drove us so hard, but it was always for our own good and we certainly respected him.'

Murphy had been a Desert Rat during the war, serving with the Royal Artillery and going through the North African campaign before arriving at Bari transit camp in Italy, where he took over from Stan Cullis as the sergeant in charge of sport and where he met Matt Busby. The son of a Welsh mother and Irish father, he was brought up in a little village called Pentre in the Rhondda Valley, and as a young man, when he wasn't playing football, he could often be found playing the organ in Treorchy Parish Church. He played for Wales Schoolboys and when he helped beat England 3-2 at Cardiff and draw 2-2 with Scotland at Hampden Park, he came to the attention of English league clubs. He joined West Bromwich, where he played from 1928 until the outbreak of the war that signalled the end of his playing career. He was the youngest player in the Welsh team of his day at the age of 21, and in all he was capped 22 times as well as captaining his country. When he teamed up with Busby at the end of the war, Murphy said: 'Old Trafford was bombed out and was little more than a rubbish dump. The club just didn't have any money either. We used to give the team their lunch on a matchday, only it was across the bridge in an old wooden hut called the United Café. They used to get a poached egg.

'As we progressed, we started to have lunch at the Trafford Hotel and the food went up the social scale as well with perhaps boiled chicken on the menu. Later, we moved to Gorse Hill and really went up in the world with lamb cutlets, even a steak, but it still wasn't like eating today in the Old Trafford Executive Suite!'

Murphy was Busby's first and best signing as Matt freely acknowledged in later years: 'I saw Jimmy Murphy talking football to a crowd of players when we were both in the army during the war in Italy, and I decided then that if ever I needed someone to help me in management, he was my man. We had a wonderful and happy relationship. He was never a "yes" man which was a good start, and our natures seemed to join to produce commonsense. He was straight, honest and loyal.'

They were totally different people, even as players. Both were wing-halves after failing as forwards, but that was the end of their resemblance because while Busby was the gentle giant, his right-hand man was the archetypal Welsh dragon, breathing fire and fury. Perhaps the choice of Murphy as his lieutenant was an acknowledgement by Busby of the lack of aggression in his own make-up.

His team talks were vintage stuff, and watching from a distance it seemed he was conducting some Welsh choir, with his arms and hands punctuating the air to emphasise the effort needed for victory. It was undoubtedly his skill as a motivator that took little Wales through to the quarter-finals of the World Cup in 1958 where they lost narrowly 1-0 to Brazil, the ultimate winners of the tournament. It was a run that has never been bettered by his country, nor is it ever likely to be.

Sometimes, he was not too fussy about how he motivated his teams. His players tell of one Welsh game against Germany, in a friendly after the war, when he delivered the usual talk on tactics and wished them luck. Then, just as they were about to walk out of the dressing room, he called after them: 'And don't forget it was Germans shooting at your fathers not so long ago!'

Munich marked the start of my own adventure with Manchester United, as I replaced Tom Jackson, who like his local rival

Alf Clarke, was among the eight journalists who lost their lives in the crash. Keith Dewhurst and I were in competition, but we became friends, too, and we both agreed that valiant though Jimmy Murphy and his players had performed for the remainder of the season after the crash, at the end of the day it wasn't quite enough. We both knew that a lot of rebuilding and hard work lay ahead if Manchester United were ever to regain a premier position in football. Keith left his United correspondent's job the following season to pursue a successful writing career. I think, by then, I knew that though my editor had switched me from politics to football duties as a purely emergency and temporary move, I was in for the long haul in football with Manchester United.

4

Recovery with the Lawman

The period after the Munich air crash was perhaps the most significant chapter in Manchester United's bid to become a major force in the game again. Bobby Charlton was back in action and proving an inspirational figure. Jimmy Murphy had performed football miracles, fulfilling Matt Busby's instruction to keep United moving forwards, and chairman Harold Hardman's determination that the club should survive had received a ready response from staff, players and supporters. And not far off on the horizon, Busby's best-ever transfer deal would see Scotsman Denis Law, the second of the immortal trinity, make the journey to Manchester from Italy.

Law would prove the catalyst that moved United to the next level. Then later, when George Best arrived on the scene to complete the trinity, the Reds really took off. In the meantime though, it was all down to Charlton to supply the magic that even in the rebuilding period would give the Reds a distinctive aura.

The period between the crash of 1958 and the European Cup victory ten years later was hardly spectacular for United in terms of winning trophies – two league championships and one FA Cup – at least not compared to the conveyor belt of success enjoyed more recently under the management of Sir Alex Ferguson. For me, though, it was always compulsive viewing as I watched Matt Busby pick up the reins again and patiently rebuild his shattered club round players like Bobby Charlton. I was gripped by the drama of a club fighting for survival. Many thought it was the end. How could a club, not especially wealthy, carry on in the face of losing the Busby Babes, with not only eight players killed but with several more so badly injured that they never played again, at least at their previous level?

Most people felt that reaching the final of the FA Cup after the disaster was mostly down to the adrenalin triggered by the emotional background, so it came as a real surprise when the following season saw United finish runners-up in the league championship. Bobby Charlton was in dominating form, and certainly he proved a quick learner after Munich as one of the key players round whom Manchester United could build. He missed two games immediately after the crash, then resumed playing with a heightened responsibility. By the start of the 1958-59 season, he was in full flow. He scored a hat-trick in the opening game at home to Chelsea and he bagged a couple more four days later at Nottingham Forest. He stormed through the campaign for his total of 29 league goals. When he and Dennis Viollet hit scoring form together, United were unstoppable. They each scored twice in a 6-1 win against Blackburn Rovers and Portsmouth also crashed 6-1 at Old Trafford with Charlton and Viollet sharing four of the goals.

Charlton and Viollet scored a goal apiece to beat Wolves 2-1 at Old Trafford in February, so that by April the two clubs were level on points at the top of the table. But Wolves had a couple of games in hand and they finished powerfully to take the title by six points. Logically, United had no right to finish second in the First Division after the grievous blow suffered at Munich just the previous season. Such a position was really beyond their wildest dreams and even Busby admitted that it had been far better than he had expected. What made it so startling, of course, was that United had been able to find so many players from within. They also received help from an unexpected source, with amateur club Bishop Auckland offering to help, which is how Warren Bradley arrived at Old Trafford.

Bradley, already capped for the England amateur team, was born in Hyde, Cheshire. He was a schoolteacher who soon made himself at home among the professional stars. His intelligent and quiet confidence helped, qualities which later saw him become headmaster of a big Manchester comprehensive school, but he hardly ranked as a major signing, at least not as far as his fee was concerned, a modest donation to Bishop Auckland.

Bradley was perhaps not trinity material but the fans were not expecting miracles during these years of consolidation, and in any case they admired the application of their new acquisition and the way he had put his teaching career on hold to help out at Old Trafford. They always had Bobby Charlton's goals to fall back on for their thrills, as they waited for Busby to conjure up another great team. While Charlton in particular was there, there was always hope, as the new United settled down to play their part in helping to recreate the kind of football that had been held up for them by the Busby Babes.

Bradley told me his story: 'I had played for Bishop Auckland in the Northern League since leaving Durham University in 1955.

Derek Lewin, our inside-right, had trained under Jimmy Murphy with the British Olympic team of 1956, and it was he, I think, who suggested to our club that since we had been knocked out of the Amateur Cup with little left to play for, we might be able to lend [United] a hand.

'So Derek, Bobby Hardisty and myself, all amateur internationals, were loaned to United. The idea was that since they were short of players, we might be able to make up numbers in the reserve team until they got straight again.

'I had no thoughts about becoming a professional footballer. I had always wanted to be a teacher. Teaching paid six pounds a week, less than the twenty pounds you could earn as a footballer, but it offered a more secure, long-term future for a married man like me,' he said.

But by late summer, Matt Busby was back in the saddle and had liked what he saw of the nippy winger in the reserves and suggested that the player should consider taking a teaching job in Manchester to enable him to train with the senior players and become more a part of the club. So in September 1958, Bradley and his wife Margaret moved to Manchester and he began his teaching career in Stretford, signing as a part-time professional a few weeks later.

He did well, so well that he was called up by England for their tour of South America in the summer of 1959. Also in the squad was fellow United player Wilf McGuinness, later to become manager at Old Trafford. Bradley won two of his three full professional caps on that trip and McGuinness remembers clearly his style of play. 'But for the Munich crash, I doubt whether Warren would ever have come to United, and a few of us wondered how this university amateur lad would fare in the real professional world,' he explained.

'He quickly put us in our places with the kind of performances that not only got him into our first team but into the England side. I remember him for his pace, his direct running on the wing and, above all, for his eye for goal. He crossed the ball well, but also when play was on the other side he used to cut in and appear like magic at the far post. He got a lot of goals for a winger.

'United didn't get many university boys in those days, but he was popular in the dressing room because he didn't have any fancy airs and graces. We also quickly came to respect him as a player which, in the professional game, is what really matters.'

Bradley played 31 times for United in the crucial season of 1959-60; crucial in the sense that this was the recovery period after the crash. A year or so later, a combination of growing work pressures, a series of debilitating knee injuries and the emergence of Johnny Giles started to restrict his appearances, and in 1962 he left to play for Bury*.

Bradley died in 2007, aged 73, and I felt honoured when I was asked to give a eulogy at his funeral outlining the football side of a widely talented life. I know he enjoyed playing alongside Bobby Charlton, a man whose values he appreciated, and I am sure he got a lot of satisfaction from the season after Munich when United finished runners-up in the league, and did so with great panache on their way to scoring an astounding 103 goals, including 29 from Charlton, 21 by Dennis Viollet, 16 from Albert

---

* Long after his playing days, Bradley returned to serve his former team-mates and many other ex-players by becoming treasurer of the Association of Former Manchester United Players alongside David Sadler, John Doherty, Bill Foulkes the first chairman, and Alan Wardle. His influence was key to the club paying increasing attention to the work of the Association, not least in recent times by the then chief executive, David Gill, and manager Sir Alex Ferguson.

Scanlon, four from Albert Quixall and 12 from Bradley himself. It was the vintage all-scoring attack that I kept urging Walter Winterbottom to select en bloc for England. He never did – but he should have done.

In this rebuilding phase the only major concession United had made to the transfer market, following the emergency sign-ings of Taylor and Crowther, was in recruiting inside-forward Albert Quixall from Sheffield Wednesday. The blond-haired Yorkshireman was bought in keeping with Busby's policy of putting players on to the Old Trafford stage who had personality and entertainment value, as well as being able to do a job of work. Quixall was the golden boy of his day. In his native Sheffield, he had swept everything before him: captain of his school, his city, his county, his country and then playing for the full England team by the age of 18. He helped to maintain the Busby tradition for creative, skilful football in a difficult period. He had charisma, though he didn't make a fortune from football. He once told me: 'I suppose I was born twenty years too early. I remember an article on me at the time saying that my transfer fee made me worth my weight in gold. Perhaps that was true, but it didn't do much for me personally. I don't harp on about that though, because you can't translate everything into money. I achieved a lot in my teens and had some great times in football. I'm not bitter by any means.'

You could hardly blame him if he was. Working after football for years in a scrap metal yard at Ardwick in Manchester, Quixall was young enough to see near-contemporaries prosper out of all proportion with a fraction of his talent ... yet he was too old to have caught the gravy train himself.

Dennis Viollet was another gifted player who hit the heights just a little too soon to catch the explosion in football wages and finances. Viollet, a local youngster, grew up playing ball around Maine Road, and was in fact a Manchester City fan like the rest of his family. Joe Armstrong and Jimmy Murphy persuaded him to come to Old Trafford and his career straddled the Munich disaster. He was one of the Busby Babes who survived the crash to play a vital role in the rebuilding period.

He could easily have become another Denis Law in terms of ability, but he couldn't quite match the charisma of the Scot, nor was he fortunate enough to play in the era of the trinity. Charlton, Law and Best, when the trinity was at its peak, fed off each other and Law certainly fed off the fans who so admired his cavalier approach to the game, his readiness to put life and limb at risk and his willingness to fly in the face of authority. He also probably edged Viollet with the sharpness of his reactions and his spring-heeled acrobatics in the air. Viollet was a sleek ghost of a player while Law was Rob Roy from the Highlands.

Viollet, however, was a supremely valuable link from the old days to the development of a newly built Manchester United. His survival at Munich did nothing to dull a sharp sense of humour – he used to call me 'Scoop' – and a jaunty approach to life. It was as if after his escape, he seemed to be even more determined to squeeze every last drop out of life. As fellow Busby Babe and pal John Doherty put it: 'The effect of Munich on his life was that he mustn't waste a minute of what was left and he lived in the fast lane.' But that did not stop him continuing to excel on the pitch with a record performance coming in the 1959-60 campaign as United set out hoping to build on their runners-up position of the previous season. That they finished only seventh was hardly the fault of Viollet, who broke Jack Rowley's club scoring record by notching 32 league goals in a season, a record that still stands.

He was a master craftsman who scored his goals with stealth, skill and speed. He was hardly a burly centre-forward, but his rather frail-looking appearance belied his strength. He was resilient, and overall he scored 159 goals in his 259 league appearances spread over ten seasons of first-team soccer.

Ken Barnes, the former Manchester City captain and one of his many friends who played both with and against Viollet, says: 'He was brilliant at timing his runs, which, together with great finishing, made him one of the best inside-lefts in the game. He was so full of guile and craft, and certainly a crafty blighter to play against.

'One of my most satisfying moments in football was when City played at Old Trafford in 1955 and we won five-nil. I would have liked Dennis to have suffered that one but he was out with some injury, but then of course if he had been playing, we might not have got that result because he was that kind of player.'

Viollet eventually left United in 1962 to play for Stoke, and helped them win the Second Division Championship under Tony Waddington. He played in the States for a spell, then after winning an Irish FA Cup winners' medal with Linfield he settled in America, becoming involved in their football, including coaching at university level.

Viollet's record scoring season should have brought him more than just two caps for England. I remember one column I wrote concerning him that got us both the then equivalent of Fergie's hairdryer treatment from the formidable Stan Cullis at Wolves. I used to 'ghost' a weekly column with Viollet and one week we hatched a piece arguing what a shame it was that Wolves as champions were representing English football in the European Cup rather than Manchester United, whose style – we said – would be much better suited for success. The next day I got a message asking me to see Matt Busby at Old Trafford. I arrived to find Viollet there already and together we went in to see Busby who simply handed me the phone and said somebody wanted to speak to me. Mr Cullis let rip in defence of his beloved Wolves, and then it was Viollet's turn for an earful. We duly apologised and as we left the room Viollet simply turned to me and said: 'Thanks, Scoop.' Nothing fazed him, though I must say we were a little more circumspect concerning Wolves in our future columns.

United again topped 100 league goals in the 1959-60 season, with Viollet's 32 backed up by 18 from Charlton, 13 from Quixall, and eight and seven from wingers Bradley and Scanlon. Alex Dawson, a centre-forward, who also played on the wing, was forcing his way into the team and grabbed a promising 15 from only 22 appearances. Johnny Giles and Mark Pearson, pilloried by Burnley's controversial and outspoken chairman Bob Lord as a 'Teddy Boy', played occasionally.

United were too erratic to win the title. One week they would score four, the next they would concede four. Things came to a head in January when the team went to Newcastle and lost 7-3. I remember well my report in that night's *Football Pink* with the headlines naturally expected to highlight the resounding defeat along the lines of United being thrashed, but we had an editor at the time, Tom Henry, who was not only a friend of Matt Busby but a United supporter, and he didn't like the tone of the headlines written by his staff. So, using his clout as editor, he rewrote the headlines himself and gave them directly to the printers. The result was that instead of a banner slamming the team's display, the *Pink* came out that night with a streamer saying: 'UNITED IN 10-GOAL THRILLER.'

Busby was not going to be mollified by that, of course, and suddenly he swooped into transfer action to pay £30,000 for wing-half Maurice Setters from West Bromwich Albion. He wanted the bandy-legged, tough-tackling Setters to stiffen the midfield. What a contrast he made with Quixall. Their styles were at the opposite ends of the football spectrum and there wasn't much love lost between them.

During this period of retrenchment for United, Busby took to rebuilding in steady fashion. He was trying to establish a foundation and consistency that would stand him in good stead for when he was able to bring in a special player like Denis Law to add to the brilliance of Bobby Charlton. We perhaps didn't know it at the time, but this was preparation work for the eventual trinity. At the end of 1960, Busby bought again, paying £29,000 for the West Ham and Republic of Ireland left-back Noel Cantwell. The intelligent and articulate Irishman became a sound influence and the ideal captain during this period. Cantwell came from that hothouse of strategists who tried to push the boundaries of football tactics at West Ham during the Fifties. Players like Malcolm Allison, John Bond, Dave Sexton, Malcolm Musgrove, Frank O'Farrell and Bobby Moore used to gather after training at a little café called Cassettari's round the corner from Upton Park. There they would move the salt and pepper pots around the table as they discussed the finer points of the game. It was like a finishing school for embryonic managers and Cantwell was always one of the leading disciples among Upton Park's footballing free-thinkers.

Although eager to learn from the most respected, and successful, manager in the business, I think Cantwell found his move to Old Trafford something of a culture shock, because United were not that kind of club. Matt Busby didn't believe in smothering his teams with tactics, preferring instead to rely on their intuition and ability to express themselves rather than trying to recall instructions from a Don Revie type dossier. Nonetheless, Cantwell was a natural leader and successfully harnessed the leading lights of the trinity to pull for the team.

He was a natural choice for chairman of the Professional Footballers' Association and some thought he was the man to follow
Busby as manager at Old Trafford. Instead, he left to become manager of Coventry City as well as enjoying a spell as manager of the
Republic of Ireland team.

At Old Trafford there continued to be no instant success post-
Munich, with United unable to improve on seventh in the league
in the 1960-61 season, and making a fourth round exit in the
FA Cup. The 1961-62 season did bring a run in the Cup, United
reaching the semi-finals, only to lose 3-1 against Spurs at
Hillsborough. In the league, however, they slipped to 15th. Scoring
power was weakening while defensively they were leaking. Busby
knew it was time for more action. There were not enough talented
youngsters coming through fast enough. Just before the start of the
1961-62 season, he had bought centre-forward David Herd, son
of his former team-mate Alex, from Arsenal for £32,000. Herd had
obliged by scoring 14 goals, but the goal touch had deserted the
others and Herd's tally was the best effort.

So in the summer of 1962, Busby spent again and pulled off
his best-ever transfer coup. He brought Denis Law home from
Italy to capture his second man for the trinity. The signing of Law
proved a masterstroke. Busby paid a record fee for him and really
Law had nothing to prove, but his success had not come easily.
While Bobby Charlton learned his trade at Old Trafford, Denis,
three years younger, had to fight a different kind of battle, trying
to make his mark as a young footballer in his home town of
Aberdeen in Scotland.

None of the trinity came from a favoured background. Bobby
Charlton was from a working-class mining family, George Best
grew up in modest surroundings in Belfast, while Denis Law came
from a deep-sea fisherman's family. Denis was the youngest of

seven, a war baby born in 1940, in the fishing town of Aberdeen with a father who'd had a hard life. During wartime, George Law had served on the Royal Navy ships that escorted the convoys bound for Russia. The end of the war brought little respite, because he simply went back to his previous way of life on the fishing trawlers. It was a tough life for £10 a week, money was tight and the family didn't see much of their father. Denis's first pair of football boots came from a friend; he didn't have his first pair of shoes, other than plimsolls, until he was 14. The pawnbroker played a big part in the Law family.

Denis went to sea once with his father but quickly decided it wasn't for him. Football was what governed his life; he was forever kicking a ball about with his brothers, one of whom could also have made it as a professional but he broke his leg badly. When Denis went to a game, it was either down the road to watch Aberdeen at Pittodrie or local non-league football. His mother worked as a cleaner at the local school where Denis did well. In fact, he passed the scholarship to go to the grammar school, but when he discovered they played only rugby and cricket there, with no football, he went instead to the secondary school where they played soccer, and once his sports teacher had switched him from full-back to inside-left, he thrived at the game.

Denis was a member of Aberdeen Lads Club and along with Alex Dawson, a future Manchester United team-mate, played for Aberdeen Schoolboys Under-15s. Denis was also picked for the Scotland Schoolboys squad that went to Ireland, though he failed to make the team. At that time, his physique counted against him. Few would have predicted a glittering career looking at Denis Law as a youngster, when scout Archie Beattie sent him down from Aberdeen for a trial with his brother Andy, the manager of Huddersfield. Bill Shankly, who was then in charge of Huddersfield's reserves before becoming manager, said later: 'He looked like a skinned rabbit. My first reaction was to say, get him on the next train home.'

Law also suffered from a terrible squint, an affliction that ran through the family, and as he said himself: 'I was surprised I caught anyone's eye. I was a little boy, undernourished, underdeveloped and weighed in at eight stone soaking wet, and I had this terrible squint.' But he loved his football and had a flair for scoring goals which is always a winning quality. He also worked hard on the field, prepared to run back defending as well as having a go at goal.

It's true to say that Andy Beattie was not too impressed by this 15-year-old lad; in fact, he is quoted as telling his brother: 'The boy's a freak. Never did I see a less likely football prospect – weak, puny and bespectacled.' The trial lasted a week, and at the end, Law was slightly surprised to be told they wanted to sign him. Archie Beattie visited the family home to discuss the arrangements with his mother who was reassured that they would put him in digs and look after him. He was duly taken on to the Huddersfield groundstaff as an apprentice in April 1955.

At times he had played with one eye closed to offset the squint, and just how far Law would have been able to progress in the game without surgery is difficult to say, but finally came a message that after two years on the National Health Service waiting list, he had an appointment with an eye specialist in Aberdeen with a view to corrective surgery.

The operation was a traumatic moment for him, as he wrote in his autobiography *The King*: 'When I woke up, I had bandages all round my head. I must have looked like the Invisible Man for several days, and then it was just like being in one of those old war movies when someone has been wounded on the battle front: the nurse came in one day and gently unwound it layer by layer. I kept my eyes tight shut. Gradually I opened them, and the nurse told me to go and look in the mirror. I shuffled over dreading what I might see. All sort of thoughts raced through my fertile young mind. The first thing I noticed was that the eye they had operated on, the right one, was bloodshot. I immediately assumed that something had gone wrong, but then I saw that the pupil of the eye was right in the middle. I cannot emphasise enough what an incredible moment in my life that was.'

The operation completely changed things for Law. Suddenly, he had the ability to look people in the eye, something he had never been able to do with any confidence before. Even better, he was able to look at girls and not be worried that they would laugh at him. His mother explained that he had been four or five when the problem had surfaced, but now his eyes were straight, without one of them retreating to a corner as if it was in hiding. Law says that even now he still dreads looking in the mirror.

He returned to Huddersfield after a couple of weeks' convalescence, and says it was a great feeling just to go into the ground with the rest of the lads and be normal, especially playing football with both eyes open. With a new-found confidence, Law was soon in Huddersfield's youth team where he caught the eye of Matt Busby. Playing in an FA Youth Cup tie against Manchester United, Huddersfield lost, but Busby after the game offered Andy Beattie £10,000 for his 16-year-old forward, a remarkably big offer for such a young player. The bid was turned down because Huddersfield had other plans, and on Christmas Eve 1956, their promising apprentice was given his league debut at inside-right against Notts County, aged 16 years and 10 months, the youngest player Huddersfield have ever fielded.

There was an arrogance in Law suggesting he could perform

on a bigger stage and Busby, enjoying a brief spell as manager of Scotland, remembered him and capped him against Wales at Ninian Park, Cardiff, on 18 October 1958, and he marked the occasion by scoring in a 3-0 win. In December 1959, Shankly left Huddersfield to become manager of Liverpool, and speculation mounted that the up-and-coming Law would also be leaving, with Everton, Arsenal, Chelsea and Rangers all reported as interested. In the end, it was Manchester City who landed him, paying £55,000 on 15 March 1960, then a British record transfer fee.

Matt Busby later revealed that he had considered going in for Law a second time following his fruitless offer, when he had been a teenager playing for Huddersfield's youth team against United, but considered he already had enough inside-forwards in Dennis Viollet, Albert Quixall, Alex Dawson and of course Bobby Charlton. He also said that you never knew what the future would bring ... how very prophetic those words would be.

Law made his City debut in a 4-3 defeat at Leeds, and scored. He played in the last seven games of season 1959-60 to help them stay in the First Division. City had a few top players, especially wing-half Ken Barnes, with whom Law struck up a life-long friendship, but manager Les McDowall was struggling to put together a consistently winning team. City continued to slide the following season, despite 37 appearances and 19 goals by Law in a campaign that prompted the quiz question: Who scored seven goals in the Cup only to get knocked out? The answer is that Law scored six times at Luton before the match was abandoned with the sodden pitch unplayable and City leading 6-2; Law also scored in the replay but the Blues were beaten 3-1 and his six goals from the first match didn't count.

Sympathy for him evaporated quickly though, when it got into the papers that if City were relegated, he wouldn't want to go back to the Second Divison. I reckon Law's distrust of the media started when what he thought was a private conversation ended in newspaper headlines calling him a big-head and disloyal. The fans weren't happy either when towards the end of the season he had to choose between club and country, and he elected to play for Scotland against England at Wembley rather than for City in a vital league game. He perhaps had second thoughts when England hammered the Scots 9-3, but the damage had been done, with accusations from some of him being a traitor.

Although City survived again, Law knew that every season was likely to become a battle against relegation, and when Italian football came calling he was ready to try playing abroad. The Scot did not need much persuading to leave City when Torino sent their football scout to Manchester to offer him a £5,000 signing-on fee plus bonuses, such as £200 for a win, terms that compared well with the English maximum wage of £20 a week. City collected a record £110,000 fee for his transfer on 9 June 1961, but the Italian move proved a disaster. Law let it be known that he longed to return to English football and just over a year later, after a lengthy chase by Matt Busby, he arrived at Manchester United for a record £115,000 fee.

His first season at Old Trafford, 1962-63, saw United flirt with relegation, though they did pull themselves together to win the FA Cup by beating Leicester City 3-1 in the final at Wembley. The real breakthrough came the following season, with new signing Pat Crerand coming into his own to give Law improved support and help him score 30 league goals from 41 games in season 1963-64. It was a bravura performance which clinched his award as European Footballer of the Year.

Few from the Sixties will forget the Law trademark as he signalled his goals to the crowd, punching the air and wheeling away with arm raised, his hand clutching his sleeve, save for the one finger pointing to the sky to acknowledge a goal. The terrace fans would rise to his salute as to a gladiator of old. It was a long way from those early days with a squint.

Still, things weren't quite right with United. The attack looked full of goals, but they only clicked spasmodically. Busby decided that the service to the men up front wasn't good enough. So he went out to buy a player who could supply the right kind of ammunition for Law and Herd to fire. The result was the arrival, in February 1963 for £56,000 from Celtic, of right-half Pat Crerand. Busby now had the balance in the half-back line: Setters the ball-winner on the left and Crerand the distributor on the right. It was too late to pull things round in the league and the Reds ended the 1962-63 season in 19th place, their lowest position under Busby's management. But the potential was there, and it showed in the FA Cup as the Reds sailed through every round without a replay, to beat Southampton 1-0 in the semi-final at Villa Park and face Leicester City at Wembley.

For a change, because of their league position, the Reds were the underdogs. Leicester had finished fourth in the First Division and had the reputation of being a side with an iron defence. So the stage was set for a mighty match when the following teams took the field at Wembley on 25 May 1963:

Manchester United: Gaskell, Dunne, Cantwell, Crerand, Foulkes, Setters, Giles, Quixall, Herd, Law, Charlton.
Leicester City: Banks, Sjoberg, Norman, McLintock, King, Appleton, Riley, Cross, Keyworth, Gibson, Stringfellow.

From the first whistle, it was obvious that the Reds had torn up the form book. Law, in particular, was in one of those moods when it would have taken a tank to stop him. The famous Leicester 'iron curtain' was torn to shreds as Law danced through it at will.

Crerand, who had taken time to settle in the side, was also having a field day in Wembley's wide-open spaces, and it was one of his inch-perfect passes that enabled Law to swivel and drive home the first goal after 29 minutes. The longer the game went on, the more composed and confident United looked. In the 58th minute, they underlined their superiority when Herd rounded off a sweet move, involving Giles and Charlton, by sweeping the ball past Gordon Banks. The game was as good as won. In a late flurry Keyworth scored for Leicester, but Herd grabbed his second to make the final scoreline 3-1 to United.

The victory more than made up for the Reds' disappointing league finish, and finally buried the memory of their two Wembley defeats in 1957 and 1958. More than that, it indicated that from the ashes of Munich, Busby was on the way towards building another side capable of taking English football by storm.

5

George

The third member of the trinity was even further down the line, growing up in Belfast and trying to make his mark in a rough, tough game despite being, like Denis Law in his early days, under-sized, underweight and generally lacking in all the attributes you expect to find in a budding sportsman. When Mary Fullaway stood at the door of her house in Aycliffe Avenue in the Manchester suburb of Chorlton-cum-Hardy, she could hardly have imagined that in George Best she was welcoming the boy destined to become arguably the world's greatest footballer.

There he stood, her new lodger, along with another youngster straight off the boat from Belfast, Eric McMordie, coming over to play for Manchester United. 'He looked more like a little jockey than a footballer. He was puny and he was petrified,' said Mrs Fullaway of Best. The pair of them were like fish out of water, with the 15-year-old McMordie particularly homesick, and that night he persuaded George to go back to Ireland with him. So back they went but George's dad, Dickie Best, took his time and spoke with Matt Busby. Between them they persuaded George to give it another go, and so the move was made with David Sadler to share digs with him at Mrs Fullaway's. McMordie didn't return but later joined Middlesbrough.

There is no doubt George Best was quite overwhelmed by Manchester United. He found the other players intimidating and he was in awe of the first-team stars like his Northern Ireland international hero Harry Gregg. 'I didn't know what to say to him,' says George who felt isolated and alone but determined now to stick it out. Little had happened in his life to prepare him for the ordeal of Manchester and playing for a major football club. The Best family, with two boys and four girls, lived at Burren Way on Cregagh's housing estate. George was the eldest and his brother was called Ian Busby in tribute to Sir Matt.

There's a blue plaque these days on the council house where they all lived, not that George spent too much time indoors because he always had a fascination for kicking a ball about. Nobody, though, could see for him a future as a professional footballer, because he was too lightly built, too thin and too small.

He passed his eleven-plus at Nettlefield School but didn't like his senior school, Grosvenor High, because they were rugby focused. He played truant and was transferred to Lisnasharragh Secondary Intermediate. He joined the school team but it was at the local youth club where his football prospered. At Cregagh Youth Club, he came under the tutelage of Hugh 'Bud' McFarlane who made the willing George one of his favourites. 'He was my boy at the club. If I wanted a message delivering, I just called on George and off he went, taking a ball out of his pocket and dribbling it all the way and back,' says McFarlane. He thought young

George had a future, and in order to get him more noticed he arranged a match between his Under-15 youth club side and the Northern Ireland Schoolboys team. 'We beat them two-one. The idea was to put George on view and in my opinion he was the best forward on show.' The Irish Schools selectors still considered him too light and small, though. The big club scouts all took the same line except one, Bob Bishop, United's legendary scout in Northern Ireland, who apparently phoned Old Trafford chief scout Joe Armstrong to say he had struck gold.

Plans for Best to become an apprentice compositor in the *Belfast Telegraph* newspaper office were abandoned after another game, especially arranged so that Bob Bishop could have a look at him. 'Bob was connected with another club that played in a different league, so I arranged for Cregagh to play Bob's team, Boyland, and George scored two of the goals in a four-two win,' says McFarlane.

Best went home to tell his dad: 'I think they are pulling my leg. Bud says there is an English club interested in me and I can go for a trial if I want.' Nobody was kidding, though, and Best duly took the boat to England, leaving Cregagh Youth Club to spend the transfer fee – a £150 donation. Not a bad deal for Manchester United then!

The boy still only stood 5ft high and weighed a lightweight eight stone, but if United were worried about him not growing and putting on a little more weight, they were not left in any doubt about his awesome skill. In fact, it was a story leaking out of the training ground that first alerted me, as the local evening paper correspondent covering Manchester United, that there was a special talent developing in the junior teams.

Harry Gregg volunteered to play with the juniors one afternoon at The Cliff training ground when one of the youngsters he later described as 'the skinny one' brought the ball up to him and scored by sending him diving the wrong way. Harry explains: 'A little later he wriggled clear again. I called his bluff and got the same result, a humiliating trip to terra firma with the ball at the other end of the goal. When he had the audacity to do it a third time, I got up and joked: "You do that again and I'll break your bloody neck, son." I had a good laugh with him and the other lads. But when I left, the image of this pencil-thin lad with the breathtaking skills lingered on. Later that day, I ran across Matt Busby at Old Trafford. We chatted briefly and as he turned to walk away, I asked him if he had seen the youngster, the little Belfast lad. He hadn't, and I suggested he take a look. A few days later we met again. "I know the boy you mean. It's a pity he's so small," he said.'

Best's size was still being held against him and he was also painfully shy. In his early days, he used to walk the long way round to the dressing rooms to avoid meeting people. He wasn't happy with his life outside the training ground either. As a youngster from Ireland, he was only allowed to come to England as an amateur, which meant he had to have a job and just train part-time. So he was sent to work at the nearby Manchester Ship Canal offices because he had beautiful handwriting, but he soon became bored. He wanted to be training with the other groundstaff boys. In the end, the club sent Best and John Fitzpatrick, another youngster in a similar situation, only from Scotland, to work for a friendly employer who said they need only work in the afternoons, which meant they could train with the other lads in the mornings.

The lack of training didn't seem much of a handicap though, as Best worked his way through the A and B teams playing in the Lancashire League and made his mark in the youth team with an occasional game in the reserves. Suddenly his career accelerated, and four months after his 17th birthday and signing as a full-time professional, he couldn't find his name on the teamsheets for either of the United junior teams, nor the reserves. It was the big break-through for George Best: he would be given his first-team debut against West Bromwich Albion at Old Trafford on 14 September 1963.

Although he had already made up his mind to give him his league debut, Matt Busby initially put Best down as a reserve for the match to spare him the ordeal of the build up and the nerves that might ensue. He needn't have bothered with such a nicety, because, as he would demonstrate many times in the future, Best was nerveless. He may have been shy, even insecure away from the pitch, but on it he had a confidence bordering on the arrogant. He might have been reluctant to meet new people, unless they were attractive girls of course, but with a ball at his feet, he could talk in anybody's language.

For his debut, Best was played on the right-wing and was up against Graham Williams, a fairly rugged Welsh international full-back. He didn't have a great game but the Irishman made his mark, and without wishing to appear too much of a fortune-teller, this is what I wrote about him in my match report for the *Manchester Evening News*:

There was also the prospect of young George Best to brighten up a dullish match. Despite the ordeal of a league debut after only three reserve matches, a gruelling duel with full-back Graham Williams, and a painful ankle injury, he played pluckily and finished the game in style.

None of the handicaps could disguise a natural talent. I know manager Matt Busby is looking forward to seeing this Belfast boy in a team with Law, to help him. I agree – it is an exciting prospect that will brighten up the dullest of games.

The game was won 1-0, with the scorer David Sadler, an England amateur at that time who shared digs with Best in Chorlton. The team line-up, with Law out injured, was:

Gregg, Dunne, Cantwell, Crerand, Foulkes, Setters, Best, Stiles, Sadler, Chisnall, Charlton.

Best claims that the lasting impression of the game for him was how easy it had been, and that he was able to go out there and do the same things he had been doing ever since he was a kid. He reckoned it all came so naturally to him, and that is certainly how he came across then, and for that matter, for the rest of his career.

Best recalls meeting Graham Williams at a function a few years after the Albion man had retired and that Graham had said to him that he wanted to look at him face to face. 'He said all he had ever seen of me was my backside and the number on my shirt. Not a hundred per cent true, but a nice compliment from a likeable and talented fellow pro.'

Even though he thought Best had done quite well, Busby, never one to rush a young player, pulled him out of the following league match to make way for the return of Ian Moir, with David Herd taking Best's position at outside-right. Best returned to the Central League reserves and was given permission to go home to Belfast to be with his family over Christmas. There was a dramatic change of plan, though, after United had crashed to a humiliating 6-1 defeat against Burnley at Turf Moor on Boxing Day of 1963. With a return against the same opponents coming up just two days later, and given the animosity between the two clubs after Burnley chairman Bob Lord's 'Teddy Boys' comments, there was a rapid change of plan. A telegram winged its way to the Best home in Belfast instructing him to return to Old Trafford immediately. Best thought he was needed for the reserves, perhaps because of injuries, but his father Dickie reckoned a telegram signified something much more serious, like selection for the first team. They had a bet on it and Dickie won.

Busby dropped his two wingers, Shay Brennan and Albert Quixall, in favour of Willie Anderson and George Best. United got their revenge with a 5-1 win that included a first league goal for Best, with Herd scoring twice and two from Graham Moore. Best and the promoted Anderson rightly held their places for the following match, a third round FA Cup tie, against Southampton at The Dell. I recall interviewing Best on the morning of the match because United, as FA Cup holders, had become a focus for television and the press, and so I asked him if he was nervous or excited by all the fuss for one so young.

'No,' he replied as he shrugged his shoulders and indicated what a daft question it had been. To him, it was just another game of football, with that same ice in his veins that we would see from him in the biggest of games. It's the cool dude approach that always marked him out before matches, standing outside the players' entrance chatting to friends until half an hour before kick-off, while his team-mates would be going through their various pre-match rituals and endeavouring to keep the tension under control.

United won the cup tie with a performance from Best that clinched his place in the team until the end of the season. With Denis Law back to fitness and Bobby Charlton now a fixture in the team, Best's call-up meant that the trinity made its debut together at West Bromwich Albion on 18 January 1964, and they made an immediate impact from then until the end of the season. Charlton made 40 league appearances that season and scored nine goals. Law was in his scoring prime and scored 30 in 30 league games, plus rattling in 16 goals in the Cup. Best finished his first season with

17 appearances and four goals to his name, an excellent start to his senior career.

The famous football litany of Charlton, Law and Best had now come together, though at this stage Best was very much the junior partner, with Law the star. By the end of the season, the three were playing regularly together. It doesn't seem like 50 years ago to me, such were the vivid pictures they began to paint on Old Trafford's receptive canvas.

Busby was still tinkering with the team. He changed goal-keepers at one point, replacing Harry Gregg for a spell with David Gaskell. Halfway through the season, he switched Tony Dunne to left-back in place of Noel Cantwell and brought in Shay Brennan at right-back. Inside-right was causing him problems, with one of his youngsters, Phil Chisnall, dropped in favour of Graham Moore, the Welsh international. David Sadler was in and out, still search-ing for his best position. Nobby Stiles was brought in at left-half to take over from Maurice Setters and give nothing away in terms of matching fire with fire. Ian Moir played half a season on the wing. There had probably been just a few too many changes to get the better of Liverpool, who proved their right to be champions by winning 1-0 at Old Trafford in November and then beating United 3-0 at Anfield on the run-in for the title. Only four points sepa-rated the two teams at the end of the season.

All in all for United, it was a marked improvement on the previous season's 19th position, and they had also fought some sterling battles in the FA Cup, especially against Sunderland in the quarter-final. The fans had enjoyed a spectacular 3-3 game at Old Trafford and then admired a stout 2-2 draw after extra-time at Roker Park. United proved to be the team with the stamina as Sunderland finally collapsed and went down 5-1 in the second replay at Huddersfield.

The semi-final took United to Hillsborough on an exceedingly wet day to meet West Ham and they didn't play well as they slid to a 3-1 defeat. Geoff Hurst scored the decisive third goal after a splendid run down the wing by Bobby Moore. The Hammers' theme tune of 'I'm Forever Blowing Bubbles' had an appropriate twist as the London fans sang their heads off in the rain while United's followers trekked miserably back across the Pennines. The Hillsborough hoodoo – not United's luckiest semi-final venue – had struck again. But there was happier news on the Cup front at youth level as the club gathered momentum again. The kids won the FA Youth Cup after a seven-year gap, heralding the arrival of more promising youngsters.

George Best, Willie Anderson and David Sadler had already played in the first team. Other players from the successful youth team who went on to play in the league side were Jimmy Rimmer, the goalkeeper, full-back Bobby Noble, winger John Aston and wing-half John Fitzpatrick. United were blooming again, especially at youth level, accompanied by imaginative development off the field. Plans were announced for the building of a new cantilever stand in readiness for Old Trafford as a venue for the 1966 World Cup in England. The bulk of the finance was to be raised by a football pool run by a development association on a scale not previously seen in soccer. There was a buzz about the place again, though Busby knew he needed a more settled side than the one which had just chased Liverpool home, and despite his many changes he felt he needed a top-class winger. So during the summer of 1964, he bought the experienced John Connelly from Burnley for £60,000. Equally at home on either flank, Connelly had already won league and FA Cup medals at Turf Moor and it proved to be an inspired signing.

Connelly was the final piece in the jigsaw which turned a team of runners-up into champions. The whole thing fell into place as the Reds swept to success in season 1964-65, pipping Leeds United for the title. In the days when goal average, rather than difference, settled issues, United won by the narrow margin of 0.686 of a goal. The significant aspect was that they were champions for the first time since Munich, with Bobby Charlton and Bill Foulkes the only crash survivors remaining in the team. John Connelly more than played his part, scoring 15 goals from outside-right, while Best dazzled on the left to score ten. Charlton, now operating in a midfield role, scored ten, while Law led the scoring with 28, supported as usual by 20 from Herd. But while the forwards attracted the headlines, they owed a great deal to the defence. Bill Foulkes, the centre-half, and the two full-backs, Shay Brennan and Tony Dunne, were ever-presents. They conceded just 39 goals to help provide their personable new goalkeeper, Pat Dunne, with a championship medal. Pat was to flit quickly across the Old Trafford stage. A modest £10,000 signing from Shamrock Rovers, he spent less than three seasons at United. He seemed to come from nowhere and disappear almost as quickly, but he played his part.

The team's championship qualities had not been immediately apparent when only one win had come in the opening six games, but they soon picked up, dropping only one point in their next 14 games. The highlight was a 7-0 thrashing of Aston Villa at Old Trafford, with four of the goals down to Law. They dropped a few points in mid-season, but put in another searing run of 10 wins in 11 games to take the title. United had an all-round strength now that also saw them do well in other competitions. They were, in fact, chasing a treble for most of the season. They reached the semi-finals of the European Fairs Cup (later the UEFA Cup), and at the same time stormed through to the semi-finals of the FA Cup and an appointment with their deadly rivals from Elland Road. Leeds United were coming to the height of their powers under Don Revie, but not everyone admired their methods. Manchester United had more than an abrasive streak as well, so it was a volatile mix when the two teams met at Hillsborough.

League points had been shared, each side winning 1-0 on their own ground, and the atmosphere for the cup tie was hostile. The match was fierce and bad tempered and could have done with stricter refereeing. There were no goals and the replay was staged at Nottingham Forest's ground. Referee Dick Windle, perhaps conscious of his leniency at Sheffield, tightened up considerably, and the players also held themselves in check better, knowing full well that one or two of them had been fortunate to stay on the field for the full 90 minutes in the first game. But it was still a mess of a match that constantly had to be stopped for fouls. It was reckoned that Manchester United had conceded more than 20 free-kicks in the original game, and almost as many in the replay. They finally paid the penalty for trying to play Leeds at their own game. With less than two minutes to go, they gave away one free-kick too many and their former inside-forward Johnny Giles, who had failed to hit it off with Busby after coming through the juniors, punished them. His cleverly flighted kick into the goalmouth was headed home by Billy Bremner, the Leeds ball of fire. So Leeds went to Wembley, leaving the Reds to contemplate their third semi-final defeat in four years.

The other leg of the treble collapsed as well, with semi-final defeat in the Fairs Cup after a play-off third game against Ferencvaros in Budapest long after the official end to the season. Nevertheless, it had been a mighty year with some memorable games on the three fronts, and they had made their mark with the championship trophy back at Old Trafford. The victorious team that played together most often was: Pat Dunne, Brennan, Tony Dunne, Crerand, Foulkes, Stiles, Connelly, Charlton, Herd, Law, Best. It was a well-balanced strong side built round the trinity, and a clear indication that Busby was winning the fight to get his club back among the honours.

In 1965 Bobby Charlton was at the height of his powers, George Best was starting to fulfil his huge talent, while Denis Law was on fire, more than just grateful to Busby for bringing him home from his nightmare in Italy. As Law said at the time: 'I'm not one for the high life. All I wanted in Italy was to be treated like a human being. It wasn't long before I realised I had made a ghastly mistake. It all finally blew up when Torino refused me permission to play for Scotland. That was the end as far as I was concerned. I stormed out so quickly that I left all my clothes behind. I never saw them again.'

Law soon had other things to think about, and for the next decade the Lawman ruled over his Old Trafford kingdom. The United fans respected the skills of Bobby Charlton, they revelled in the genius of George Best, but they worshipped Denis Law, the hero of the Stretford End. The trinity had arrived and was flying high. Said Law: 'What I walked into from Italy, was the finest football club in the world, with the finest manager. Matt Busby always stuck by me through thick and thin. Your problems at home, your illnesses, any little worries – they were all his business. That's what made him so different. That is why you gave everything for him on the field.'

Not that Law was always the apple of Busby's eye. Three times between 1963 and 1967, his fiery temperament landed him in serious trouble with referees. Twice he was suspended for 28 days, and that is not the kind of record guaranteed to endear you to Busby.

He had a head-on clash with the manager in 1966, when he grandly told the club in a letter that unless he was offered better terms, he would ask for a transfer. Busby refused to be blackmailed, though, even by one of the main jewels in his Old Trafford crown. He called his bluff and transfer-listed him. A few days later, a sheepish Law was paraded at a press conference to make a public apology. Some said that in return for eating humble pie in front of everyone, he duly received better terms.

But the good times outweighed the bad. Law helped the Reds win the league title again in 1967, as well as collecting an FA Cup winners' medal in 1963. He was voted European Footballer of the Year in 1964. Injury forced him to miss playing in the European Cup final, which is perhaps why one of his fondest memories at Old Trafford remains the 1963 FA Cup final against Leicester.

Law: 'It was one of the greatest games I played for United. I can see Paddy Crerand now hitting me with a perfect ball from the left wing. I turned quickly and hit the ball into the net, past Gordon Banks's right hand. It was the first goal, and one I had always dreamed of scoring at Wembley.'

The King was electric near goal. When he jumped he seemed to have a personal skyhook, so long did he hang in the air above defenders. His razor reflexes and courage brought him 171 goals from 305 league appearances in his 10 years at Old Trafford. In the FA Cup, he had a remarkable return of 34 goals in 44 matches, while European competition gave him the even more impressive scoring rate of 28 goals in 33 games. The Stretford End took him to their heart. They loved not just his goals but also the streak of villainy that ran through his game.

The player who knitted the trinity, and indeed the whole team together was undoubtedly Pat Crerand. Sir Matt once said that when Crerand played well, Manchester United played well. He was right, too, and I doubt whether Charlton, Law and Best would have flourished the way they did, if it hadn't been for their play-maker. It wasn't just blind love and admiration on Crerand's part, as he spelt out at the time: 'You can't tell Bobby, Denis or George what to do when the ball is at their feet . . . instinct does that. We had three of the best forwards in the world.

'The first time I saw Denis play, I thought he was the most arrogant so-and-so I had ever seen on a football field. He didn't just act as if it was his ball, but his *stadium*. When someone took the ball from him, he glared at them, as if they had a damn cheek. Even when he scored a goal, he made you wonder if anyone had ever scored a goal before.

'There are two sides to him. There's the Denis Law you see on the field, all gestures and genius. Then there's the Denis Law his public wouldn't even recognise.

'His timing is fantastic. His reflexes on the ground are uncanny. His reading of the game is brilliant. He is the greatest player in the world today. It is his ability to read a game that gives him the edge on others, like Bobby, George, Eusebio and Pele. As well as setting a high standard for himself, he sees every mistake made by others and can recall these in detail when the game is over. He will show his annoyance if you fail to do what he can see is the obvious thing to do with the ball . . . which doesn't make him the easiest bloke to play with.

'Denis, for instance, could be very hard on David Herd. Denis was a world-class player, and he thought that every pass should be perfect. I told him that he had to be a bit lenient. Denis couldn't fathom it, but when David was out of the side for a few games, Denis began to miss him, and he realised the truth of what I'd said.

'The most amazing thing about Denis, of course, is the way he alters the moment he pulls off his jersey, and changes into a lounge suit. Frankly, he's better with kids than adults. He has fantastic patience and can keep them amused for long enough. Basically, he has a great sense of humour, which pops up when you least expect it, like the day when we were playing Burnley at Turf Moor. Priests often come to talk to me before a game. Most of them are keen on football, and I know they are hoping I will introduce them to some of the boys. That day, I was talking to a priest when Denis approached. I grabbed his arm and said, "Father, I would like you to meet Denis Law." Denis stuck out his hand and with a deadpan expression said, "Pleased to meet you, Father. Do you know, you're the five-hundredth priest I've met since Paddy joined United?"

'He would rather have a beer in a quiet pub with some ordinary blokes than mix with celebrities at a cocktail party. In fact, he takes a lot of trouble to avoid the limelight. He makes few public appearances, and would rather have his own privacy than the fees he could pick up.

'While Denis will talk to me about most subjects, there are one or two things that he rarely discusses; for instance, the attitude towards him from Scotland, his own country. Strange as it seems, there was always a certain section of the public and of the press in Scotland that was happy to see Denis left out of a Scottish team. In some way, they seemed to resent the fact that he played all his senior football in England or Italy. He didn't talk about it, but I'm sure it hurt him, because nobody is more passionate about Scotland; and nobody got a bigger kick out of pulling on a dark blue jersey over his head.

'Denis Law, the flamboyant extrovert on the field, bears no resemblance to the family man who leads a very private life away from the game. People didn't realise that he could be nasty on the pitch. He had to be because a lot of defenders believed the only way you could stop great players was to kick them and Denis was not prepared to put up with that!

'Bobby Charlton was equally dedicated to football, his club and his country of course. Football was his life and still is. As a player, he wanted to have the ball all the time because then he was helping the team and this is what mattered most to him.

'He and I were completely different characters. He was quiet. I wasn't. People did and still do think he's dour. He could be, but the public image of Bobby is not the real him. He's not an outgoing man, but he's a nice fella who loves United as much as any fan. He's great for the club, and an accomplished ambassador.

'In his playing days, Bobby was only comfortable with certain people, like Shay Brennan and Nobby Stiles, when he was happy-go-lucky. He was a practical joker but he was easy to get back; all you had to do was deprive him of a cream cake.

'Bobby was an honest player and football was his life. When he had the ball in the pre-match warm up, he was like a kid with a new toy. He never got over the thrill of having the ball at his feet. We had a good understanding in midfield, which came naturally. He was an easy player to play with. He was an artist of a player and looked like a ballerina compared to a clogger like me.

'We did have the occasional problem because we played close to each other, and we both wanted the ball all the time. Such was our desire to get it, we almost fought. We didn't but we'd scowl, and have our own little battle for midfield domination.'

As for George Best, although he'd made his first-team debut, he was, of course, still only 17 and young enough to play in the United Youth team. He missed the early rounds of the FA Youth Cup because of his first-team commitments, but he was brought in for the final. He played in both legs against Swindon Town to win 5-2 on aggregate and claim the 1964 trophy. Best scored in the first leg for a 1-1 draw at Swindon and then watched his house-mate, David Sadler, grab a brilliant hat-trick, which, with a goal from John Aston, gave United a 4-1 win on the night and their first success in the youth competition since the Munich air crash. United had won the competition for five successive seasons from its inception in 1952 and this was a long-awaited return to those halcyon days and a further indication that Busby was getting his grip back.

Sir Alex Ferguson's class of '92 that won the FA Youth Cup was rightly hailed as a triumph, with players like David Beckham, Ryan Giggs, Gary Neville, Nicky Butt and Paul Scholes who went on to form the backbone for both United and England. But the Best era was an important stepping-stone along the way to complete recovery from the Munich calamity, with six players coming through to the first-team squad. Best, David Sadler, John Aston, John Fitzpatrick, Jimmy Rimmer and Bobby Noble all went on to play senior football at Old Trafford with two more, Willie Anderson and Albert Kinsey, also playing for the first team before going on to successful careers with other clubs.

The jewel in the crown of this sparkling surge of youth, though, was undoubtedly George Best, as he drew ever closer to the personal triumphs that played such a big part in creating one of Manchester United's most successful eras. Best was ready for big things, not only for United, but at international level where he was capped for Northern Ireland after only 21 first-team games.

Many aspects of life in Britain were undergoing rapid change as the post-war years swung into the Sixties. Prime Minister Harold Wilson referred to the white heat of the technological revolution as he tried to steer the country into new industries, and professional football had certainly been stuck in a timewarp, positively feudal in its relations between employers and its workers.

Clubs had a stranglehold on players with a maximum wage fixed by the Football League and contracts that limited their opportunities to move and better themselves. But in keeping with society generally, things were changing and in 1961 the Professional Footballers' Association gave notice to strike to end the maximum wage. Three days before the strike notice was due to expire, the Football League backed down. The players, led by PFA chairman Jimmy Hill, had won, and soon afterwards, thanks to George Eastham's challenge in the High Court, the feudal retain and transfer system was overturned as well. Footballers now had freedom of contract, and couldn't be retained indefinitely by clubs simply holding on to their registration.

The changes had been long overdue, but at least the professional game had shown its readiness to cast off the old cloth-cap image and move with the times that, for instance, had seen Harold Wilson establish the Open University to give wider access into higher education. Football was ready to embrace the new liberties on offer in social behaviour, fashion and music. Indeed, in George Best they had a trendsetter who was soon in the thick of the action with his own clothing boutique and nightclub along with a seemingly non-stop parade of lovely ladies from the ranks of Miss England and Miss World.

Bobby Charlton and Denis Law were certainly not among the movers and shakers; they still represented the more old fashioned values that you saw among the Busby Babes in skipper Roger Byrne and the trilby-wearing, pipe-smoking Mark Jones, growing up in the tradition of 'gentleman' Johnny Carey who never seemed complete unless puffing away. Matt Busby himself, an innovator in terms of the game's technical know-how, came from the generation whose principles had been formed as a pre-war player and as a soldier during the war. He helped change football in so many ways but he could also be old fashioned. He used to tell his players: 'Don't go chasing the money, because if you are good enough the money will find you.' To a certain degree, it did, but that's hardly the philosophy of today's agents and millionaire footballers who make grotesque fortunes with the help of the money poured into the game by television.

That's another story, though, and while I'm sure the trinity would not plead poverty, they played too soon to reap the riches of today's game. What's not in doubt, is that they played their part in the advancement of football because they were highly talented; they excited people, they entertained them, and they were in the vanguard of those who took the game to a new and higher level.

6

Jimmy and Bobby

Looking for players and developing the youngsters in the reserves was Jimmy Murphy's special responsibility and, because he was the key element in the emergence of Bobby Charlton and the Busby Babes, when the Munich crash occurred it hit him hard. As far as he was concerned, they were his boys, and of course he had watched these little acorns grow. Ever the optimist, he also used to insist that the sun was always shining . . . and if you protested, and said you couldn't see it, he would reply that it would still be shining, even if it was behind the clouds! That was his philosophy, though even Murphy must have wondered, in the aftermath of Munich, whether the sunshine would ever return to warm his soul.

Although he spent his career as an assistant, a role that suited his partnership with Sir Matt, he didn't hesitate when the call came after the devastation of Munich to step up to the plate and lead from the front. He proved the saviour of Manchester United.

Some would say that being a right-hand man, without the ultimate responsibility, suited him better than being the number one. The aftermath of Munich suggested otherwise, but as John Charles, the great Welsh international who was one of the first to join the foreign legion abroad to play for Juventus, discovered, Jimmy Murphy had a loyalty and dedication to Manchester United that contributed so much to establishing Old Trafford as a special place, a club with family values where people wanted to play.

Juventus in particular had been impressed by the way he had held Old Trafford together during the chaos that followed the disaster and while Matt Busby was battling for his life in hospital. The Italians had also admired the way that as the manager of Wales he had taken the mixed bag of players who made up his Welsh team to the quarter-finals of the 1958 World Cup in Sweden. Juventus used John Charles as their intermediary and authorised him to offer Murphy £20,000 on their behalf to become their manager. Charles, talking about his attempt to lure Murphy to Italy, says: 'He was being offered what was a fortune in those days, but he wasn't interested and turned Juventus down.' Murphy explained to him: 'I have got to help Matt pick up the pieces and start all over again; we have to rebuild after losing ten players at Munich. Besides, John, how can you put a price on loyalty?'

So Jimmy Murphy stayed with United for the rest of his career, even turning down an offer to manage Arsenal. It took years before the club fully acknowledged his role in United's history, with a bust of the man unveiled at the North Stand where I met up with Keith Dewhurst, who was the *Evening Chronicle*'s United reporter immediately after the crash, before going on to write *Z-Cars* scripts for television, and is still writing plays and books. Dewhurst became particularly friendly with Murphy in those difficult days and straightaway realised the enormous work he did behind the scenes and on the training pitch. As he wrote in his book, *When you Put on a Red Shirt*: 'Look at what he did with Bobby Charlton, repeating again and again his instruction: "Just hit the ball. Don't look up for the ball. Just hit it." He would roll balls from different angles for Bobby to hit again and again, until the action became instinctive and turned him into the most spectacular sharpshooter of his day, the goal against Mexico being a classic instance.

'He also had Wilf McGuinness banging a ball against the perimeter wall first touch with alternate feet . . . The energy of this, the determination, the willingness to impose and re-impose one's personality in the pursuit of small faults and of making another person perfect, is extraordinary. It is the energy that was poured out, week after week, year after year; the energy that after Munich he never quite recovered; the energy that was barely acknowledged in public but was taken for granted and then forgotten in the myth that Matt allowed to grow around himself.'

The relationship between Busby and Murphy fascinated Dewhurst at the time, and he has long wondered whether Busby could have delivered the goods on the field without Murphy. Probably not, he concludes. Could Murphy have done what he did without the protection of a Busby figure? Again, almost certainly not. For Murphy to have managed Wales in short-term bursts was one thing; to have coached in detail as he did, and at the same time undergone the day-to-day stresses of club management, would have been quite another, and probably impossible for anyone.

The partnership was in fact a dream ticket that worked well for the club generally, and certainly for the players like the trinity who cut their teeth in a superb academy, long before the term was introduced to football.

Bobby Charlton, of course, went on to become a distinguished international, a United director, a man of influence and a senior figure in football, knighted and admired by people ranging from football fans to others, like the late Sir Alf Ramsey, England's World Cup winning manager, who said: 'Bobby's probably the best known footballer in the world. He has been a wonderful ambassador for England, not only as a footballer but also in the way in which he has upheld the prestige of his country in every possible sense. He also introduced so much thought and consideration into his game. I mean consideration to the team and those around him.'

I certainly agree with Sir Alf's reference to Bobby's world renown which was born out for me when I travelled with United to a European Cup game against the East German army team Vorwaerts in 1965. This involved flying to West Berlin and then finishing the journey by coach through 'Checkpoint Charlie' to the rather forbidding East Berlin. We were naturally held up at the checkpoint where unsmiling soldiers checked the bus and inspected all the passports and crossing papers. It seemed to be taking a long time, a situation not helped by one of our number filling in his form as '007' and signing it as 'James Bond'. Stern faces grew sterner until the border guards checking the coach suddenly caught sight of Bobby Charlton. Suddenly, it was all smiles as the guards dashed for pieces of paper to get his autograph and take photographs. From then on, we were quickly waved through, all thanks to our popular global ambassador.

Michael Parkinson, the television chat show king and presenter, as well as one-time sportswriter, had a similar experience: 'I was once in the Arctic Circle making a documentary when a peasant guarding a herd of reindeer approached and said: "Manchester United, Bobby Charlton number one."'

The players' view of their long-serving team-mate was probably best summed up by Pat Crerand when he said: 'Bobby has artistry. Even when he was having a bad game he would still come looking for the ball, a one hundred per cent honest player. Football is his life.'

In the stress of actual combat, all is not necessarily sweetness and light, but Wilf McGuinness makes the point that there was no resentment among the stars. He recalled: 'I remember Bobby shouting at me to call for the ball when the goalkeeper was looking to throw the ball to a team-mate. I responded by shouting back: "No, you call for the ball, because if I get it and lose it we are in trouble, whereas if you lose it, I'm behind you and can stop them."'

Charlton, as the years went by, became an elder statesman in the dressing room, which was perhaps slightly daunting for the younger players. As his team-mate David Sadler explained to me: 'Bobby was the popular hero when I arrived, the golden boy of English football. He had been through Munich and come out the other side, and I can't even begin to imagine how he felt.

'People wondered whether he should play at inside-forward, centre-forward or outside-left. There was confusion because he could do all those things so magnificently. He had terrific pace, great ability to beat people, he could hit crosses from anywhere, and he could shoot with power and accuracy. So where best to play him?

'Eventually he became a central midfielder. With the emergence of George Best wide, and with John Connelly, Denis Law and David Herd up front, there was a need for someone in the middle to hit passes. Maybe it was not a conscious decision to move him there; it might have just evolved through team needs.

'Perhaps he was rather wasted when he played wide, in that

he didn't get enough of the ball. Our idea was to get the ball and give it to the top players. The longer that Bobby, Paddy, George and Denis spent in possession, the more damage we were likely to do.

'But everywhere Bobby played in an attacking situation, he would come up trumps. For example, he was a far better header of the ball than he was given credit for. People talk of his aerial work as a weakness, but it simply wasn't the case. There were some great headed goals early in his career, and, of course, the one he glanced in – from a David Sadler cross, it has to be said – to open the scoring in the 1968 European Cup final.

'Mind you, he was not a great defender, although he was extremely industrious. Perversely, though, that very industry could cause problems. Bobby played in an almost innocent, naive sort of way. He wanted to be wherever the ball was, almost like a lad in the playground. Quite often as a defender, you would be lulled into complacency because you'd see Bobby on the right side of an opponent and think he was covered. But the next moment, Bobby might be gone, attracted by the ball. After a while, you'd get used to it and not take anything for granted.

'Nobby Stiles and Bobby were perfect together in this way. Nobby would never, ever accept that in a dangerous situation Bobby had things covered. That said, while Bobby would have poor games, like everyone else, you could never lay down lack of commitment or effort as a reason for it.

'Without question, Bobby Charlton was an all-time great. There has never been a better ambassador for Manchester United and England. He sits on a pedestal alongside the likes of Pele and Beckenbauer, which speaks volumes of his continuing stature in the game.

'As a player he was totally instinctive, going where the game and the ball led him. There was a natural grace and ease about everything he did. He was gifted with exceptional talents: he could hit passes that nobody else could hit, he had the vision to know where and when to deliver them, the ability to score fantastic goals with either foot and with his head. Bobby could beat players on either the left or the right, however he wanted. He didn't carry the ball as close to his feet as George Best; he wasn't a dribbler in the accepted sense. Instead, he flowed along at high speed, and it was incredible to watch him. He provided a spectacle.

'Off the field, Bobby was mature, a senior player when I arrived. As a result, I was a bit in awe of him and, inadvertently, he gave the impression that he was not approachable. People are different. Paddy Crerand, for instance, exudes "come and talk to me" the moment he walks into any room, but you don't get that from Bobby.

'So it can take a while to get to know him and be accepted by him. But once you get beyond that, he's got a terrific sense of humour and is great fun with people he trusts. After football, I worked for him when he was manager of Preston North End, and then in his football schools company. He is a true friend and I have untold admiration for all he's achieved.'

Personally, of all the goals Charlton scored, I treasure the memory of the one in the FA Charity Shield against Spurs in 1967 as he wellied in a pass squared to him by Brian Kidd. Right to the end of his days as a player, he didn't lose either the readiness or the strength of his shooting. His team-mates, Law and Best, also scored freely but the beauty of the trinity was that they each had their own approach and trademark goals, as we will see later.

One of Charlton's greatest admirers was undoubtedly the late Geoffrey Green, the eminent sportswriter of *The Times* newspaper, whose daughter Ti has Bobby Charlton for her godfather.

Geoffrey, a delightful man, described by Charlton as the foot-baller's favourite journalist and friend, once wrote of him: 'It was the explosive facets of his play that will stay fresh in memory. His thinning hair streaming in the wind, he moved like a ship in full sail. He always possessed an elemental quality; jinking, changing feet and direction, turning gracefully on the ball, or accelerating through a gap surrendered by a confused enemy, he could be gone like the wind.'

But at this stage of their story, great and popular though Charlton and Law were in the eyes of the fans, it was really George Best putting the magic into Manchester United. David Sadler knew Best better than most. He told me: 'There was nothing com-plicated about George, certainly not in the early years. All he wanted to do was to play football. He and I were very much of an age, although by the time I arrived he had been to Manchester, returned homesick to Ireland and then come back to Old Trafford. We signed as professionals at about the same time and became pals, eventually sharing digs for about six years and rooming together when we travelled.

'We were both part of a successful United youth team, and in 1964 we won the club's first FA Youth Cup since pre-Munich days. Although I made my senior debut ahead of George, I was in and out for some years, but once George stepped up he was on an esca-lator to the skies.

'The minute you started playing with him, even in a kick-around, it was blatantly obvious to everybody that he was special, and nothing was ever a surprise afterwards. He was born to play football.

'Nominally he was a winger, but he enjoyed a free role and just played the game. He was never restricted to supplying crosses or hugging the touchline – that would have been foolish. My main thought when playing was: "Let's get the bloody ball to him as quickly as we can, because that's the most likely way that we're going to earn a bonus!"

'George's greatest strength was that he didn't have a weakness. Bobby Charlton, for instance, was a great player but not a good tackler. George was. In fact, there was a time when he could have played anywhere in the team and been the best in that position. It sounds incredible, but by the middle to late Sixties, he could do everything better than everybody else.

'He could tackle and defend as well as anyone; he was instinctive but understood the technical aspects of the game; he could shoot and beat people, and he knew when to pass (usually!). True, some people thought he was greedy on occasions, but as he matured everything fell into place.

'When you make your debut, the best you can hope is that you fit in and do your bit, that you don't let the team down. George did that from the word go. There was never the slightest doubt that he was worth his place.

'Whatever is said about George Best, I am certain of one thing – he was the greatest footballer I ever played with or against.'

Best could certainly bewitch people, opponents as well as admirers, but there was only one king of Old Trafford, and that of course was Denis Law. The Lawman was the people's champion because he brought together flair and fire. He was slightly built, but there was venom in his play that made him a hero and which at times could bring him into confrontation with opponents as well as referees.

It all added to his status, though, and his followers certainly liked the streak of villainy which ran through his football and which saw him serve two lengthy six-week suspensions in the course of his career. The fans loved his willingness to fly into the thick of the action. He was daring, cocky, impudent and abrasive, which together with his lightning quick football, his perception for being in the right place at the right time, and his prolific goal scoring, was an explosive mix.

Law flourished in front of goal, where his scoring rate made him the most deadly marksman of all the famous players to perform on the Old Trafford stage. The terrace fans would rise to Law signalling yet another goal as to a gladiator of old. His strike rate was phenomenal in league, FA Cup and Europe. He scored 171 goals from 305 league games, 34 FA Cup goals in 44 appearances and 28 goals in 33 European Cup ties. Sir Bobby Charlton scored a record 198 times but it took him 604 games to do it, while for all his magic, George Best had a ratio of 137 goals from 361 appearances. David Herd hit 144 goals in 263 appearances, which was impressive, but nobody could quite touch the Lawman in terms of the ratio of goals per game.

Ruud van Nistelrooy was rapidly closing in on Law before his departure from Old Trafford and had already matched his European total by scoring 28 goals and, significantly, done it in four fewer games. Van Nistelrooy's league strike rate was also impressive, with 81 appearances yielding a superb 62 goals, but he still had some way to go before reaching Law's career tally.

United had emerged from the dark days of Munich and a recrafting of the first team to become a great club again, thanks to the trinity but also, in no small measure, to a supporting cast of players who were stars in their own right.

7

The Supporting Act

Although Charlton, Law and Best were iconic players during this successful period of the mid- to late-Sixties, United were by no means a three-man team. There was a balance to the side that Sir Matt Busby had created. One of the newcomers was goalkeeper Alex Stepney. I remember asking Sir Matt what had been the key factor in their 1967 championship success, and he replied without hesitation: 'Signing Alex Stepney. I only saw him play once for Millwall but it was enough. I kept the picture at the back of my mind so that when I decided we needed a new goalkeeper, I knew he was the man. He was the final piece in the jigsaw.'

The London-born Stepney had started his career in the amateur ranks of Tooting & Mitcham before being snapped up by Millwall, whom he helped get promotion to the Second Division. Despite being out of the top flight, Stepney's talent stood out and he was called up for three England Under-23 appearances. He also caught the attention of Tommy Docherty, then manager of Chelsea, who signed him for a record fee for a goalkeeper of £50,000. After a brief four months at Stamford Bridge, in which Stepney made just one league appearance – the Doc had signed him as insurance cover for an unsettled Peter Bonetti but then Bonetti made up his mind to stay – Busby brought him to United and put him straight into the team in mid-September to succeed Harry Gregg and David Gaskell, and watched United race away with the 1966-67 title. In the following year's landmark European Cup campaign, Stepney's presence in goal proved vital, especially when he pulled off a remarkable save against Eusebio in the final against Benfica. As Sir Matt said: 'I thought as Eusebio raced towards him, that all my dreams of winning the European Cup were going to be shattered. He shot with all his power but Alex held it.' In 12 seasons at Old Trafford Stepney made 433 league appearances and played in another hundred cup games. He also achieved the rare distinction for a goalkeeper of scoring two league goals, both from penalties.

In front of Stepney in those days, Busby had two speedy attack-minded full-backs in Shay Brennan and Tony Dunne to complement a particularly rugged and effective central defence of Bill Foulkes and Nobby Stiles. Brennan, one of the most popular players in the dressing room, was a particular pal of Bobby Charlton, and always used to claim that he made the goal that won the European Cup. He would acknowledge that Best was the scorer two minutes into extra-time, and if pushed, would concede that it wasn't a bad goal. In fact, as we all know, it was brilliant, but Brennan preferred to dwell on the build-up. With tongue firmly in his cheek he would say: 'I got this ball and knocked it back to our goalkeeper. Alex Stepney kicked it down the field, Brian Kidd headed it on and Bestie raced away to score. But I started the move, and if I hadn't laid back that pass to Alex Stepney we wouldn't have scored ... would we?'

That was Shay Brennan, a man with a bubbling, infectious sense of humour, but essentially he was a modest, retiring soul who did his best to avoid publicity. However, in the dark days immediately after Munich, from being an unknown junior in the reserves Brennan was suddenly thrust into the senior side as Jimmy Murphy desperately put a team together to replace the Busby Babes. Having been a forward in the team which had won the FA Youth Cup in 1955, Brennan was played at outside-left in the patched-up side that met Sheffield Wednesday in the fifth round of the FA Cup at Old Trafford in the club's first game after the Munich crash. He scored twice in a remarkable 3-0 win and stayed in the team for his league debut against Nottingham Forest three days later. Although he had lost his place for the FA Cup final at the end of the Munich season as more senior players recovered from their injuries to start playing again, he shared in the success of the Sixties by winning two league championship medals and playing in the historic European Cup final victory as a right-back. In all, he made over 360 first-team appearances for United and won 19 caps for the Republic of Ireland. He was always happy to play a supporting role from his right-back position: nothing too fancy, nothing too risky, with an acceptance that there were more skilful players in the team like the trinity better suited to create the magic.

His full-back partner, Tony Dunne, was also a quiet man in the pecking order, though not so happy always being cast as a lesser light playing a supporting role. Dunne was certainly not a headline hunter, he just got on with his job. He was so efficient that he rarely stood out. He was hardly ever injured, even more rarely booked and hardly ever scored. He just didn't attract attention to himself, yet in terms of a player's contribution to the cause of Manchester United, few have a better record. He made over 400 league appearances, played in 54 FA Cup ties and appeared in 40 European ties during one of the club's most successful eras.

A lack of recognition certainly used to rankle with Dunne. I remember on a pre-season tour on the continent catching him staring at a poster in our hotel advertising a forthcoming match. In big letters it said: 'Manchester United with Bobby Charlton, Denis Law, George Best etc.' He turned and said: 'It's nice to be on the poster,' to which I said I couldn't see his name. He replied: 'Yes, there I am ... Etc Dunne. Nice name, isn't it?' He had a point, because second billing was invariably his lot. Yet once you broke through the reserve, he invariably had much to say for himself. The Irish FA certainly thought so when he was part of a deputation that went over to Dublin to campaign for the appointment of a manager rather than relying on a committee to select and run the team. As he told me at the time: 'We want Irish football to be taken seriously.'

Dunne was also a trailblazer in the development of full-back play. For years, the traditional backs had been strapping guys with often more strength than finesse. Even his predecessor, Noel Cantwell, was a well-built man, but with the arrival of Tony Dunne came a new breed of defender: small, wiry and exceedingly fast.

He credits Jimmy Armfield for the emergence of what he described as 'little people' for the full-back position. 'Jimmy was not exactly small, but he was no giant and he was certainly fast. He used his pace as part of his defence and also in the modern style to get forward down the flank to link up with the attack. He did this for England and was one of the first to be noticed, because he took his style of play into the spotlight. I think he influenced a lot of managers.'

Bill Foulkes, at the heart of the defence, was never regarded as a pedigree footballer but Sir Matt picked him for a then record 556 league appearances, and the great man wouldn't have done that if he'd had the slightest doubt about his reliability and consistency. Foulkes, hard as nails, often used to greet me with what he considered to be a playful punch on the arm. He didn't know his own strength and I usually had a battle to stop my eyes from watering. Big Bill was the rock on which Sir Matt built the recovery of Manchester United after the Munich disaster. He was the symbol of the rebuilding because he had been in the crash himself. He emerged somewhat traumatised but physically without a scratch, and along with Harry Gregg, carried on playing for the club.

Other survivors joined in later in the season but Foulkes was there at the start to become a key player in the dramatic struggle to keep Manchester United going. He and Gregg were the foundation blocks for a recovery which was so incredible that Sir Matt Busby was able to return and create another outstanding team.

Foulkes bridged the gap from the Busby Babes destroyed at Munich and through the rebuilding years to complete the circle and enjoy the European triumph of 1968. As he told me at the time: 'I had come the whole way with the boss trying to make Manchester United the champions of Europe. I thought the destruction of our team at Munich would have been the end of it, but he patiently put together another side. I'm proud to have been a part of it, and for those of us who lost our friends coming home from a European tie in 1958, our victory seemed the right tribute to their memory.'

Perhaps it helped that Foulkes came from sturdy stock, his father a miner at St Helens as well as playing rugby league for the town team. Foulkes Jnr also worked down the mine and was recruited playing for Whiston Boys Club at the age of 17, though only as a part-timer. Two years of national service delayed his career, but eventually he made a debut against Liverpool and went on to set his appearance record, until overtaken by Bobby Charlton. He scored only nine goals in his United career, but one of them was against Real Madrid in Spain to win the 1968 European Cup semi-final on aggregate and put United through to the final and ultimate glory.

David Herd played very much in the shadow of the trinity, the workhorse of the attack who never received the acclaim he should have done. Goals always came naturally to Herd, who had the distinction as a 15-year-old of playing in the same Stockport County side as his 39-year-old father, Alex Herd, who in turn had played in the same Manchester City team as Matt Busby. After five years at Edgeley Park, Herd moved to Arsenal for £8,000 where he spent six years, before Sir Matt paid £35,000 to bring him to Old Trafford in the summer of 1961. He was bought to replace Dennis Viollet as the process of rebuilding at United continued, and the new striker obliged by becoming top scorer that season with 14 league goals. Although Denis Law arrived a year later, Herd still reeled off seasonal goals totals of 19, 20, 20 and 24 before breaking his leg the following season. Team-mate Pat Crerand says: 'David Herd was one of the most under-rated players ever to play for Manchester United.'

Herd was one of a select band of strikers who averaged better than a goal every two games. In all competitions for United he scored 144 goals in 263 appearances. Two he will remember especially came in United's 3-1 FA Cup final victory against Leicester City in 1963, and he went on to become an important player in the championship successes of 1965 and 1967. His broken leg in

March 1967 saw him fade from the picture before the European Cup success of '68, and it was perhaps typical that his injury happened in the act of scoring, as he hit one of the goals in a 5-2 league win against Leicester. Always a tremendously hard hitter of the ball, he dispatched the shot with his usual venom only to catch the boot of Graham Cross as his opponent came sliding in. You could see his foot hanging at an angle and his United career was as good as over.

Another of the supporting acts working in the shadows for the big three was undoubtedly David Sadler. Such was his athleticism and intelligence in his playing days that he was equally comfortable playing in either attack or defence, or indeed anywhere in between. Allied to an equable temperament and loyalty to his club, he took his shifting positions without complaint to prove himself a truly versatile player, though one wonders whether he might have achieved more than his four full England caps had he specialised in the defensive centre-back role which did not become his regular position until relatively late in his career.

Sadler first came to the fore as a centre-forward with his local side, Maidstone United, when he was so outstanding that he played for the England amateur team at the age of 16. He was a much sought after youngster and Matt Busby turned on all his charm to bring him far from home to Old Trafford, where he played as an amateur for his first three months. Still a forward, he scored a hat-trick in the final of the FA Youth Cup against Swindon in a team which also featured George Best, his fellow lodger in digs with Mrs Fullaway in Chorlton-cum-Hardy.

He soon made his first-team debut, replacing David Herd for a spell and then filling in for other forwards, so that he made 19 league appearances and scored five goals in his first full season of 1963-64. He had a quiet couple of years, but then with the help of the versatility that saw him filling a number of roles, he became an integral part of the team that won the 1967 championship and the European Cup the following year. As a forward, at first he didn't like the idea of playing in midfield and defence, and as he explained at the time: 'I didn't want to become a "basher" which playing centre-half can sometimes make you, but at the same time I wasn't unduly worried because at least I was playing in the first team.

'I became a jack-of-all-trades and in our league championship success I played in three different positions. The following season saw me in five different shirt numbers,' he said.

Eventually, after an injury to Nobby Stiles, he settled into what he describes as his best position, playing in defence alongside the centre-half. He played right through the successful European Cup campaign of 1968 and stood in at different times for Bill Foulkes, Stiles and Denis Law on the way to the final. Looking back, he says with typical modesty: 'There is something very special about belonging to the elite eleven Manchester United players who won the European Cup all those years ago, but it is time to hand some of the European glory from the days of Sir Matt Busby over to Sir Alex Ferguson's team.'

In his early days, rather like Tony Dunne, he admits to being irked by his role as a support act for the superstars. 'After my initial breakthrough, for several years I would come in and play when the likes of Denis Law or David Herd were not available. The Lawman spent a lot of time in the treatment room, but in the days before a match, Sir Matt would never state that Denis was not going to be fit. If there was a doubt, it was always left until as late as possible before making a decision.

'After all, if you said at the start of the week that Law was out, then you could take some off the crowd. Matt wouldn't miss a trick. Quite often I wouldn't know until a couple of hours before a game that Denis had failed a fitness test. So, as we walked out on to the pitch they would announce that Sadler was replacing Law, and believe me, it was hardly a great welcome to walk out to some sixty thousand people booing because I had replaced their hero.

'Not that I could blame them – I would have booed too,' he explained.

Alan Gowling also suffered from unflattering comparisons when he was trying to break into the United team. 'Whenever I got a chance in the first team, it was in place of one of the crowd's favourites like Denis Law, the King, or Brian Kidd, another hero on the terraces. It was hard work getting myself accepted,' he told me. His team-mates used to call him 'Bamber' with reference to Bamber Gascoigne, host of BBC TV's *University Challenge*, because he had gone to Manchester University and come out with an economics degree. I nicknamed him in one of my reports for the *Evening News* 'The Galloping Chip' with reference to his rather tall, gangling physique and loping run. I don't expect he felt flattered at the time, but now he laughs about it and perhaps feels all the more gratified that he achieved so much despite lacking the grace of Bobby Charlton, the dancing feet of Best and the whiplash reactions of Law. He was certainly a hero when he followed up a fine game against Spurs in 1970 by scoring four goals in a 5-1 win against Southampton, including a hat-trick in eight minutes. Big John McGrath, the Saints' centre-half, gave him a right battering and said afterwards: 'The lad is certainly brave!'

Gowling was perhaps a player who suffered from comparisons with the mighty trinity, but when he moved to Newcastle United in 1972, after six years at United, he went on to outscore and out-shine the Geordie hero, Malcolm 'Supermac' Macdonald.

Sir Matt always liked wingers and he persevered with John Aston Jnr, the son of John Aston, one of the full-backs in his 1948 FA Cup winning team and later a club coach as well as scout, for longer than some would have done. But his faith was well rewarded in the final of the European Cup when young Aston turned on so much style and pace against Adolfo, the luckless Benfica right-back, that in many people's eyes he was man of the match. It was certainly a rewarding experience for Aston because not all the fans appreciated his style and at times had not been slow to express their displeasure. His problem was that he was playing in an attack featuring three European Footballers of the Year. Who wouldn't look a little ordinary at times in comparison with Charlton, Law and Best? As he says himself: 'For me, it was a bit like being a work-horse alongside thoroughbreds. It did get to me and at times I had tremendous problems with the crowd.'

On the occasion of the final though, everything came right just when it mattered most and he says now: 'It is one of the few things in my life that never diminishes with time. I remember the George Best goal, a great Alex Stepney save and I can remember playing well. But they were all very secondary to what it all meant. It was Matt Busby's and Manchester United's greatest night. That's what makes me very proud.'

His other memory is more personal. 'We wore blue in the European final, and blue is a good colour for the Astons. My dad wore a blue shirt when he won an FA Cup medal with United in 1948,' he explained. All quite humble words, but then that is typical of a modest and unassuming man whose career at Old Trafford was set back by a broken leg the season after the European success, and in 1972 he was transferred to Luton, later playing for Mansfield and Blackburn. More recently, he's been pleased with United's success in the Champions League, and perhaps the massive time gap of 31 years between his team and the Treble-winning side points up the merit of his own big day. As he tellingly puts it: 'People look at me now, a bald-headed man with a beard, and it reminds them just how long it is since we were European champions. It was about time.'

The other rather junior member of the 1968 European Cup-winning team, in fact the babe of the side, was Brian Kidd, home grown and later to play an important role in the development of the club under Sir Alex Ferguson. Kidd joined United as a youngster from St Pats, the famous football school in Collyhurst which also launched Nobby Stiles, and Sir Matt Busby gave him his head after a tour of Australia. A strong, well-built striker, he scored United's third goal in the 1968 European Cup final against Benfica. There can surely be few better ways of celebrating your 19th birthday.

Yet it always seemed to me that the hero-worship of the famous trinity sat uneasily with Kidd, who once told me as we travelled to a match on the team bus: 'It seems there is one set of rules for certain players and another set for the rest of us.' I have no doubt he had George Best in mind, as United tried desperately to keep the Irishman on side and pandered to his moods in an effort to keep him in a red shirt.

As a still young player, Kidd seemed to become overwhelmed by the managerial strife that followed Sir Matt's retirement, and Tommy Docherty sold him to Arsenal for £110,000 following relegation for United in 1974. His career picked up again and he figured in three more big-money transfers to Manchester City, Everton and Bolton. He played for a number of teams in the States before management took him to Barrow, Swindon and Preston. He seemed to be going nowhere significant, however, and he returned to Old Trafford to work in community football. That led him into youth development with the club itself and a key role when Sir Alex Ferguson decided to revamp the scouting and coaching setup.

United were lagging behind Manchester City in the youth stakes, but Kidd worked hard and used his local knowledge to lay the foundations for the sudden rush of talent, which would later supply half the United and England teams in the shape of David Beckham, Gary Neville, Paul Scholes, Nicky Butt, plus a few more including Ryan Giggs. When assistant manager Archie Knox suddenly upped sticks and went back to Scotland to join Rangers as coach, Brian found himself asked to take over. He began to take the first-team coaching sessions and by the time of the 1991 European Cup Winners' Cup final against Barcelona in Rotterdam everything was functioning smoothly again.

Ferguson officially appointed him assistant manager and coach, and said: 'It was a big shock when Archie decided to leave, but I reached the conclusion that Brian Kidd would grow into the job. He had done a fantastic job for me signing local schoolboys and I thought he could handle senior coaching. He was a big player himself which helps win the respect of senior players. His training routines were always excellent and he played a key part in our championship successes.'

He certainly enjoyed the respect of one very senior star who said: 'What a joy it is to train under him. There is more than quality in what he does. There is love,' declared Eric Cantona.

In the year 2000, after flirting with the possibility of becoming Manchester City's manager, Kidd left Old Trafford to manage Blackburn Rovers only to quit after relegation. He came back into football as youth coach at Leeds, later promoted by David O'Leary to coach the first team, and then after beating prostate cancer became an assistant to Roberto Mancini at Manchester City. He survived the cull that came with the departure of Mancini and now assists new manager Manuel Pellegrini at the Etihad.

Important though the megastars were, the trinity never regarded themselves as untouchables and all three would certainly be happy to pay tribute to the contribution Nobby Stiles made to their team. Stiles danced his way into the hearts of football fans everywhere when he celebrated England's World Cup victory over Germany at Wembley in 1966. With his socks round his ankles and an ear-splitting grin revealing the absence of front teeth, the Manchester United man jigged joyfully round the pitch into the affections of people who knew they had just seen a footballer who had played his heart out for his country.

While never the most elegant of performers, it was the only way Stiles knew how to play, and coupled with his outstanding ability to read the game, he was a key member of United's defence through the successful Sixties. Sir Matt valued him enormously, and so did Sir Alf Ramsey who consistently selected him to knit together the more sophisticated talents of his World Cup winning team, just as he did for United. Ramsey played him just in front of his central defenders, Bobby Moore and Jack Charlton, whereas Busby had him mostly alongside Bill Foulkes. In both roles, he was a ball winner and the provider of the simple pass, always showing an uncanny knack for spotting an attacking threat. Of course, he snapped at a few heels to do it and undoubtedly had a fierce tackle, though Bobby Charlton always used to insist that some of his mistimed efforts were down to poor eyesight. 'He didn't tackle people so much as just bump into them,' said Charlton. Matters improved after Stiles discovered contact lenses.

Stiles played first-team football at Old Trafford for 11 seasons after joining as a young apprentice and making his debut at the age of 18. He played nearly 400 games before suffering the effects of two cartilage operations, which brought his United career to an end at the age of 27. He was far from finished though, and he went to Middlesbrough for £20,000. Unlike the hostile reception accorded to most players returning to their old clubs, there were welcoming banners for him when he arrived back at Old Trafford and he was given the warmest of welcomes, still as popular as ever. He moved on to Preston from Middlesbrough where he was successively player, coach and manager. He also coached in Canada and at West Bromwich before Sir Alex Ferguson brought him back to Old Trafford as a junior youth coach.

It's strange how so many players from the Sixties era have settled in the Manchester area, as if their ties with Old Trafford had become too strong to break, and it's their era that has supplied the leading lights in the club's old boys' club. Pat Crerand, for instance, is a passionate Scot who played for Celtic, but today he lives in Sale and has even closer links with Old Trafford as a full-time pundit for Manchester United TV, travelling all over to commentate at matches, and not just for the first team. He is intense with his feelings about United and if the trinity was ever to become a quartet Pat would be the best qualified to be next up on the pedestal. For this was the man who made the trinity tick; the man who became the heartbeat of the European Cup team.

Despite signing Denis Law, Busby knew there was still something missing. He needed more creative ability in midfield, and so he raided Celtic in February 1963 to bring Paddy Crerand to Old Trafford. The attack, featuring David Herd and Denis Law, had looked full of potential but had failed to provide a consistent scoring level. Busby decided that he needed to improve the service to the front men. It was one of his shrewdest decisions. With the arrival of Crerand, he now had the right balance in the half-back line with Maurice Setters, the ball-winner, on one flank and

Crerand, a player of vision, on the other side who could pass the right kind of ammunition for Law and Herd to fire home.

Crerand arrived too late in his first season to do much about United's league position. Indeed, he struggled to fit in at first, but in the FA Cup that season there developed a pattern and a glimpse of better days ahead. United got through every round without needing a replay and after beating Southampton 1-0 at Villa Park in the semi-final they faced Leicester City in the final. Leicester, doing well in the league, were clear favourites, and were expected to swamp a team heading for a finishing place of 19th in the table.

It was the match which saw Crerand come into his own. He destroyed the Leicester midfield in a link-up with Law, which was a firm indication of things to come. It was a perfect pass from Crerand which saw Law score the first goal, with Herd going on to score twice for a 3-1 victory. Manchester United and Pat Crerand were on their way, as they visibly showed the following season by finishing runners-up in the First Division and reaching the FA Cup semi-finals again. The next three seasons brought United two championships and the European Cup, with Crerand at the heart of their super side of the Sixties.

It was sometimes said that Crerand was slow, and a favourite jibe from after-dinner speakers these days is that he had two speeds: slow and stop. But the remark doesn't do justice to his superbly creative skills. The Scot also had his fiery moments. He wasn't a hatchet man, but if fouled, his retribution tended to be dramatic and swift. He once escaped a ban for fighting with an opponent, on the grounds that he had only struck him once and that hardly constituted fighting; what was not mentioned was that nothing more was ever really needed.

After a brief spell as assistant manager to Tommy Docherty at Old Trafford and a few other coaching posts at the end of his playing career, including managing Northampton, Crerand remains an ardent United fan whose passion for the team now spills out of our television screens.

As the Sixties gathered pace, Bobby Charlton and Denis Law were proving the driving force for United. In fact, the trinity was prospering as a unit, and it was George Best moving more and more to centre stage.

8

El Beatle

Season 1964-65 was a key period in the development and emergence of the trinity as a major force in football as the big three refined their roles in a tactical reshaping of the team. Prior to George Best winning a regular place in the side, Bobby Charlton had played for three years on the left wing. He didn't particularly like being out wide because he felt he didn't see enough of the ball, but Matt Busby had been short of a first-class winger and also felt that Charlton at that point lacked the positional sense to run a game from midfield. He persevered and felt his plan worked because Charlton was still able to maintain his high scoring rate. But when Best arrived in the team, the obvious place for him was on the wing, though with a freedom to roam to capitalise on his genius to throw the opposition into disarray. At the same time, Charlton was ready to demonstrate his maturity as a play-maker in midfield as well as retaining his ability to surge forward with his foot on the trigger.

Best was now asserting himself as a bone fide member of the trinity as United steadily moved to great achievement. In fact, Nobby Stiles rated 1964-65 as the top season of his time, for not only did United reach the semi-finals of both the FA Cup and the Fairs Cup in 1965, they won the league championship as well.

It was a magnificent all-round effort on three fronts, and despite a long and gruelling finish to the campaign, prolonged by reaching the last four of the Fairs Cup involving replays, United were able to clinch the championship with the help of a flurry of goals.

Denis Law, playing brilliantly, led the way, with a tally of 28 goals in the league and a magnificent 39 in all, while there were 18 in all competitions from Bobby Charlton and 14 from George Best. As Stiles described it, their forward line was dripping with goals, with the trinity leading the way.

United's run in the Fairs Cup is probably the least remembered of all their campaigns in Europe, but Stiles reckons the team never played better. 'People recall our European Cup win and the famous encounters with teams like Real Madrid and Benfica, but in my time at Old Trafford we were at our peak in the Fairs Cup. We played some cracking football and scored five or six goals in every round, sometimes even away from home. We opened cautiously enough with a nil-nil draw against Djurgardens in Sweden but we demolished them six-one in the second leg at Old Trafford with the help of a hat-trick from Denis Law.

'We then went to Germany and won six-one in the first leg against Borussia Dortmund, this time with a hat-trick by Bobby Charlton. For good measure we saw them off four-nil at Old Trafford.

'The next round we were drawn against Everton, which was a

Bobby Charlton was the first of the trinity to join United and, having made his debut earlier in the month of October 1956, shows the fierce shot that would become his trademark, as the Everton defenders duck for cover. (Getty Images)

Denis Law signs for Manchester United in July 1962 watched by Gigi Peronace, the Italian agent who handled the transfer from Torino, Matt Busby, assistant Jimmy Murphy and secretary Les Olive. (Getty Images)

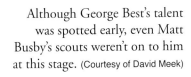

Although George Best's talent was spotted early, even Matt Busby's scouts weren't on to him at this stage. (Courtesy of David Meek)

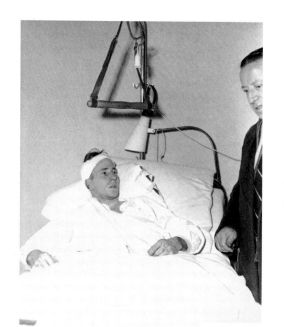

Jimmy Murphy checks on Bobby Charlton, still recovering in hospital from his injuries at Munich. (PA)

Astonishingly, United bounced back from the tragedy to reach the FA Cup final that season, the phoenix on Charlton's shirt symbolising the club's rebirth. Sadly, they were unable to win at Wembley, losing 2-0 to Bolton Wanderers. (PA)

Five years later in 1963, the Reds were back at Wembley, and with two of the trinity now in place, United won their first trophy since Munich. While Charlton and Law were gearing up for action, George Best looked on from the stands. (Mirrorpix)

George Best displays perfect balance as he evades a challenge during United's fifth round FA Cup tie at Barnsley in February 1964 on his way to scoring his first-ever goal in the competition. (Getty Images)

Denis Law receives the trophy as European Footballer of the Year in 1964, after scoring a club record 46 goals in 1963-64. (Getty Images)

Bobby Charlton shoots for goal during the Inter-Cities Fairs Cup game against Strasbourg in May 1965. United were eventually knocked out in the semi-finals, but by then they had already won the league title – the first trophy for the trinity. (Getty Images)

George Best transforms himself into 'El Beatle' after his stunning performance against Benfica. (Getty Images)

Law flies through the air in an effort to beat Tony Macedo in the Fulham goal. This time the ball went over the top and United drew 2-2 in March 1967, but soon after the Reds were champions again. (Getty Images)

The trinity surge to the attack with Law, Charlton and Best in the thick of the action against West Ham. (Courtesy of David Meek)

Piccadilly Gardens in Manchester, when there was still some grass to sit on, proved a suitable location for the author to interview the young players of Manchester United in the 1960s. Left to right: Shay Brennan (standing), Bobby Charlton, David Meek, Wilf McGuinness, Bobby English and Tony Stratton-Smith (journalist). A repeat of such an event in 2013 is extremely unlikely. (Courtesy of David Meek)

A young George Best interviewed by a young *Manchester Evening News* football reporter. (Courtesy of David Meek)

I reported on Matt Busby's United for many years, and it was his vision that helped to bring together United's trinity of Best, Law and Charlton.
(Courtesy of David Meek)

Denis Law gets treatment from Jack Crompton while Nobby Stiles and referee Jack Taylor look on. Sadly, the knee injury was eventually to keep him out of the European Cup final. (Getty Images)

Bobby Charlton and George Best celebrate after beating Benfica in the 1968 European Cup final; between them, they had scored three of United's goals in their 4-1 victory. (Mirrorpix)

George Best scores his first goal during United's 8-2 romp against Northampton Town when the Belfast Boy scored a club record six goals in a single game. (PA)

The trinity pair up

Football isn't all glory and glamour as Denis and Bobby take a breather from the slog and sweat of training.
(Courtesy of David Meek)

This way Bobby, says George.
(Courtesy of David Meek)

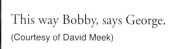

Denis jokes with George after his testimonial match. (Getty Images)

The United Trinity

George Best joins team-mates Denis Law and Bobby Charlton in becoming European Footballer of the Year. (PA)

Law, Charlton and Best reunited in 1995 to launch Sky Sports Gold. (PA)

The trinity immortalised in bronze outside Old Trafford, the ground they lit up for a wonderful decade together. (Getty Images)

shame, and understandably the scores were tighter: one-one at Old Trafford, with a two-one win for us at Goodison. There seemed to be no stopping us when we went to France and beat Strasbourg five-nil. The home leg was goalless but we had certainly scored some goals overall, and we were confident about the semi-final against Ferencvaros.

'The only doubt in our minds was the fact that it had been an extremely long season. We didn't even play Strasbourg until a fortnight after the end of the league season and it was June before we tackled Ferencvaros. I know that by then I had played sixty-six games, including England Under-23 appearances and an FA Cup semi-final involving a replay against Leeds that we lost one-nil. We had also become league champions after a run of ten wins in eleven matches, and the long, tiring season was perhaps beginning to have an effect, and we didn't play particularly well in the first leg against the Hungarians.

'Denis Law scored a penalty, and though a fellow called Novak put Ferencvaros level we seemed to be OK after two goals by David Herd to lead three-one. But then we gave away a silly goal, Pat Dunne misjudging a long lob that bounced into our net. So the trip to Budapest was always going to be difficult with just a slender one-goal advantage.

'The journey was awful, to say the least, delayed in London by a strike and with another hold-up in Brussels, but we were ready to give it a good go. Ferencvaros had a good player, Florian Albert, and he had a real tussle with Bill Foulkes. Just before the interval, he got the ball to Varga who let fly with a shot. I flung myself to block it and stopped it with my shoulder. The referee gave a penalty against me for handball. I thought it was a harsh decision. Novak scored with the spot-kick, and though we tried hard in the second half we lost the game one-nil to finish on aggregate three-three. They didn't have a system of away goals counting double in those days, so it was a play-off – and we lost the toss.

'We had to go back to Budapest, with me feeling terrible as the player responsible for the penalty which had forced the third game. The journey by road from Vienna to Budapest seemed never ending and by then it was 16 June when most footballers were on holiday. But we played well. In fact, we paralysed them, only to lose two-one because we couldn't put the ball into the net. So success in Europe, albeit only the Fairs Cup, eluded us for yet another season, though I still look back proudly on that period. We had won the championship at least and we certainly had a good team normally bursting with goals.

'We had five players in double figures in the league. It was an attack oozing scoring power and I shall always remember that season for some great football. It was a very good team and great to be part of it. People said we used to play off the cuff, without any tactics or planning, but in reality we were well organised and we had good players, which at the end of the day is what it's all about.'

The bonus, of course, was that thanks to winning the league in 1965, United were back in the European Cup competition for the first time since the Munich season, and what's more they had a good team that gave them every hope of a successful campaign the following season.

Despite the long and gruelling finish to the season they had been able to clinch their championship by reeling off seven successive wins with a flush of goals. Matt Busby and Jimmy Murphy had been back to the drawing board in the years since the crash, and with the help of some notable transfers plus the fact that their rebuilt assembly line was again supplying talented home-produced youngsters, United were back in business.

But the magic still centred on the trinity, with George Best now the inspiration, despite arriving at Old Trafford looking like a lost waif. Best brought his young genius to bear on the left wing, though often roaming far and wide for the ball, while the more orthodox John Connelly supplied penetration on the right flank. Law and Herd fired in most of the ammunition. Charlton and Crerand generated ideas and movement but the whole pattern was based on solid defence. Centre-half Bill Foulkes was rightly proud of his department's contribution and pointed up the increasingly effective role of Nobby Stiles. After winning the 1965 championship, Foulkes said: 'The forwards are the glamour boys, especially the ones who scores goals. But I would say we are stronger in defence now than we have ever been since I joined the club seventeen years ago.'

Bill felt that the career of Nobby Stiles was an example of how hard it is for a defender to steal the limelight, and went on: 'Nobby must be one of the most under-rated players in the game. He is regarded by most people as a destroyer and indeed this is an important role in any team, but he also has skills which can be overlooked. For instance, he is a fine reader of a game. He brings aggression to the team and without some aggression you might as well stop in the dressing room. He probably didn't help himself in his early days by getting into trouble, though if you knew him off the field you would find it difficult to imagine. His nickname for instance at the club was always "Happy". Fortunately, his behaviour improved and Alf Ramsey was able to see his real worth. In fact, England need more players like him. It's all very well having a team full of highly skilled individualists, but not all those kinds of players are noted for hard work and someone has to supply the steam for the outfit to function. If you had eleven Nobby Stiles in a team, you would not need to worry about losing. He is a player in the real meaning of the word. I think he and I struck up a good understanding in our championship season.

'Tony Dunne and Shay Brennan were strong full-backs who didn't lack courage, but they were not exactly bruisers. They fitted into the modern concept which calls for defenders to have the skill of forwards with an eye for going up in attack.'

Stiles's tackling improved when he began to wear contact lenses. They obviously improved his social awareness too. It's said that he once left a football banquet in a big hotel for a break, returned, sat down and took a long time to realise he was in a different room and at someone else's dinner.

Bobby Charlton and Nobby Stiles brought great credit to Manchester United with the way they performed for England at the World Cup in 1966. What did not reflect so well on Old Trafford around this period was the number of times United players were in trouble with referees. George Best was one of the main offenders, and Denis Law rarely finished a season without being sent off, to leave the third member of the trinity, Bobby Charlton, upholding the finer principles of the game.

In the 1963-64 season, Noel Cantwell, David Herd, Denis Law and Pat Crerand were all sent off, while Albert Quixall was dismissed playing for the reserves and Bobby Noble was sent off playing for the youth team. The following season, on the way to the championship, Law received the second of his four-week bans after clashing at Blackpool with the ego of York referee Peter Rhodes, who was determined to make clear who had the last word in such matters.

Gregg and Crerand received marching orders in season 1965-66 while the following year Stiles was sent off and suspended for three weeks for accumulating too many bookings. Law survived the season but managed to get himself dismissed on a summer tour in Australia.

The European Cup triumph in 1967-68 was accompanied by another six-week ban for Law following a spectacular bust-up and very early bath along with Ian Ure of Arsenal. The pair of them squared up almost from the kick-off, a dismissal just waiting to happen. That season John Fitzpatrick, Brian Kidd and Carlo Sartori were also sent off.

So cautions were numerous and revealed an undisciplined trait in the make-up of an otherwise gloriously successful period. The villainy contrasted vividly with the man at the helm, a manager who throughout his career represented all that was fair and sporting in the game of football.

United, of course, were playing more games than most in this period, many of high tension, and a lot of their offences occurred in retaliation. Crerand, for one, couldn't abide cheats and if he felt an opponent was taking a liberty with him, he was more inclined to take an immediate swing at him than wait in the time-honoured way to get his own back with a tackle. Law was a highly-strung character who reacted fiercely to provocation and like Stiles couldn't tolerate poor referees and linesmen.

Busby never went in for the dubious tactics and gamesmanship of Don Revie at Leeds, but possibly after the experience of Munich he was prepared to turn a blind eye to some of the excesses of his players in his ambition to make Manchester United a power in the game again. He was not getting any younger, and he was now a man in a hurry. In any case, United could always point to Bobby Charlton as the upholder of the noble game and of United's reputation.

I can still see him now ... slicing through the Benfica team as if they were so many training cones, to plant the ball firmly past goalkeeper Costa Pereira. George Best was on his way into football folklore as 'El Beatle', a new superstar who went on to give me, and countless others, such joy to watch.

It hadn't been planned, far from it, but it was the defining moment for the 19-year-old boy from Belfast. For once the senior members of the trinity, Bobby Charlton and Denis Law, were in supporting roles. The occasion was the quarter-final of the European Cup in season 1965-66 with Manchester United in Lisbon after winning the first leg 3-2 at Old Trafford. The Benfica party looked quite happy after the match in Manchester, because they didn't think a one-goal lead for United would be enough to shoot down the high-flying Eagles on their own ground. Few, in fact, gave United much of a chance and Matt Busby planned accordingly, ordering a cautious start in an effort to hang on to their precious but slender advantage.

But he hadn't reckoned with George Best stamping a personal fearless imprint on the game, against a team who had been unbeaten in 19 European ties on their own ground. The United team, which started in Lisbon, was:

Gregg, Brennan, Dunne, Crerand, Foulkes, Stiles, Best, Law, Charlton, Herd, Connelly.

On this night of Wednesday 9 March 1966, there were 80,000 people crammed into the Estadio da Luz, most of them expecting to hail a Benfica triumph, and why shouldn't they have anticipated victory after watching their team win 18 and draw one of their previous European contests, scoring 78 goals in the process and conceding only 14? Never had a visiting foreign side scored more than two goals in a match there, and the mood of the home crowd was one of noisy confidence as the 10pm kick-off approached and rockets shot into the night sky to celebrate the presentation of a statuette to the great Eusebio to mark his selection as European Footballer of the Year.

Within 12 minutes, he should have handed over his award to the brilliant Best, who produced such shimmering skills and spectacular craft that the home fans in the Stadium of Light were plunged into gloom. He scored his first goal with a header from Tony Dunne's pinpoint free-kick, leaving goalkeeper Costa Pereira stranded. His second followed a huge goal kick from Harry Gregg that David Herd headed back and down into the path of the Irish youngster. Best streaked away, past three white-shirted Benfica players as if they were statues, before slamming a right-foot shot low into the corner of the goal. Denis Law masterminded the third as he worked the ball in from a deep position to draw two defenders before slipping a pass to Best who promptly played it further across to present John Connelly with a goal.

Early in the second half, Benfica got a goal back, but Law laid on a fourth goal by finding an unmarked Pat Crerand on the penalty spot, and near the end Bobby Charlton sailed through for a fine fifth goal to avenge the five-goal drubbing they had received in Lisbon just two years previously in the European Cup Winners' Cup. Revenge was now complete, as back home England prepared to hail a new hero and salute the player who the press saw as English football's answer to the music of the Beatles. He was a mere stripling, playing in only his third season of league football, but Best's mesmerising performance in Lisbon that night heralded the emergence of a cult figure from football representing the Swinging Sixties.

As for the team tactics, Sir Matt Busby laughed afterwards and said: 'I couldn't believe it. Out this kid comes as if he's never heard of tradition and starts running at them, turning them inside out. I ought to have shouted at him for not following instructions. But what can you say? He was a law unto himself. He always was. I was cross with him . . . almost!'

Best told me afterwards that he had fallen in love with the place where United stayed in Estoril, just down the coast from Lisbon, and the sunny, beautiful sandy beach, lovely park, and luxurious hotel.

The atmosphere had been set for me the day before, when the players and the British press toured around Lisbon and came across the massive white stone sculpture built in tribute to Portugal's intrepid explorers like Prince Henry the Navigator and Vasco da Gama. Somehow, I persuaded Sir Matt to let his players off the team bus to pose for an iconic photograph alongside the statue on the eve of another bold explorer breaking the bounds of football. Stone explorers and flesh and blood footballers were all pictured gazing out to sea and fresh horizons. Certainly for George Best, his life was to change dramatically.

Although Best stole the headlines in the Lisbon game, the other members of the trinity were not far behind, as Denis Law said later: 'It was unusual for the three so-called stars, Charlton, Law and Best, to turn it on in the same match, but we did in that match.' Law is being modest, except to say that in Lisbon that night all three of them were peerless, and that didn't happen every game of course, even for the trinity.

In the dressing room before the game, Pat Crerand, warming up with a ball, banged it against the mirror. The glass shattered, and no one said anything, but all his team-mates were thinking about was seven years' bad luck. It certainly didn't help the mood, yet they went out and were three goals up on the night in the first quarter of an hour. It was incredible and one of United's best performances in Europe. Law says he found it a beautiful experience and a joy to share in a splendid team effort.

Sir Matt Busby called the performance in Lisbon that night 'our finest hour'.

Best reckoned the Lisbon fans had never seen their team so humiliated. He remembered counting the United players during the match because they seemed to outnumber the opposition. Every time he looked up, there seemed to be nothing but a United man to pass to. Best said he couldn't go wrong.

After the match, a man rushed up to Best brandishing a knife. It was an alarming moment until the stranger explained that all he wanted was a lock of the hero's hair in memory of a fantastic performance. Best said: 'I had a feeling of total warmth afterwards. That is the only way I can describe how I felt when I walked off the field at the end of the game, knowing I had done something that no one else could have done, or is ever likely to do again. I was suddenly the best-known sportsman in Britain.' Best also showed that he had instinctive flair off the field, as well as on it. Hunting for souvenirs the morning after the match in Estoril, he bought himself a huge floppy sombrero. He carried it through all the airport formalities and stuck with it on the journey home. Then as the team walked off the plane in Manchester, he put the hat on his head. The press photographers were already looking for the game's scoring hero and now they were being presented with a publicity dream: an unusual and distinctive picture opportunity which duly hit the next day's papers in a big way. The *Daily Mirror* had him on both the front and back pages wearing his giant sombrero. Best later admitted that it was in his mind that later in the month he was due to open a boutique and that he thought the sombrero would be good window dressing and publicity. He was right ... the picture went round the world!

The groundwork for winning the tie had of course been laid in the first leg at Old Trafford. It was only a 3-2 win, but from the United perspective they had shown they could hold their own against Europe's top team. A full-house 64,000 crowd enjoyed it so much that they applauded both teams back on to the pitch for the second half and again as the players went off at the end.

Benfica had started and ended with a flourish. They scored first when Eusebio bent an inswinger from the corner flag on to the head of Augusto. United responded with goals from Herd and Law for a half-time lead, and then, with half an hour left, Noel Cantwell crossed from a free-kick for Bill Foulkes to head the Manchester team into a 3-1 advantage. Benfica finished as well as they started though, and with a touch more magic from Eusebio, the towering Torres scored to reduce United's lead to a slender one goal. As the headline in *The Times* summed up: 'PRECARIOUS LEAD PLUCKED FROM MAGNIFICENT MATCH.' The report paid tribute: 'Here was a match played at a sizzling speed, full of creation and movement. For Manchester, Charlton was world class, the equal on this occasion of Eusebio, needing no space in which to move, a dark flash who shoots like a thunderbolt from all angles and at any range ... Herd was a bombardier, pressed on by the fluid movement of the darting Law and a delicate Best.

'For Benfica, there was, of course, Eusebio; lazy, almost casual, in movement, but eating up the ground as he changed direction, sending the defence one way and moving the other; little Simoes also jinking down one flank; and the long-striding giant Torres, at centre-forward, another player with lazy strides, but seven league boots and a head that can almost reach a ball from the over-hanging clouds. One goal in the bank may not be enough for Manchester United. But at least this night cannot be taken away. It was something to remember.' But *The Times* was wrong with their estimate. The trinity were in full throttle for the return as

United went to Lisbon to win the second leg 5-1 and stand football logic on its head.

The earlier rounds in Europe had given little indication of what was to come in 1966, though United certainly started well enough. After winning the first leg of their preliminary round against Helsinki 3-2, with Law to the fore, they romped home in Finland 6-0 with a hat-trick from Connelly, two goals from Best and one from Charlton.

The first round proper saw United drawn against the East German army team, ASK Vorwaerts, clearly a harder task, if only because of the unknown nature of the opposition. The game in East Berlin was played on a frozen hard pitch, with sleet falling on a huge bowl of a ground where only the band was undercover, and the absence of floodlights meaning the match took place in the afternoon. United won 2-0 with Law leading the charge, making one and scoring the other himself, but it is the memory of the German players taking our players and press out after the match that sticks more in the mind, especially the toasts to friendship through football between East and West. Vorwaerts were certainly ready for the Wall to come down. The second leg was a comfortable exercise with a hat-trick for David Herd in a 3-1 win.

United knew they were in for a more searching examination in the quarter-finals against a team that had reached the final of the European Cup four times in the previous five seasons, winning twice, but as we know United hit the heights against Benfica. The significance for Best was that he had carried his domestic achievements on to a global stage and given notice that here was a player worthy of consideration for European Footballer of the Year.

Matt Busby laughed afterwards and said: 'George must have had cotton wool in his ears when we made our plans. I told them to play it tight for a while, for twenty minutes or so, until we got their measure. George just went out and destroyed them. I couldn't believe it and Benfica most certainly couldn't until it was too late. They were also prepared to play it tight for a while, which is what used to happen in European Cup games.'

The player himself described the match in one of his books: 'I felt superb. The atmosphere sent the blood coursing through my veins, adding power to my muscles, imagination to my brain.

'Why I played the way I did that night is one of those inexplicable things. Genius, and I believe on the football field I had it, is something you simply can't begin to explain.'

Best was always a target for interviewers and seemed to fascinate American journalists for whom analysis was of the greatest importance. Why do you do this, and how? It all seemed so important to them, whereas to Best it was natural. He never really thought about it, he certainly couldn't explain it, as I also discovered whenever I tried to probe him for his secrets. For George, football was simply a simple game.

Even the jeering Benfica fans before the game didn't upset him, holding up five fingers to the coach windows as a sardonic reminder of the 5-0 defeat by Sporting Lisbon two years earlier in the Cup Winners' Cup quarter-final. He said with satisfaction: 'We gave them five goals all right, and we put a stop to their damn firecrackers and rockets. They had been masters of Europe but we showed them how to play the game.'

The morning after the match, every bikini-clad lady on the beach wanted his autograph. The men were just as eager. He was having his first taste of pop-star treatment and he was clearly enjoying it.

After their dazzling feat in Lisbon, United were immediately established as favourites to go all the way and become the Champions of Europe, but fate had a cruel trick to play. The hero of Lisbon twisted his leg in a tackle in an FA Cup tie against Preston a fortnight later. He had a cartilage problem in his right knee and without warning it would lock. It needed an operation but Busby asked the player to carry on playing for as long as they remained in the European Cup. He was rested for one league fixture and then brought back for a run-out which persuaded the club he was worth a gamble for the first leg of their European Cup semi-final against Partizan Belgrade in Yugoslavia. Best by now had become integral to success. While Law and Charlton were still key components of the team, it was the much younger Best who more and more contributed to the match-winning moments.

So Best was strapped up and sent out against a team that proved to be far more accomplished than had been acknowledged. Partizan had in fact seven internationals in their side and with a record for springing shock results. In the quarter-final, for instance, they had lost the first leg against Sparta Prague 4-1 but had roared back to win the second game 5-0.

United certainly found them a tough nut to crack, although as early as the fifth minute Best missed a chance and Law hit the bar from only five yards out. It was downhill soon afterwards when Best felt a stab of pain return to his knee and he faded to become little more than a limping passenger, though many at the match thought overall he was still United's most dangerous player. That didn't say much for the rest, and indeed, as Peter Lorenzo put it in the *Daily Herald*: 'The same team whipped Benfica 5-1 in the last round but tonight they had no punch, sparkle or rhythm.'

Law hammered another cross against the bar but in the second half United were made to pay for their careless marksmanship. Two minutes after the interval, a long cross from Partizan right-back Jusufi seemed to catch Harry Gregg in two minds and he was beaten by a fierce header from Hasanagic. Partizan, through to the semi-finals for the first time, clinched their 2-0 win after an hour when Vasovic fed the ball forward for Becejac to hit a sharp low shot into a corner of the net.

The Yugoslavs had acquired a useful lead for the second leg, but just as big a blow for the Reds was that it had become pointless to persevere with the injured Best. As soon as the team got home, he was sent into hospital for a cartilage operation and it seemed that when Best dropped out, the magic went with him.

Partizan defended powerfully at Old Trafford. Tension rose as the game dragged on, with United unable to score. In the 70th minute, Pat Crerand and Mihajlovic were sent off after exchanging blows and United's goal finally came three minutes later when Nobby Stiles crossed from a short corner to catch goalkeeper Soskic unawares. He could only palm the ball into his own net. United redoubled their efforts but there was precious little time for the further goal they needed to force a play-off.

Partizan went on to lose in the final against Real Madrid, who exposed the limitations of the Yugoslavs, and Manchester United were left regretting even more deeply their failure to account for a relatively average team after their heady success against Benfica. Busby was devastated because he knew his team was at its peak and that after finishing fourth in the league it would be at least two more seasons before he could make another attempt to conquer Europe. He said: 'I was at the lowest ebb since the Munich air crash and it was in my mind to turn my back on football altogether. It seemed the fates had conspired against the club and myself, and I remember telling Paddy Crerand: "We'll never win the European Cup now."'

Busby had a right to be concerned because his team was not getting any younger, but he was speaking out of frustration because he knew it was a missed opportunity. The truth was that he still had a first-class team, as future events would show. The trinity were still looking good, and Crerand recalls telling his manager: 'We'll win the league next season, boss, and the European Cup the season after.' He later admitted that he had said it more in hope than judgement, and because he realised Busby had been so utterly devastated by the defeat against Partizan. It turned out to be a brilliant forecast, but, more significantly, it also perhaps reflected the team's determination now to let nothing stand in the way of making Busby's big dream become a reality.

Denis Law found it a bitter sweet season, and remembers: 'Benfica in 1966 were the cream. They had been in three European Cup finals and had taken over from the legendary Real Madrid as top dogs. We beat them three-two in the first leg at Old Trafford but as they left the field their players were smiling because they didn't think one goal would be enough for us in the second leg in Lisbon. How wrong they would prove to be!'

'By rights we should have gone on to win the European Cup that year, but we played badly in the semi-final against Partizan Belgrade . . . So we missed out on final glory and Matt Busby was bitterly disappointed, but it was nevertheless an exciting period in the club's history. I think we saw football at its best. I was privileged to play in a great side. Matt Busby had recovered after Munich and I came home from Italy to join the team he had rebuilt. It was a splendid team, too, with players like Pat Crerand, Bobby Charlton, Nobby Stiles and George Best. Over a period of five years, United were outstanding for entertainment and goals.

'We always felt that if the opposition scored one, we could score two, if they scored two we could get three. It didn't always work out that way, but that was the feeling, and it was all very special for me.'

United overcame their Partizan disappointment and launched into the 1966-67 season with a renewed vigour, especially the trinity who hit top form to win the championship, finishing four points in front of Nottingham Forest. They were particularly strong in the second half of the season, perhaps helped by the fact that they were not in Europe and that they had been knocked out of both the FA Cup and League Cup in early rounds. They clinched the title with a flourish, beating West Ham 6-1 in London to take the honours with a match to spare. It was the biggest away win of the season in the First Division. They were unbeaten at home, where they were watched by a league average crowd of 53,800. They were in relentless mood right to the end. As Nobby Stiles said afterwards: 'Just after we had scored our sixth goal at West Ham, I trotted over to Bill Foulkes and said: "Congratulations, Bill, on your fourth championship medal," for which he gave me a rollicking and told me to concentrate on the game.'

Charlton scored after only two minutes, while Crerand, Foulkes and Best added goals to give United a four goal lead in the first half an hour. Law scored twice in the second half, one from the penalty spot, for a swashbuckling finale. It was a crashing climax to a season in which the Reds paced the title with a perfect sense of timing and a remorseless last lap that was too good for their opponents. This was a championship won on the classical formula of winning at home and drawing away. Starting in January, they marched on to a run of eight away draws backed by eight home victories. This was the solid base, consistent and relentless, from which they sprang to tear West Ham to pieces and take the title.

Nottingham Forest provided a late challenge and they got within a point at one stage. The decisive game came when Forest played at Old Trafford. There was a 62,000 attendance with the gates locked. It took United until five minutes from the end to crack Forest, but Denis Law, the maestro, banged in the winner. This was the season when David Herd broke his leg in March in the act of scoring his 16th league goal. It could easily have been Herd's best-ever scoring season with United and it was with some anxiety that the manager waited to see whether the team could get by without any more goals from him.

But Law remained the leading spirit in United's sparkling attack. Charlton came back to his best in the second half of the season and after Herd's injury stepped up his scoring rate, notably with a fine pair against Sheffield Wednesday at Hillsborough. United also had the dazzling play of George Best to stretch the opposition and supply a steady stream of goals. The United manager also helped cover Herd's absence by switching Stiles into the attack to add more fire, while bringing in the versatile David Sadler back from the forward line to form a redoubtable centre-half pairing with Bill Foulkes.

Stiles – now wearing his dental plate for matches because he considered that his fierce, toothless appearance, as seen on television during the World Cup, frightened referees and got him into trouble – finished the season in fine form.

Foulkes had started the season with many people wondering whether the club should have bought a new centre-half, but he supplied the answer himself with some uncompromising displays.

Every player played his part, including Tony Dunne, brilliant at full-back and Irish footballer of the year, and Pat Crerand, the architect of so much of United's midfield play, along with players who came in for brief but vital periods like Noel Cantwell, John Fitzpatrick and Jimmy Ryan. They made an attractive team to watch, with over a million piling in for the home league games, the highest since the war, with many fans travelling to bring record gates at a number of away matches.

Matt Busby gave notice he would be there to lead the next campaign into Europe. 'I'm too young to retire,' said the then longest serving club manager in the game, a quote that resonated in more recent times as Sir Alex Ferguson prepared for his retirement as manager in charge at Old Trafford.

It wasn't just winning the championship that brought the crowds flocking to watch United at home and away in such numbers; it was the personalities packed into their team, not least the compelling trinity. George Best had become a cult figure by this time. He took your breath away with his finesse on the field and he certainly took away the breath of the girls idolising him. He was a new breed of footballer with a following more like that of a pop star. I vividly recall girls sobbing as they stared with emotional frustration at him through the windows of the team coach. Writers flocked to his door to question the magic of not just his play, but of his appeal to beauty queens and actresses. I remember on a preseason tour in Scandinavia being asked by a stunning blonde, as I left the hotel to get onto the team coach, if I would give a note to Best who was already on board. The note of course contained her phone number and was the start of his relationship with Eva Haraldsted. It was a love that led to an engagement and a subsequent breach of promise action; at least Best didn't ask the bearer of the note that started it all to contribute to the damages.

Busby had already declared: 'George has the lot. He's a world-class footballer'. Alf Ramsey was sighing: 'I wish he had been born in England.' In 1967 he was simply a brilliant player, well worth his place in the United trinity.

The players all had their own ideas about how the team came to win the championship that put them back in Europe. Bobby

Charlton said: 'We won it because we believed right from the start that we could do it.' George Best added: 'If the championship was decided on home games, we would win it every season. This time our away games made the difference. We got into the right frame of mind.'

Noel Cantwell, no longer a regular, summed up the success that had given United another tilt at the European Cup after falling to Partizan Belgrade two years previously, when he said: 'It's simply that Matt Busby has built another great team.'

9

Champions of Europe

The trinity were now on a mission to complete what most people felt was Manchester United's destiny and become champions of Europe. They were back on the European stage, with the first half of Pat Crerand's promise to win the league again fulfilled. Now there remained the truly difficult part of realising Matt Busby's vision, a vision shattered at Munich in 1958 and then frustrated by Partizan in 1966. The big three of Best, Law and Charlton had already showcased their talents in Europe, with Charlton also sharing in England's World Cup victory of 1966. Could United finally clinch the European Cup? The trinity were ready as senior players to play a pivotal role.

Not everyone grasped the significance of Continental competition when the European Cup was launched in 1955, but Matt Busby was always pro-Europe. 'It always seemed to me the logical progression that the champions of England should pit their abilities against the best of Europe. You cannot make progress by standing still,' he used to tell me.

Busby had every right to feel his team were ready for a wider challenge after creating the youthful Busby Babes and winning the league with flair. Indeed, United made an impressive European debut in the 1956-57 competition, beating Anderlecht, Borussia Dortmund and Athletic Bilbao. The adventure only came to an end when they faced the majesty and experience of Real Madrid in the semi-finals, but the flame had been lit and the enthusiasm of the fans had been captured. Even though the tragic events in Munich the following year would stall their progress, European football had arrived in Manchester as the ultimate challenge and ambition.

Just as Busby was committed to rebuilding Manchester United on the pitch after Munich and had in George Best a glittering new star, so the club itself were looking to move forward and improve and develop their flagship stadium. The trinity needed and deserved a platform worthy of their talents and Charlton especially shared a sense of history and appreciation of the need to keep the club at the forefront of football both on and off the field. Those behind the scenes had been looking for continuous growth and improvement ever since John Henry Davies, a wealthy Manchester brewer, rescued the club from bankruptcy in 1902, changed the club's name from Newton Heath to Manchester United and gave them their famous red shirts. The new chairman triggered the club's first era of success, and after winning the league in 1908 and the FA Cup the following year, he felt emboldened to put up £60,000 to provide a new stadium. This was built in Manchester's industrial heartland at Trafford and the new ground staged its first match on 9 February 1910, when a crowd of 50,000 saw the home side beaten 4-3 by Liverpool. A local reporter, struggling to convey the impressive nature of the ground, described it as 'a wonder to behold,' a sentiment echoed by Sir Bobby Charlton in more recent years when he described Old Trafford as the theatre of dreams.

The ground's proximity to the Trafford Park industrial estate meant that during the last world war, two German bombs fell on United's home during the night of 11 March 1941. The main stand was virtually destroyed by the first bomb, and the second hit the terracing on the other side as well as damaging the pitch.

The return of league football in 1945 saw United forced to play their matches at Maine Road, courtesy of Manchester City. Eventually Old Trafford was rebuilt and the Reds returned home in August 1949, to beat Bolton 3-0. Even then they had to return to Maine Road to play their first season in the European Cup on City's ground, because they didn't have floodlights.

After their inaugural season in Europe, United rightly felt their stadium worthy of hosting a major European final. But it was Wembley that hosted the 1968 European Cup final, with Busby's cavaliers ready to do battle. It was, of course, much more than the final of the European Cup; for United it was a date with destiny, a feeling that there was a final chapter to write after the chilling tragedy of the Munich air crash.

We didn't have a fancy name for it in those days, but what we were all looking for – and by 'all' I mean the club, the players, the supporters, and me as the local newspaper reporter – was closure. It had been 10 years since Munich had wiped out the Busby Babes and left the manager at death's door and this was clearly going to be Sir Matt's last opportunity to try to bring the great European adventure to a happy conclusion.

The responsibility of taking his brilliant Babes into Europe with its disastrous outcome in 1958 had always weighed heavily on Busby's mind; at least winning the competition now in 1968 would perhaps offer some small justification. The players certainly felt that way, especially Munich survivors Bobby Charlton and Bill Foulkes.

The preliminary round was not particularly testing. Hibernians, a team of Maltese part-timers coached by a local priest, Father Hilary Tagliaferro, even lost one of their players on the way to Manchester for the first leg. As the players broke their journey in London to take in an Arsenal match, 17-year-old winger Francis Mifsud went to buy an ice cream, wandered off and got lost. The party had to travel on to Manchester without him. He couldn't remember the name of his hotel in London, but he knew they were on their way to Manchester, so he caught a train to Piccadilly on his own and with the help of a girl he met on the journey he was eventually reunited with his team-mates and Scotland Yard were able to call off their hunt.

Denis Law and David Sadler scored two goals apiece in a 4-0 win and Father Hilary said he was happy to have kept the score so low. He added that the United players might find the conditions in Malta a bit of a shock. He was right about that, with the Gzira pitch in Valletta a rock-hard surface of sand, gravel and lime. The ground had few facilities and I discovered to my horror that the telephone link the *Manchester Evening News* had asked to be installed hadn't materialised. With no floodlights, it was an afternoon kick-off, so the intention was to phone-in a running report like the Saturday afternoon reports I did for the *Football Pink*. My solution was to knock on a few doors of a block of flats that overlooked the ground. Eventually, I found one with a flat roof and spent my time running up and down stairs from there to the phone in the hall to send my report through in bursts.

Fortunately in a way, not a lot happened. It was extremely hot and it was perhaps the combination of the weather and pitch conditions that saw United give a very stilted display in a goalless game. The Maltese spectators, many of them United fans, didn't know whether to laugh or cry. On the one hand, they were pleased that their team had held the mighty Manchester United to a draw, but at the same time they were disappointed that such distinguished visitors had failed to thrill and entertain them. However, there was no doubting the warmth of the welcome, which started with a cavalcade of cars and motorbikes, horns blaring, escorting the team bus at breakneck speed from the airport to the Hilton Hotel, with yet more enthusiastic supporters throwing flowers at the players. The United Supporters' Club, which has always thrived on the island, threw a big party for the officials, players and press.

The first-round draw brought more testing opposition and pitted United against Sarajevo, the champions of Yugoslavia, who were based in the historical city where Archduke Ferdinand had been assassinated to trigger the First World War. In the first leg, the home side proved a tough and ruthless team, but United kept their heads in the face of some scything tackles on Francis Burns, George Best and Brian Kidd. Trainer Jack Crompton was on the field so often, treating injured players, that Pat Crerand commented afterwards: 'I bet half the crowd thought Jack was playing.' Their composure, as much as the goalless result, was an indication of United's growing experience, and as Matt Busby summed up: 'I was pleased with the result but even more with the way the players behaved under extreme provocation.' Best and Law had their moments of reckless behaviour, but in this kind of situation the trinity was not just about silky skills, they were also physically and mentally tough.

United returned home quite confident about the second leg, though Sarajevo were equally optimistic. The first capacity crowd of the season, with 62,801 packed inside Old Trafford, saw United open the scoring in the 11th minute through John Aston, after George Best's header from a Brian Kidd cross had been palmed out by goalkeeper Muftic. The Yugoslavs were slowly getting back into the game until a decisive moment in the second half when Best took a swipe at Muftic after the pair had collided. Best lost his cool, because as the goalkeeper helped him up he dug his nails into him, and Best explained afterwards that it had hurt. The irony was that it looked like an ungracious gesture to an opponent offering a helping hand, and the Yugoslav players clearly didn't like Best's reaction. The result was that they lost their heads. One of their players, Fahrudin Prljaca, hunted Best down in revenge and kicked him so blatantly that referee Roger Machin had no option but to send him off.

The Sarajevo tempers were even more inflamed, especially when Best made the score 2-0 after the ball had looked to have gone out of play. Eventually the visitors got back to playing the ball rather than the man and even pulled a goal back through Delalic, but it was too late and United emerged 2-1 victors. The nastiness spilled over as the players went up the tunnel, and when it looked as if Muftic was coming for Best, Pat Crerand intercepted, and in his own words: 'I gave him such a clout I nearly broke my hand.'

Busby stepped in to sort things out in his usual diplomatic way. He was cross with the players over the tunnel incident, but couldn't conceal his satisfaction at winning through to the quarter-finals as he switched back to the domestic programme during the European midwinter break of three months. In January, he saw his team knocked out of the FA Cup in a third round replay at Tottenham but with his boys going well in the league and looking forward to resuming battle in the European Cup, it was proving a good season. Shortly after the domestic Cup knockout, United took revenge on Tottenham by beating them in the league to move into a five-point lead at the top of the First Division. Realistically speaking, they had enough on their plate without an FA Cup run, so nobody was complaining.

Back on the European trail in February, United were up against Gornik Zabrze, the dark horses who had knocked out Dynamo Kiev, conquerors of Celtic, the European Cup holders. At the end of the first leg in Manchester, with United 2-0 winners, the home players stopped at the top of the tunnel to applaud their opponents off the pitch – a gesture later to be repeated in Poland – because it had been that kind of game, a refreshing tonic after the previous round. Best got the first goal, after an hour's play, when Florenski turned his shot into his own net, and the second when Brian Kidd flicked in a shot on goal by Jimmy Ryan. It looked a comfortable lead, until United arrived in Silesia for the second leg to be greeted by biting cold and snow.

Busby toyed with the idea of asking for a postponement because he said they had not come this far in the competition to go out on a farce of a pitch. His hand was rather forced though, when Concetto Lo Bello, Italy's top referee, went missing on the day of the match, perhaps conveniently to avoid confrontation and controversy over whether the match should go ahead. The players waited and consoled themselves with another brew of tea in their room at the Katowice Hotel after taking their own kettle. Pat Crerand had remembered a trip there with Scotland three years before and had unhappy memories of being unable to get a decent cuppa!

The pitch was deemed playable, the tie went ahead, and in the event United performed brilliantly on a snow-covered surface and for half the time in a mini-blizzard. John Fitzpatrick, replacing Jimmy Ryan for the second leg in the absence of the injured Denis

Law, gave the team a more defensive look, a plan that was put into operation with great discipline.

Danger man Lubanski, who had played for Poland at the age of 16, scored for Gornik 20 minutes from the end to win the match 1-0, but the Polish champions went out 2-1 on aggregate, to give Manchester United their fourth appearance in the European Cup semi-finals.

The semi-final brought them up against much respected adversaries from their early days in Europe. In United's eyes, Real Madrid, under their great president, Don Santiago de Bernabeu, were the team that had set the standard. There had developed between the two clubs a close sporting friendship, and indeed the Spanish club had been particularly sympathetic after the Munich air crash. It was practical sympathy, too, waiving their normal match fee to play a friendly at Old Trafford to help ease United's financial strain and keep alive the tradition of European football in Manchester. Later on, when United celebrated its centenary in 1978, there was only one choice to bring over as opposition to mark the occasion, and that of course was Real Madrid. But in 1968 it seemed appropriate that United should be meeting the club which pre-Munich had just proved a step too far for the newcomers to the European scene.

The first leg was played at Old Trafford in front of a full-house 63,000 crowd who constantly roared their side forward. Indeed, United supplied most of the attacking play but, for all their possession, could do no more than force a 1-0 win. The goal came 10 minutes from the interval when Brian Kidd put John Aston away down the left wing. As the winger pulled the ball back from the by-line, it was met with a thundering left-foot shot from George Best into the roof of the Real net.

Pat Crerand had already hit the woodwork, but against some

masterly defensive play by the visitors there were few real chances. It was a nerve-tingling match of high technique, and played in the kind of spirit associated with a club who were friends as well as foes. Indeed, the Russian referee commented later: 'The number one footballer and gentleman on the field for me was Bobby Charlton, and I have never had more pleasure in taking such a match.'

The Spaniards, so well versed in the arts of two-legged ties in Europe, seemed quietly confident about overhauling United's slender lead in Madrid. Their optimism seemed justified as they went into a 2-0 lead. Their first goal came after half an hour when link man Pirri headed in Amancio's cross. Ten minutes later, Gento, the left-wing flier, came out of the blocks to beat Shay Brennan and score from a very narrow angle. The lifeline for United came just before half-time when Zoco panicked under pressure from Brian Kidd and turned the ball into his own net. No sooner were United back in the hunt, though, when Amancio made it 3-1 and not many in the crowd of 120,000 would have given a peseta for United's chances of recovering from that kind of deficit in the second half. The faint-hearted had not allowed for the shrewdness of Busby under pressure though, and the manager made good use of the few minutes he had at his disposal during the interval.

As he explained later: 'Although we were three-one down on the night, I reminded the players that the aggregate score was three-two and that we were, in fact, just one goal down. I told them that if they were three-two down at half-time in an FA Cup tie, they wouldn't consider that the match was over and that they had no chance. I told them simply to go out and play.' And this is what his team did with such flair and force that the Spanish champions crumbled and lost their grip on the game. With attack once more at the forefront of their tactics, United were a different proposition. David Sadler left his defensive duties and started to advance upfield, to such telling effect that in the 70th minute he was on hand to turn in a header from George Best following Pat Crerand's free-kick.

Level now on aggregate, United had their tails up and just five minutes later they stunned Real with a winner courtesy of one of the players least likely to score. Bill Foulkes played first-team football for 18 seasons at Old Trafford and in all competitions played around 700 games, but in that time he scored only nine goals, certainly none of them as important as this one. He rarely strayed over the halfway line, but something dragged him forward as Best began a run down the right wing. As Best jinked his way closer to goal, Foulkes steamed down the middle of the pitch, and when Best turned the ball back he sweetly side-footed it home. As Best described it: 'I saw a red shirt on my left and just pushed the ball inside. When I saw it was Bill Foulkes, I wished I had hung on to it, because I expected him to lash at it. I was quite wrong. He was really calm and just placed his shot past the goalkeeper.'

Pat Crerand said: 'Bill Foulkes of all people – goodness knows what he was doing so far upfield. All I know is that people have talked about providence and about fate evening things out after Munich ten years previously.'

What was hard fact was that United had become the first English club to reach the final of the European Cup and take Matt Busby ever closer to his dream of conquering Europe.

Bill Foulkes had been in at the start of Matt Busby's European quest and it was entirely fitting that he should score the winning goal to take the Reds to the final against Benfica at Wembley. It was only his second goal in Europe out of a total of 52 appearances.

Sir Matt was always entranced by the artistry of players. For instance he loved the super skills possessed by the trinity, but he knew the importance of defensive strength, too. Some didn't think Bill Foulkes was a good enough player to be in the United all-stars, but Busby picked Foulkes to play 679 competitive games for him, which is testament to how he rated his centre-half. Foulkes linked the Johnny Carey era of the early Fifties with the Busby Babes, survived Munich, shared in the European Cup triumph and played until 1970. Some record for a man supposedly not out of the top drawer!

'I still don't really know what possessed me to go forward and score the winning goal. After so many games with no thought of scoring, it seems unbelievable as I look back,' says Foulkes. 'I was even lucky to be playing. I was rarely injured, but that season I was out from about January. I had missed the first leg against Real Madrid and had played only two league games when the manager picked me for the return in Madrid.

'I think Matt went for my experience, because I wasn't really fit. My knee had blown up at Sunderland on the Saturday and the European tie was just four days later. My knee was strapped up and I seemed to be hobbling everywhere. I think I only got by, thanks to some brilliant defending and covering by Nobby Stiles and Tony Dunne.

'We had gone to Spain with that precious one-goal advantage and at half-time, when we were three-one down on the night, it didn't seem anything like enough. We were struggling. George Best was double-marked. Bobby Charlton and Pat Crerand, who normally ran the games for us, hadn't shown and at half-time we were all a bit depressed.

'But Matt, with his typical logic, pointed out that on aggregate we were only one goal behind and that at least a replay wasn't beyond us. His reasoning made an impression and we went out again thinking: "We can do it."

'Perhaps Real Madrid sat back a little as well and gave us more room to play. For suddenly George began to figure, and Brian Kidd, too. We got a corner after the ball had hit David Sadler's heel. It seemed to me then as if both sides stopped playing, perhaps too frightened of making a mistake and losing. Nothing much happened for us, until we got a throw-in on the right. Paddy Crerand was taking it and nobody seemed to want the ball. I shouldn't have done, but I called for it. Paddy looked and then decided not to bother, sensibly perhaps.

'He threw it to George instead who promptly shot off down the wing to elude three or four tackles. Perhaps it was moving slightly forward to call for the throw-in that prompted me to keep running forward.

'Anyway, I reached the corner of the box and again found myself calling for the ball. George saw me and I thought I was going to be ignored again – you must appreciate I was never renowned for my attacking and shooting skills.

'So I thought George was going to do what he usually did and have a shot, but instead he cut back the most beautiful of passes to me. It was perfect and I just had to side-foot the ball in at the far side.

'There wasn't a sound from the Spanish crowd. My first thought was that it was so quiet, it wasn't a goal, but I realised it was when all the lads piled in and I was trying to get out from beneath all the bodies.

'There was still ten minutes to play, but we hung on and scoring that goal remains as probably my most precious moment in football. It opened the door to the final for us, the beginning of the end of the rainbow for us.

'I had come the whole way with the boss and I thought the destruction of the team at Munich would have been the end of it, but he patiently put together another team. When we finally did it, I thought that for those of us who had lost our friends at Munich coming home from a European tie, it was the right tribute to their memory.'

Now they were in the final, Matt Busby was convinced the European Cup would be won as much by character as ability. He described the need for the kind of fighting spirit that his team had shown to pull the game out of the fire in Madrid, and he would find it significant that only three men in that season's European campaign had come to Old Trafford on big fees. That is not to belittle players like Denis Law, Alex Stepney and Pat Crerand, recruited in the transfer market, but to recognise that the bulk of the side was fashioned in his own image.

Before the final at Wembley, in their hotel at Egham in Surrey as they prepared for their big night against Benfica, Busby quietly summed up: 'Their heart is right and that is the important thing.' His belief was to be tested.

The teams for this European Cup final at Wembley on 29 May 1968, with United wearing an all deep blue strip, were:

Manchester United: Stepney, Brennan, Dunne, Crerand, Foulkes, Stiles, Best, Kidd, Charlton, Sadler, Aston. Sub: Rimmer.
Benfica: Jose Henrique, Adolfo, Humberto, Jacinto, Cruz, Jaime Graça, Coluna, Jose Augusto, Torres, Eusebio, Simoes. Sub: Nasimento.

It was hard going against the Portuguese champions, with tension seeming to cramp the style of both teams. Perhaps because the match was being played on 'home' soil, United were the first to settle and establish themselves as the team taking the game to their opponents.

Crucial duels were taking place all over the field. Bill Foulkes knew he had to win the aerial battle with the towering Torres, and Nobby Stiles was certainly aware that his marking of the elusive Eusebio was critical. Benfica, from their point of view, knew they had particular players to mark and the rugged Cruz became George Best's watchdog, several times bringing him down without hesitation. When Cruz missed him on one occasion, Humberto sailed in and was booked.

United's persistence in attack took a long time to find a chink in the visitors' defence but finally, in the 53rd minute, David Sadler crossed from a deep position on the left for Bobby Charlton to leap and glance the ball over the goalkeeper into the far corner of the net. That was the signal for Benfica to throw caution to the winds, to step up their own forward momentum and draw on the experience garnered from playing in five European Cup finals. Nine minutes from the end they pulled level through a finely worked goal. Augusto put the ball in for Torres to nod down. Eusebio made a run which drew the defence and it was midfielder Jaime Graça who latched on to the ball to score with a fierce shot from a narrow angle.

This was the moment when United needed all the heart they could muster. Benfica stepped up the pressure and twice Eusebio broke through to test Alex Stepney. His last effort brought him face to face with the United goalkeeper and he unleashed a rocket which Stepney saved with such brilliance that even his opponent applauded. Pat Crerand, while giving credit to his team-mate, was critical of Eusebio and said: 'Only Stepney stood between Eusebio and the goal. It didn't look like the kind of chance he, the Black Prince of Portugal, would miss. All he had to do was side-step the keeper and push the ball into the net. For a player of his calibre, it was a piece of cake. Then, when he did shoot, there was that wonderful feeling of relief when he hit the ball straight at Stepney, who clutched it to his chest with a great save. But Eusebio wanted to score a spectacular goal ... If Bobby, Denis or George had been in Eusebio's boots at that moment, it would have been a goal, because they would not have been thinking about the crowd. Their only concern would have been to put the ball in the net by the surest method. But then, they don't have ego trouble like Mr Eusebio.'

It proved a definitive moment because United were faltering, and as Stiles put it later: 'If the game had gone another ten minutes without a break, I think we would have lost. We suddenly realised how tired we were. For me, it was like the World Cup final all over again when Germany pulled level just before the end. It came close to knocking the stuffing out of us.'

When the whistle came for the completion of normal time, Busby seized his chance to massage the patient's heart back into active life again. 'I told them they were throwing the game away with careless passing and hitting the ball anywhere. I said they must keep possession and start to play their football again,' he explained later.

Extra-time opened dramatically as United played with renewed vigour to sweep forward and score twice in two minutes. In only the third minute, Brian Kidd headed on Alex Stepney's clearance to Best who immediately headed for goal. He took the ball round the defenders in a splendidly curving arc and then past the goalkeeper before popping it into the empty net. It was the Irishman at his best, and Kidd was quick to match him with a goal to mark his birthday. His close-range header from David Sadler's cross was blocked by Henrique, but as the ball came out the youngster got in a second header which this time looped over the goalkeeper. Kidd then laid on a goal for Bobby Charlton and United triumphed with a 4-1 victory.

Charlton and Best had delivered with goals but everyone had raised their game, none more so than John Aston who made his critics eat their words with a dashing display down the left wing. Although unsung and an unappreciated player, many people made him man of the match. He was certainly an unlikely hero with the way he tormented Adolfo, the Benfica right-back, repeatedly going past him. Aston was only 20, a stripling compared to most of the others on the pitch, yet here he was modestly explaining how he came to open up Benfica's right flank: 'Adolfo was a decent right-back but he had no pace, so I was on a winner from the start.' He went on to offer an insight into the Busby style of management. 'In my early days I had tremendous problems with the crowd getting on to me, but never did he [Busby] offer to help me. To me, he was never a father figure, but I accepted it because that was the way the club was run. It worked on a star system. He got what he considered to be the best players and he put you in the side and you performed, or you didn't. To put it another way, he taught you to swim three or four strokes and then threw you in at the deep end. You sank or swam. I was one of those who did several lengths that night at Wembley.

'Matt Busby wasn't a tactician, he was a great handler of men, a manipulator of people. People don't believe me when I say this, but I never received any coaching. Nobody did. We had a trainer, Jack Crompton, and that's what he was, not a coach. We never worked on tactics, we never practised a throw-in or a corner.

'Matt always believed he'd win and made you believe too. He was a very powerful speaker and had a great gravity about him. When he spoke his voice seemed to come from the middle of his chest. He could say: "Let's have a cup of tea," and it sounded like an edict from on high.'

Although Eusebio was always a threat in the final, Nobby Stiles came out on top in his fourth game against the Portuguese star – three for United and one for England – and, what's more, he played him cleanly. 'One newspaper said Eusebio had asked for more protection from the referee, but I don't believe he ever said it. I never went out to kick him. I respected him and found him all right,' said Stiles.

Brian Kidd, the babe of the side but fast catching up on the trinity in terms of influencing the course of a game, said: 'I honestly felt it was something that was meant to be. We arrived at this old hotel at Egham just outside London for the final with everyone convinced that we just had to win. We knew we had to do it, if only for Sir Matt who had patiently created another great side.'

Kidd, son of a Manchester bus driver who spent a lot of his working life driving the number 47 route past Old Trafford, thought the first half was a slight disappointment in a match that didn't come alive until extra-time. He said: 'When their equaliser came, you could sense the game slipping away from us. We were exhausted.

'But Sir Matt talked to us and urged us to start playing our football again. My moment of glory, I will never forget . . . a goal to celebrate my nineteenth birthday. What a present!'

Bobby Charlton was unashamedly in tears at the end of the game. Like Bill Foulkes, he had survived Munich to fight back with Matt Busby. Later that evening, he missed the celebration party at the team's London hotel, too exhausted, physically and emotionally. Looking back, he says: 'My thoughts on the day of the European Cup final were that we just wouldn't lose. I can remember thinking that we had come too far and had been through too much for us to fail in that final match.

'The European Cup had become like a mission for Manchester

United and I think the older players felt as if we had been pursuing a sort of golden fleece of football. We had everything going for us of course, playing on our own patch at Wembley. We also had a good record against teams from Portugal, and after coming from three-one down in Madrid to win the semi-final, I thought it would be impossible for us to get beaten.

'It was very humid during the day and I knew it would be hard work, but I also knew that we would find something extra. That's something British teams have always had, this resilience, especially in extra-time. This is what England had produced to win the World Cup two years previously.

'I thought there was no point me worrying because Benfica had a lot more to worry about. I knew it would come one day, but it was in the nick of time. Without being disrespectful to the players involved, the 1968 team was probably no longer at its best. We had faded in the league to let Manchester City win the title and a lot of us were past our peak. I, for one, wasn't going to get another chance and about half the team were in the same boat.

'So we were all pretty determined and, as I say, defeat was never in our minds. Our first goal confirmed that idea because I scored it with a header – and that didn't happen very often!

'We felt some despair when they equalised to force us into extra-time, but even then, I thought our background of stamina training would stand us in good stead. We knew they must be tired as well.

'Then came that sparkling ten minutes in which we scored three goals . . . George Best, Brian Kidd and myself.

'Benfica were a formidable side going forward but I thought their defence might creak, and that's how it worked out. Our own defence rose to the occasion, with some key saves from Alex Stepney against Eusebio, and steady displays from Bill Foulkes,

Shay Brennan and Tony Dunne. Nobby Stiles was an important cog in that team, too. He used to tidy up for us. He seemed able to sense trouble and where danger was going to come from. So he was always there ready and waiting, a great reader of the game. He was a bit like a sheepdog keeping everything under control. If one of the sheep tried to break away, he would dart into action and put the breakaway back in the pen.

'Johnny Aston had a particularly good game in the final, running the legs off their full-back down his wing to produce some great crosses. At the same time he was pulling their defence wide, which gave the rest of us more room.

'When the final whistle went I remember thinking that it was the ultimate achievement, not just for the players but for the club and Sir Matt Busby. I suppose I can't speak for everyone, but I think I probably do, when I say that we felt winning the European Cup had been a duty to Manchester United. For some of us it had become a family thing. We had been together so long.

'I missed most of the celebrating that night. I was absolutely drained and kept fainting. My wife Norma told me the next day that Matt had got up late in the evening to sing "What a Wonderful World" and I guess that just about summed it up for all of us.'

Manchester United's success had not just bowled over local media like myself but had similarly impressed the more neutral – and perhaps less biased – national press, like *Guardian* football writer Albert Barham, whose report the next day put the achievement into a national perspective but was humming with admiration.

Albert wrote: 'At last the European Cup comes to England from Manchester United's triumph at Wembley last night. They won just as they promised they would, not so much for themselves but for their manager, Matt Busby.

'And what a victory it was. They were taken to extra-time by Benfica but in seven minutes of it the Portuguese were crushed by three goals ... What finer player could there be to score United's first goal than Bobby Charlton. This was his first goal in European Cup football since the previous, and up to now greatest triumph, of United – against Benfica in the Stadium of Light two years ago. It also fell to him to score the last. And in between was a goal taken as coolly as on the practice pitch by Best, and one from Kidd.

'But goals apart, this again was a great triumph of teamwork and team spirit. Every player gave his all from Stepney, who three times was United's saviour from the powerful shooting of Eusebio, to Foulkes, who has missed only three of United's matches in their eleven years of waiting for this supreme moment. And there was too the covering of the backs, the prompting of Crerand, and the sight of Aston enjoying himself on the wing, and Best so often cruelly hacked down in full flight.

'Otto Gloria, Benfica's manager, had feared the speed of United. "They all come forward and they all go back," he said, "and the speed could upset my team." So it turned out.'

Denis Law watched the game from a hospital bed in Manchester. He had more than played his part in getting the Reds to the final, making nine appearances in that season's competition, but had missed the big occasion itself in order to have a long overdue operation on his troublesome knee. Overall, he'd had a frustrating season and at one point the club thought the pain he complained about was more in his head than his knee. After his operation, Law couldn't resist having the offending piece of irritant bone pickled in a jar and labelled: 'From my head!' As for the final, Law said: 'The nurses at St Joseph's were United supporters. A few of my pals came in too, and along with the nurses we watched the match in my room and got bladdered together on a case of McEwan's. It was a great emotional night for everyone.

'I took the congratulations from my friends, the nursing staff and other patients, but it wasn't about me; it was about Sir Matt, a decade after he had lain on what he must have thought was his deathbed. The cheers were soon mixed with tears as Matt Busby finally held aloft the European Cup.'

Winning the European Cup brought entry into the World Club Championship, a competition played home and away between the champions of Europe and the winners of the Copa Libertadores in South America. This meant a match against Estudiantes of Argentina and something of a culture shock. The first leg, played in Buenos Aires, was summed up the following night by the headline with my report that simply read: 'SAVAGERY.' The *Daily Mirror* carried a banner that said: 'THE NIGHT THEY SPAT ON SPORTSMANSHIP.'

Argentina had been badly upset by England manager Sir Alf Ramsey during the 1966 World Cup when he had described the players in their national team as animals. The quarter-final when England knocked out Argentina and their captain Rattin had been sent off had provided a provocative background.

Everything started well enough, with United's arrival in Buenos Aires marked by presentations of flowers, great hospitality, and even a specially staged polo match for the players, officials and English press to watch. The first indication that the South Americans meant business came on the eve of the match, when both teams were invited to an official reception. Matt Busby wasn't keen on taking his players to what he expected to be a long drawn out affair and hardly the best preparation for a big game, but he agreed in the interests of goodwill and courtesy to the hosts. His unease was confirmed when the Estudiantes team failed to turn up and their coach, Osvaldo Zubeldia, said the next day: 'This is a game for men. I see no point in teams kissing each other.'

Ironically, I got a scoop for the *Manchester Evening News* out of the situation, because the national morning papers had assumed the party would take place, and because of the time difference between Argentina and home, they had written reports describing it in imagined detail. I had time on my side, and of course my report talked about the snub, much to the embarrassment of the nationals.

The United manager became even angrier when he had the local newspapers translated to discover the Estudiantes manager had been quoted with some hardly welcoming comments. He was reported as saying that Nobby Stiles was 'an assassin', and Estudiantes even ran an article in their match programme saying that Stiles was 'brutal, badly intentioned and a bad sportsman'. Stiles, of course, had been in the England team which had beaten Argentina in 1966, and he was the focus and hate target for the Estudiantes supporters. The hostility for Stiles actually started as he walked off the plane in Buenos Aires and an excitable commentator announced the arrival of the United players over the loudspeaker system as they walked through the airport: 'Bobby Charlton . . . El Supremo,' he shouted. 'George Best . . . El Beatle,' he declared. Then his voice went up an octave and there was a great answering roar as he went on: 'Nobby Stiles . . . El Bandido!'

The pre-match scene was surreal, with steel-helmeted riot police armed with batons and tear-gas guns waiting behind the goals, while out on the pitch, pretty girls in colourful national costume gave delightful dancing displays. As the players came out, a bomb releasing a thick cloud of dense red smoke lent a nightmarish touch, as the United players struggled to retain their composure.

Stiles was headbutted early on, and did well to keep control in the face of some fierce tackling until he was finally sent off 10 minutes from the end of a 1-0 defeat to the accompaniment of loud jeering. Charlton, who had needed stitches in a shin wound, said: 'Their ideas and interpretation of football are just different from ours. We didn't really get a chance to play.'

After the match Nobby Stiles got the fright of his life as he was coming out of the stadium. He describes the scene: 'It was dark and shadowy, when I suddenly felt something thrust into my back with a voice whispering into my ear: "Now then, El Bandido . . ." I thought my end had come until I realised it was Brian Kidd!'

Stiles had something of a chequered career with disciplinary issues, though as Bobby Charlton said previously, he didn't so much tackle people as bump into them, and that of course was down to poor eyesight that he kept hidden from the club because he thought it would damage his career. It was Harry Gregg who came to his rescue after noting his struggle to see properly when they were playing cards. He went to see Busby and said: 'You know boss, you just have to do something about Nobby's eyesight. The kid is really struggling; he is putting the wrong cards down when we are playing. It must be affecting his play, too.'

The club finally sorted him out – remember this was in the days before United had a specialist optician on hand for this kind of problem. So began the trademark big black specs and the ritual of contact lenses for training and playing. It brought about a marked improvement in his game, though his new look didn't evidently impress England colleague Jack Charlton. Stiles wrote in his book, *Nobby Stiles: After the Ball*: 'It was in the dressing room before playing for the Football League that I first met Jack Charlton. We eyed each other across the room and I was not thrilled when he recalled for the world his first impression of me. He said in his book he saw this "little Japanese-looking bastard fitting these bloody great things into his eyes."' Not very politically correct these days, I suppose, but then it was a few years ago and that was what life in the dressing room was like.

Bobby Charlton once wrote that Stiles was his favourite footballer, and not just because he was a pal. He simply admired him as a player, and it's my guess that Nobby Stiles is arguably the nation's favourite, certainly among those who witnessed his toothless and joyful jig round Wembley after England had beaten Germany to win the World Cup in 1966.

Stiles can certainly look back with pride . . . he and Bobby Charlton are the only two Englishmen to hold winners' medals in both the World Cup and the European Cup. That's a bit special isn't it?

The second game against Estudiantes at Old Trafford wasn't really a good night for George Best or for Denis Law who had to quit the game for four stitches in a gashed knee that saw him take no further part. Best didn't finish the match either, sent off with Medina 10 minutes from the end for swinging a punch at the man who had just tackled him heavily.

Willie Morgan scored late for a 1-1 draw but it was an aggregate defeat for United. The competition was further marred the following year when Estudiantes had three players jailed for 'acts of hostility' in their second leg in Milan. A number of European clubs subsequently refused to take part and the competition lost its stature.

Defeat in the World Club Championship couldn't take the gloss off what had been a tremendous 1967-68 season, as United finished runners-up to Manchester City in the championship and topped that by clinching their holy grail, the European Cup, at the home of football. A breakout year for George Best had seen him score 32 goals in all competitions en route to the European Footballer of the Year award – completing the award hat-trick for the trinity – while Bobby Charlton and Denis Law had contributed a further 31 goals between them. Manchester United, Sir Matt Busby and the trinity had forever etched their names into European club football's record books.

10

Idols

Time undoubtedly lends enchantment to our heroes and as fans gaze at the statue outside Old Trafford and pay homage to the trinity in all their bronze glory, they must seem like demi-gods. For many people they were, and still are, but they were also revered and respected by their peers and contemporaries. It was certainly daunting for young players coming into the team to play alongside the anointed ones, as Sammy McIlroy explained to me after casting his mind back to his first-team debut, aged 17, in 1971.

'To begin with, I felt let down. I had been looking forward all week to playing in the reserve-team derby at Maine Road on the Friday evening before the following day's league match. I was upset when Bill Foulkes, the reserve-team coach, told me I wouldn't be playing for the reserves as usual because I had to report the next morning for duty with the first team at Old Trafford.

'I had been looking forward all week to playing in the mini-derby, and I didn't think it was fair that I would have to go with the first team to help carry the kit baskets.

'But of course, I had to do as I was told, and it came as a bit of a shock the next morning to be told by manager Frank O'Farrell that Denis Law had failed a fitness test and I would be making my debut. Talk about excitement. The only problem was, I wasn't told until 11am, so I didn't have time to tell my parents, but it was good in a way because there was no time to get nervous or over-awed by the occasion.

'This was the era of Charlton, Law and Best, as well as players like Brian Kidd, and I would also be playing against people like Mike Summerbee, Colin Bell, Francis Lee and Neil Young.

'Both sides were full of big names and it was a marvellous experience, especially the way it worked out. To score on your debut is great, but to do it in a derby made it even more memorable. Brian Kidd set it up with a cross from the right to George Best. He couldn't control it properly because Tony Book was pulling his shirt, but he did manage to get a pass to me and I was able to put it past Joe Corrigan.

'Before the match, George promised me a bottle of champagne if I scored, and with his help that's exactly what I did, and on the Monday morning a celebration bottle duly arrived for me. I kept it for years, because I worshipped him and it was so precious to me.

'You see, I was in awe of George because of our Northern Ireland connection, though I felt a great respect for both Bobby and Denis as well. It wasn't that they tried to frighten you, but they had achieved so much compared to the likes of me just starting out in the game.

'I played a few games in the same side with all three of them; in fact I remember scoring against Pat Jennings in one game and all three came up to congratulate me. I saw it later on television. It was like a dream. I couldn't believe it and I would love to have had a photograph of that moment. That was against Spurs. As I say, I scored, and Denis got two.

'I had a few games with Denis in the team when I deputised for Brian Kidd, but he was beginning to get his knee problems [in the Seventies]. Even so, I got glimpses of his brilliance in the penalty area, his movement and his spring in the air . . . quite unbelievable.

'Bobby was a totally different character compared to Denis and George. Bobby was the serious one. He just got on with the game, even in training, and the five-a-sides had to be played properly, no fooling around. He wanted everything to be right. While Denis and George would want fun, nutmegging opponents just for the lark of it, Bobby had no time for that kind of thing. If you were slacking, he would tell you off and you wouldn't dare cheek him.

'Not that you took liberties with Denis and George. Remember, I was only 17 and they were senior players of great distinction, though I must admit that George didn't exactly look it, with the boots he brought with him for a Northern Ireland international fixture against Iceland at Windsor Park. They looked as if he had picked them out of a rubbish bin; goodness knows where he had got them from. He must have been in a great hurry and taken them from a pile due to be thrown out by the kit man.

'Anyway, he started complaining about the left one that he said had nails coming through. We took roughly the same shoe size, so I said try my left one. It fitted so I took his and we both played in odd boots. At least George's didn't have nails sticking in his feet. Why was I so generous? You have got to bear in mind that I was in awe of him, and it just didn't seem right that he should play in boots that were hurting him.

'I just went off and got some extra inner soles and everything worked out fine, with me scoring in a three-nil win. I remember playing another international with George in the team against Holland, a two-two draw in Amsterdam.

'I admired the others too and went to some trouble to make my boots look like Denis Law's. One day, I noticed him taking the Adidas stripes off his boots because he was contracted to Puma and should have been wearing their kit, only he preferred his old Adidas boots. I rather liked the look of his doctored all-black boots, so I ripped the stripes off mine just to be like him and I wore Puma for the rest of my career.

'I learned so much from the three of them, and not just about sponsorship,' he added.

McIlroy, who had joined United as a 15-year-old in 1969, learned his lessons well and went on to play in United's first team for 11 years under five different managers as the Reds hit a turbulent part of their history. He marked the end of an era, the last of the Busby Babes to roll off United's production line and build a future at Old Trafford.

His favourite time at Old Trafford was under Tommy Docherty, the manager who followed Frank O'Farrell. He told me: 'It was an unforgettable spell under the Doc. You just never knew what to expect from one day to another. We were relegated, but the team that came out of the Second Division mirrored his image. It was all-out attack and to hell with the consequences. We may have been unpredictable but we must have been exciting to watch – runaway champions of the Second Division and FA Cup winners too.'

McIlroy, who won a total of 89 caps for Northern Ireland, left United after Ron Atkinson had succeeded the Doc and joined Stoke for a £350,000 fee. He was briefly at Manchester City, and after working abroad joined Bury and found out that there is always something new to learn in football.

'At Gigg Lane, we had to take our own kit home after training to be washed, and that's when I learned a new skill . . . how to work the washing machine,' he explained. Nowadays, McIlroy is a familiar figure again around Old Trafford, part of the former player network helping to entertain corporate guests and also working as a pundit for the club's television network.

Naturally, opponents had good cause to respect George Best, especially the defenders who had the job of marking him, as Tony Book, the former Manchester City manager and full-back in Best's day, explained to me: 'I was always quite quick as a full-back, so I was always the one asked to mark George when we played a derby match against United.

'I recall one particular game when I dropped a clanger very early on. I made the mistake of letting the ball bounce and George was in like a flash to stick it in the back of the net. The next time, he had the ball running down the wing and I was running beside him waiting for my chance to tackle him, saying to him: "Pass the ball, George, pass it!" He later asked me why I'd said that. "Because if you haven't got the ball, you can't hurt us you little blighter!" I was very conscious at the time of the way, not long before, he had hurt another member of the Book family when he had put six past my brother Kim, the Northampton goalkeeper, in an FA Cup tie.

'I always had a great respect for him because he was a marvellous player,' Book said.

The City man who knew the Irishman best was undoubtedly Mike Summerbee, because the pair of them were pals, even though they played for fiercely rival clubs. Says Summerbee: 'I first met George soon after arriving in Manchester as a local lad from Swindon feeling a bit homesick and lost in a big city. I went into the Khardomah Lodge in the centre of town for a coffee. I was sitting on my own when I spotted George at a table, also on his own. The only thing we had in common was in a blonde girl, Georgina, who turned out to be the daughter of Ruth Ellis, sitting at a table between us, also on her own. Naturally we competed for her attention, and that was what brought George and me together.

'We became good friends, enjoyed some great holidays together and George was best man at my wedding. We never spoke about the game, and when we played against each other we were on opposite sides of the pitch and so it was easy to keep away from each other. He could easily have come over to my side to show me up, but he never did. He could have done, because I was a footballer and he was a genius.'

George Best, a European Footballer of the Year of course, certainly had international admirers, like the leading Dutch sportswriter, Marcel van der Kraan, who writes for *De Telegraaf.* In a recent interview for the English Football Writers' Association website, he was asked by then FWA chairman Chris Davies for the one moment in football he would put on his personal soccer highlights DVD. His answer: 'George Best playing in the De Kuip stadium in Rotterdam for Northern Ireland in a 1976 World Cup qualifier. He ran the show against a team with Johan Cruyff, Johan Neeskens, Wim Jansen, Arie Haan ... That same Dutch team went on to play in the 1978 World Cup final in Argentina, but they were held to a two-all draw in Rotterdam that night. I was a young kid, at the match with my dad, and all I can remember is watching George Best for ninety minutes. It was like watching Jesus in football boots. Absolute magic.'

His trinity colleagues certainly admired him as a footballer, even though they might have had reservations once he had taken up the drink. Denis Law: 'You think of Maradona, and you think of Di Stefano and Puskas in my day. There have been many great players, but Bestie was definitely up there. He will be remembered for all the magnificent ability that he had and he was definitely one on his own.'

Sir Bobby summed him up: 'Manchester United's glorious history has been created by people like George Best. Anyone who witnessed what George could do on the pitch, wished they could do the same. He made an immense contribution to the game and enriched the lives of everyone who saw him play.'

Sir Matt Busby once told me, as he tried to keep George on the straight and narrow: 'I'll sort him out, if it's the last thing I do.' For once in his life Busby failed but he had no hesitation in his appreciation of him as a footballer. 'George was gifted, with more individual ability than I had ever seen in a player. When you remember great names like Matthews, Finney and Mannion, I can't think of one who took the ball so close to an opponent, to beat him with it, as George Best did.'

Denis Law also had the charisma and personality to impress people. You just have to talk to Fred Eyre, who after football became an extremely successful Manchester businessman, but who 50 years ago was a young hopeful on Manchester City's groundstaff, to appreciate the effect the Lawman could have on those around him.

Fred, who also made a career in after-dinner speaking by selling himself as a failed footballer and wrote the bestselling book *Kicked into Touch* describing his experiences, prospered in the stationery business but his heart still lies in football and Manchester City. Looking back to those early days at Maine Road, he says: 'I remember the first time I saw Denis Law and can tell you exactly what he was wearing. Along with other lads like Neil Young and David Wagstaffe, I was there to watch a reserve match against Huddersfield Town. Denis wasn't playing because he was in their first team by then, and we weren't playing because we were still in the junior teams.

'He was standing in the tunnel leaning against the wall and he was wearing a black Italian suit, slim tie and winkle picker shoes. I decided he was already a superstar and that if I ever made it in football, that's how I would dress. As a young man, you couldn't help but be aware of him. His face was alert and alive, he just stood out. I had seen all the stars like Puskas, the Busby Babes like Duncan Edwards, but Denis just stood out both on and off the field. I thought, that's class, and said to myself if and when I got to that level, that would be me. He was so different and already a superstar in my eyes.

'Denis was supremely confident of course, but off the field, at any rate, he wasn't cocky and he was brilliant with us kids. There are always defining moments in your life when you are young and one of them for me came shortly after I had left Ducie Avenue School to join Manchester City and had cadged a lift from train-ing with Denis and [team-mate] Roy Cheetham in Roy's car. When we drove past the school, I was waving to my old school mates and singing the Sinatra song "What a swellegant, elegant party" which is how I felt sitting in the same car as Denis Law. Denis was in good voice, too, little knowing that just four days later he would be at Wembley playing for Scotland in the team beaten nine-two by England. I doubt he would have been quite so breezy if he had known what was in store for him!

'Of course, in those days as kids we were always in awe of foot-ballers. I remember going to school each day from Blackley on first the number eighty-eight bus and then the seventy-six to Ducie Avenue, which is just one stop from Maine Road, and always on the same bus would be Joe Hayes, the City inside-forward famous for scoring the opening goal in the 1956 FA Cup final. We used to fight to get to sit next to him, though we never tried to speak to him because we were too scared. Then came the day I was reporting to Manchester City for my first day's training and so stayed on the bus after all my mates had got off at the school stop. I saw Joe Hayes give me a funny look because I was still on the bus, an even funnier look when I got off at the same stop as him, and even more so when I followed him across the forecourt at Maine Road and then through the door into the ground. He must have thought I was stalking him, at least until he turned into the first-team dressing room while I went the other way to find Jimmy Meadows, my new boss.

'Most people remember Denis Law as a striker, but when he first came to City he was an all-action inside-forward. He had the energy to be everywhere. I had never seen a player like him before.

'I have got to say though that there was one aspect in training where myself and the other groundstaff lads put Denis in the shade. It was the custom in those days at the close of training for Laurie Barnett, the trainer, to suspend a football on a rope from the roof of the tunnel leading from the pitch to the dressing room area. He would set it swinging and then the lads in turn would run up the tunnel and head the ball. It was tricky until you got used to the ball moving about. We juniors had been doing this for some time, and we were pretty good at timing our runs to give the ball a good thump, but not Denis. He never got the hang of it and he had to take some terrible ribbing.

'Out on the pitch in a match situation, there was nobody better at heading the ball. He was famed for his ability to get up there and hang in the air to make marvellous contact and score stunning goals – but not in that tunnel!

'For me though it just made him human, which he certainly

looked on his 21st birthday when he came into the ground with a big smile on his face, and again I can recall exactly what he was wearing. This time he didn't look quite so slick wearing a bottle-green jumper with three buttons at the neck. I can see him now. I suppose it must have been quite fashionable at the time.

'What is nice, though, is when great players are great people, and Denis Law certainly falls into that category. I will always remember starting out in the stationery and office equipment business because after playing for different managers and coaches at many clubs I realised I needed to do something else in the way of making a living. Even I had to admit that I was running out of clubs, so after experience working for Chris Muir, a City director, in his Caldwells shop, I decided to start out on my own. I was so excited when I got my first big order involving desks, tables and chairs. I hired a van and the wholesale people I had bought from helped me load up. I then drove to King Street in the middle of Manchester to deliver to Horizon Travel who were on the first floor. As I pulled up, it hit me for the first time, how on earth was I going to manhandle all this furniture up the stairs all on my own? I was sitting on the tailgate wondering what to do when Denis came strolling by. After the usual "how are you doing" exchanges, I admitted I had a problem and explained it to him.

'Without a word, he took his jacket off, threw it into the back of the van and said let's get started. He helped me shift the whole lot and later I heard one of the girls in the office say: "Fred must be doing OK in his new business because he's got Denis Law working for him part-time." What a guy!'

Yes, Denis Law was some player and some character, and clearly not an easy man to follow into the team. Yet like the other members of the trinity, he couldn't go on forever, and with Tommy Docherty now at the helm, the Doc went for another Scot to play striker and signed Lou Macari for £200,000 from Celtic. And just to make sure that there was no doubt about what was expected of him, he gave Lou the number 10 shirt for his debut in a 2-2 draw against West Ham with Law, much to Lou's embarrassment, given the number 4 shirt.

Says Macari: 'I was a young player from Scotland and didn't realise until later that this was a shocking thing to do. The number ten shirt belonged to Denis Law right through his career at Old Trafford, and looking back I can only think the Doc was making mischief. If I had appreciated it at the time, I would have refused to take the ten.

'The thing was, Denis didn't make the kind of fuss that some players would have created in that situation, and I stayed United's number ten right the way through. I saw Denis recently and reminded him of what had happened, but typically of him he just laughed.

'He was sitting having a pot of tea at the time, which is also typical; he always loved a cup of tea. When I first arrived at United, I was just delighted to be training and playing with Denis because that's how you learn. At Celtic, I had learned from the older Lisbon Lions who had won the European Cup and then at Old Trafford I had the chance to pick up stuff from a great striker.

'When you play up front, it's a tough position and you have to look after yourself or you will get knocked from pillar to post, particularly if you are a little fella! Now I had the chance to learn from a man who was capable of being Mr Nasty on the football field, if he thought it was necessary. What he told me was music to my ears.'

Macari says he found Law, Charlton and Best all willing to help the younger players like him. 'Learning from the pros is what it is all about,' he told me.

'People said about George Best that he was a drinker, and maybe he was at the end, but during my time at Old Trafford I never regarded him as a drinker. He went into clubs and people assumed he had a jug of gin on the go, but half a lager lasted him ages. I don't drink, still don't, and so I notice these things, and in my view a lot of people had the wrong idea about him. I found him a good pro, just like Denis and Bobby.'

Macari never quite matched Law's scoring rate, but not many did, and he was a key player up front with Stuart Pearson, leading United out of the Second Division. He made over 400 first-team appearances and scored 77 goals in his 11 years at the club – wearing Denis Law's number 10 shirt!

We've essentially been taking a nostalgic walk down memory lane, absorbing the triumphs and tragedies of the United trinity, but it is more than that for Sir Bobby Charlton who is still just as keenly involved with Manchester United as he was as a player. In his long-standing capacity as a director of the club, Sir Bobby played a key role for instance in the appointment of Sir Alex Ferguson as manager of the club, as he made clear to Tom Tyrrell and myself when we wrote a tribute to Sir Alex on completing 25 years at Old Trafford. Bobby told us: 'The appointment of Sir Alex as manager was the best thing that ever happened to Manchester United. He has led our club to the forefront of the game in England and made us the dominant force with such a stack of trophies that he has overtaken the great man of my playing days, Sir Matt Busby, as the most successful manager of all time.'

Another instance of how Sir Bobby has transposed himself from player to contemporary football man is reflected in the thrill he experienced when United completed their unique treble in 1999. He explained to me that that special night in Barcelona, when United beat Bayern Munich with two late goals, was his best ever occasion in football. I thought about the significance of his remark, and said how could it possibly be better than winning the European Cup as a player in the team, as he was in 1968? He said it was too nerve racking in '68 to be enjoyable, and watching in the Nou Camp was a far more pleasurable experience.

Indeed, that's the message that comes through when I asked him to look back at his career and talk me through from the old days to the trophy-winning empire that Sir Alex Ferguson has created. He told me: 'When I first started with Manchester United, the club won the FA Youth Cup five times in successive seasons. I think I played in three of the finals and Jimmy Murphy left us in no doubt about the importance of the youth programme. He used to tell us to forget the league and the FA Cup, the youth team is the cream of the club.

'I remember I could hardly sleep the night before a youth match, because I had been brainwashed by Jimmy into thinking it was the most important game of the season. Of course, in a way it was, because when Matt Busby started to have a few bad results he decimated the first team in the knowledge of what he had coming up behind. He didn't do things by halves, and he said: "I'm bringing in the kids."

'That's how the Busby Babes came into being, with players like Eddie Colman and Duncan Edwards who could hit the ball left foot, right foot and manipulate it any way he wanted. Duncan could hit seventy-yard passes, could defend, attack, was good in the air and was brave, a fantastic and complete player. With the Babes we had a feeling that we were as good as anyone around in the world. They were great players who were on the verge of becoming world stars. This was an age before television, but word was going round fast, look out for Manchester United.

'Then suddenly with the crash at Munich, the whole thing had gone and the future for Manchester United was not as certain as it had seemed. Matt Busby had to start all over again, which of course he did. He always stressed with his teams, both before and after Munich, that we were all good players and said that we must not be afraid to express ourselves.

'It was because of that, that George Best felt he could beat six people in one run. It was why Denis Law would try acrobatic overhead kicks and why I would try to shoot for goal from such long distances – which a lot of the time was probably stupid – but which, I might add, also led to a few great goals.

'Then in 1968 we won the European Cup ... As soon as the match was over, everyone went up to Matt to pat him on the back, and my feeling was that it was something for the lads who had died in the first attempt to become champions of Europe. It was a very emotional time.'

11

The King Departs

Nothing lasts forever, not even the great trinity, and as they moved into the Seventies it was clear that Bobby Charlton, Denis Law and George Best were all on the last lap of their careers. Just as they had taken different routes to find themselves together at Old Trafford, so their departures from Manchester United took contrasting paths.

Bobby Charlton, as you might expect, took the exit door marked 'dignity'; Denis Law, again perhaps typically, departed with a touch of embarrassment and controversy to join rivals Manchester City, while George Best went, as he had lived, with drama and tragedy played out under the spotlight.

For Denis Law, the end of the United road was a bumpy ride. His long-standing knee injury was increasingly becoming the bane of his football life. Treatment for injuries 50 years ago was nothing like as sophisticated as it is today, with all manner of technical aids as well as a better understanding of what is required now the norm, especially at the big clubs like Manchester United. When I go to United's old boys' functions, I meet a lot of former players now limping as they pay the price of their profession, very often the result of their courage playing on through injuries when rest would have been a better option. Hip and knee replacements are commonplace, and we mustn't forget those former players now suffering from some form of dementia, as it does seem to me that heading the heavy leather balls of the Sixties might well have contributed to their problems.

One of the treatments for troublesome knee injuries in the old days was the use of cortisone injections. When injected into your body, it disguised pain for three or four hours and helped restore surrounding tissue. The consensus now is not to have more than one a month, with a maximum of three or four during the course of a year, and to avoid excessive movement or stress on the joint for about a week after an injection, but players like Denis Law were injected and sent out to play without rest.

Law seemed to have them weekly. He used to come into the dressing room at half-time with his knee throbbing and he would sit in the big bath with a hosepipe spraying cold water on his knee, in an effort to deaden the pain and get the swelling down. Doing that for a year or two would inevitably take its toll. Players accepted it because they didn't know differently, and, in fairness, neither did the medical and physiotherapy staff. The culture at that time was to be ready for the next match, whatever the problem, and it was the same for all players, no matter how much they had cost the club.

Law's knee problem became chronic in 1967, so much so that he consulted and paid for a private osteopath, which, when United found out, did not please them. In the 1967-68 season, he played only 23 league games, many of them when he wasn't fully fit. United kept him going in the European Cup and he played in all rounds up to the semi-final, at which point he was forced into hospital for an exploratory operation on his knee that saw him watching the final from a hospital bed.

Injuries certainly restricted the closing chapter of Law's career at Old Trafford, and I also don't think he felt at ease with any of his three managers following Matt Busby's retirement. Wilf McGuinness was the first to drop him, which must have been a real shock, and he had an uneasy relationship with his successor Frank O'Farrell, once describing him as coming to United a stranger and leaving as a stranger, too. Perhaps Law sensed that O'Farrell did not have much faith in him either, something which the Irishman revealed when he told me that he would never have a successful team until Busby's old guard had moved on, referring to the likes of Law and his trinity colleagues as Matt's players, not his.

When Tommy Docherty took over in the United hot seat in December 1972, it seemed at first as if he would be good for Law's career – after all, the two Scots had known each other for a long time, and Law had even recommended Docherty to the club – but the Doc was no sentimentalist. He brought Law back into the team in midfield for his first game in charge, a 1-1 draw against Leeds, but was not impressed with the team's performance. Law was one of the casualties as Docherty declared war on the older players, saying that some of them were taking big money out of the club but giving nothing in return. Clearly, the trinity must have been very much in his mind. In fact, Law would play in only nine league games that season, making two substitute appearances and scoring just one goal.

Tommy Docherty had brutal plans for the trinity, and I

unwittingly figured in them. As the 1972-73 season drew to an end, I asked the manager for the customary transfer and retained list, which was when a club announced who would be staying and who was available. I immediately wrote a report for that night's *Football Pink* that included the news that Denis Law, along with Tony Dunne, were being given free transfers. It was a big story of course, and it was picked up by other news agencies, which is how Law came to read about his future on television in a bar in Aberdeen.

It came as a bombshell for Law who, rightly or wrongly, had understood that after his planned testimonial against Ajax early the next season, he would announce his retirement as a player and take up a coaching position with United. He was not impressed with the news of his free transfer, and naturally felt publicly humiliated. He returned to Manchester to join his wife Diana, who was awaiting the birth of their fifth child, and decided to have it out with the Doc. I don't think he got much satisfaction, it was all too late, and at the end of the season he duly left and signed for rivals Manchester City.

There was still the matter of his testimonial, but as Docherty had promised, the match against the Dutch masters Ajax would go ahead, with the idea that Law would swap his blue shirt for a red one again and play for United. In fact, he didn't play in his testimonial because he had been injured and Johnny Hart, the City manager, ruled against it in order to get the player fit for the Blues' game that coming weekend. I was proud to be on Law's testimonial committee and edited the match programme in which I made this tribute on behalf of the *Manchester Evening News*: 'The King lives again. He is back in the blue shirt of Manchester City but with his mane of lion-coloured hair still flying in the goalmouths, his spring-heeled menace still stalking the grounds of the First

Division.' I went on to say that United fans would never forget him and would be indebted to him forever; and that whatever he achieved for City could not wipe out the memories of his brilliance for the Reds, because, as I pointed out: 'He was one of a special trinity . . . Charlton, Law and Best. Their names trip off the tongue like a football litany. The image of the Lawman's fire and flair in the penalty area will never fade.'

The late Derek Potter of the *Daily Express* expressed similar sentiments when he said, with a memorable description: 'He is the sharpest blend of mind and muscle . . . that was Demon Denis.'

It was a chance meeting between Docherty and Johnny Hart, the City manager, at the football writers' annual dinner that had triggered the cross-town signing, and of course it completed the circle for Law, returning to the club where he first cut his teeth in the First Division. He showed that he hadn't completely lost his touch, making 24 league appearances in that 1973-74 season, and scoring nine times, the last one a goal he will never forget because it was against United, whose 1-0 defeat at the time many thought might be the loss that would send the Reds down into the Second Division.

It was a kind of half-hearted score, back-heeled in past Alex Stepney with only nine minutes of the game remaining, and this time there was no gladiatorial salute with finger pointing to the sky. Law looked absolutely crest-fallen, though he needn't have worried because the two other clubs fighting against relegation, Southampton and Norwich City, both won, so United were condemned to go down anyway.

Law still enjoyed a final international flourish and a World Cup hurrah in West Germany in the summer of 1974. Willie Ormond had recalled him after being impressed with one of his displays for Manchester City against Coventry City – 'The best centre-forward display I have seen all season,' said the Scotland manager – and Law duly helped the Scots qualify, with the added bonus of England failing to get to Germany.

Scotland's World Cup finals' campaign was short-lived, but at least there was the satisfaction for Law of bowing out at the top when new City manager Tony Book let him know that he wouldn't be figuring in his first-team plans for the following season. Book told him he could stay and help with the reserves, but Law decided to seize the moment to retire. He had a lot of offers to go abroad to places like America and wonders now if he was a bit hasty. He says: 'If I have a regret, it is that I quit a year or two too early, because you are a long time retired, and I didn't take a coaching course that could possibly have kept me in football.'

Not that the King lacked other interests. He did a lot of radio and television work after his playing career and took up a variety of jobs, ranging from working in Francis Lee's paper company to trying his luck out in the carpet business. By now of course, he also had a busy family life with his wife Diana, four sons, a daughter and grandchildren. Di Law, his daughter, became a popular press officer at Manchester United for a number of years to keep the Law link with United very much alive.

Sir Matt Busby used to describe him as a good friend and a warm-hearted family man who was never less than cheerful. More recently life tested him again, but he won through like the King he is after an operation for prostate cancer. To his great credit, this very private man went public, in the *Manchester Evening News* and other papers, with his illness because he felt it was important to increase public awareness of prostate cancer.

Denis Law was quite different as a player and as a personality. It was all fireworks on the field, but he could be abrasive off it as well. As Pat Crerand said: 'Denis can be funny and great company if he likes you, but there is no middle road with him. If he doesn't like someone, he won't even talk to him. He picks company carefully and takes a lot of trouble to avoid the limelight. He is a marvellous bloke at keeping a secret.'

Law made no secret of the fact that he was not always happy with the press, especially the *Manchester Evening News* reporter, as I remember only too clearly. It was as if at times he resented being questioned in interviews by someone who had never played the game and whom he probably felt didn't really understand it. I was quite used to this approach, best summed up by my late friend, John Doherty, one of the original Busby Babes and for many years the chairman of the Association of Former Manchester United Players. John once introduced me at a sportsmen's dinner as a man who had made a fortune out of writing about football in the paper and in books but who still knew sweet FA about the game. I put it down to dressing room banter; you certainly need a thick skin to be a local paper football correspondent! Law certainly didn't like me referring to the fact that he had spent a couple of Christmas periods back home in Scotland serving six-week suspensions, and I wrote as Christmas approached again whether we could expect a transgression to earn him a further winter break.

I explained it was a joke but he didn't see the funny side until a good few years later. Now, when we meet at former players' reunion dinners, we get on fine and he didn't even seem to mind his old boys' association making me an honorary member when I retired from the *Manchester Evening News* after many fruitful years reporting on Manchester United.

I wasn't the only one who had his moments with the Lawman. David Sadler in his early years had a rough ride when comparisons were made. He would often face the wrath of United fans when he took the place of their favourite, Law, but Sadler remains an admirer, as he explains: 'The description "great" sits very comfortably with Denis Law. Undoubtedly, he would have been one of the greats of any era.

'People have told me since we finished playing that we never saw the best of Law at Old Trafford. Now if we didn't, and there was a better Law in Torino or at City, then he really, really must have been some player.

'At United, he was an out-and-out striker but some say they saw him as an inside-forward, like Peter Doherty and Raich Carter, who could do absolutely everything, including making *and* taking goals. Certainly his knowledge and understanding of how the game should be played was second to none. You had to drag it out of him more often than not, but he had it all.

'Was there a weakness? We are talking now of a time when tackling was legal, defenders could go through forwards to reach the ball. Physically, Denis wasn't big and strong, but he would flinch from nothing. No one could intimidate him, which is possibly why he got so many injuries. Often he played with problems that would sideline footballers today.

'Denis could play deep and hit long passes and run any game, but he was considered more valuable to the team up front, scoring goals. Also, of course, it was a major factor that we had Bobby and Paddy doing the creative bit.

'The hardest part of the game is scoring goals and he did it for fun. There are countless stories of Bobby shooting from twenty-five yards and the keeper stopping the ball, as Denis closed in to tell him: 'You might catch the next ten, but if you drop one, I'll be here.'

'He had an uncanny instinct, anticipation, call it what you like.

He was quicksilver and had a fabulous football brain. While most people were thinking about it, Denis had done it. He was brilliant in the air, which for his size was the most surprising of his attributes, and he was wonderful with both feet. He was a genius and, as they say, he could look after himself. I would have hated to play against Denis Law.'

Just like the other members of the trinity, the name and fame of Denis Law lives on, even among those too young to have ever seen him play. In 2001, the United striker was crowned the Top Scot at a ceremony in Glasgow following a poll by readers of the influential *Daily Record* newspaper. Long known in Manchester as the King, Denis now reigns as Monarch of the Glen after a vote that saw him hold off the challenge of Kenny Dalglish and the ever-popular Jim Baxter. The readers named their best XI as: Andy Goram, Danny McGrain, Willie Miller, Billy McNeill, Eric Caldow, Jimmy Johnstone, Billy Bremner, Graeme Souness, Jim Baxter, Kenny Dalglish, and Denis Law.

To come out top man from that glittering array of Scottish stars says something about the enduring qualities of the Manchester United star, and naturally the readers also had Law as the decade winner of the Sixties. He was handed his award by none other than his trinity colleague Sir Bobby Charlton at the Hampden Park ceremony attended by the then Chancellor Gordon Brown and fellow proud Scot Sir Alex Ferguson, who incidentally delighted the tartan army when he said that the greatest-ever Scottish team would beat any all-time England side and referred to the strike partnership of Law and Dalglish as made in heaven. He said that Law or Dalglish would score in the first minute, then they would give the ball to Jimmy 'Jinky' Johnstone and the other lot wouldn't be able to get it back off him. Incidentally the United manager was voted the greatest ever Scottish manager!

Law, 60 at the time of his newspaper award, said: 'At this stage of my life, it's fantastic to receive such an honour. When I think of all the great players who have graced the Scottish jersey, and I have played with many of them, like Jim Baxter and Kenny Dalglish, then I'm thrilled the *Record* readers have chosen me.'

Apart from a long connection with the Association of Former Manchester United Players, Law has lately become much more involved with the club again. Early in 2013, United made him one of their ambassadors in a select group that includes Sir Bobby Charlton, Andy Cole, Gary Neville, Bryan Robson and Peter Schmeichel. Law is delighted with his new role which has seen him once again working in tandem with Sir Bobby Charlton. He says: 'Being an ambassador has been enjoyable. It's been great meeting fans, young and old, and it's brought back a lot of good memories. Just before Christmas, I attended a dinner for the club's oldest season ticket holders. Some had been going to matches for over fifty years. It was nice to meet them; some even remembered seeing me play. I'll be honest though, I couldn't remember half the goals they were asking me about!'

More recently, his duties have taken him to more glamorous places, such as Bahrain where he represented United at their academy there. I can also reveal that there are moves afoot to redress an omission that has seen countless other sportsmen awarded a CBE or MBE but nothing of that kind for Denis Law, one of the most successful and popular footballers of all time. He certainly doesn't seek public acclaim but quietly he has done a lot for charity. He used his prostate cancer experience to try to make men more aware of the problem and he has certainly worked hard to support the meningitis charity since one of his sons, Andrew, was struck by the disease. The Association of Former Manchester United Players has been active in both England and Scotland with letters to the appropriate authorities urging long overdue recognition for a major sportsman who has been a credit to his profession both on and off the field. Let's hope the association is successful.

12

Epitaph for George

George Best's descent into retirement was protracted, gripped by drink, gambling and a fading ability as his life began to unravel. Season 1968-69, saw George score 19 goals from 41 appearances and he helped United to the semi-finals of the European Cup in the defence of their title. Reaching the last four in Europe was a good effort but they looked vulnerable when they came up against AC Milan. They had been knocked out of the FA Cup in the sixth round by Everton and with Busby starting to lose his impetus, the weakening of the team was reflected in their finishing position of 11th in the First Division. The club were heading for a period of uncertainty and troubled times.

A change of manager seemed to speed up the last act for all three of the trinity, with season 1969-70 a period of transition for Manchester United generally following Sir Matt Busby's decision to move upstairs as general manager, with Wilf McGuinness taking over as chief coach. Busby had become aware that he needed to give the players fresh impetus and that it had become more difficult for him to supply it. As he put it: 'The demands were such that I was neglecting the all-important thing, the team. United are not just a football club any longer, but a kind of institution. So many things need attention that I felt my move to general manager was the right thing to do.'

I'm sure that Matt, approaching his 60th birthday, also felt that the club needed a younger man to stay in tune with the new breed of footballer like George Best, and that in the 31-year-old McGuinness he felt he had a natural successor, steeped in the tradition of the Old Trafford family and possessing great qualities of confidence and drive.

McGuinness had been outstanding as a young player, his qualities of leadership demonstrated in the early days as he captained Manchester Schoolboys and England Schoolboys. He played for England Youth, the Under-23 team and had won two full caps before breaking his leg in a reserve game against Stoke City at Old Trafford in December 1959. United appointed him assistant trainer when it became clear that he would never play again, and he was ready in the wings for the call to follow in the footsteps of Sir Matt.

Three games into the season, McGuinness made his first decisive move as new man in charge and dropped both Denis Law and Bobby Charlton. The whole forward line had been stuttering, and after losing successive home games to Everton 2-0 and Southampton 4-1, he brought in Don Givens and John Aston to take over from the two legends. He also swung the axe in other directions, with Paul Edwards brought in for a league debut in place of Bill Foulkes. In what turned out to be his final game, the centre-half had played against Southampton and had been given the run-around by Ron Davies, though nothing should distract from his fantastic record of 563 league appearances made over 17 seasons. Not long after, McGuinness went into the transfer market to pay £80,000 for Ian Ure of Arsenal to become his new centre-half. Ure steadied things at the back and the team went eight matches without defeat, despite McGuinness also controversially dropping Pat Crerand for a three-month sojourn in the reserves.

As the trinity and the team generally disintegrated, Best, perhaps feeling isolated and vulnerable, didn't score until the seventh game of the season, though he then hit a rich spell for a couple of months when he found his scoring touch again. In a run of 14 league and cup games he scored 13 goals, but then they dried up with the next 15 games bringing him only one goal. In keeping with his now erratic form, Best, still only 23, ran into discipline problems. He was cautioned for kicking the ball away at a free-kick and then was reported by referee Jack Taylor for knocking the ball out of his hands as they left the field. It was an offence that brought him a month's suspension. Following the Jack Taylor incident, he was sent off a second time that season playing for Northern Ireland, when he was reported for throwing mud and spitting at referee Eric Jennings. This time, amid much acrimony, he escaped punishment with the support of the Irish FA who wanted him available for the next international.

Behind the scenes, Best was becoming increasingly difficult to manage. He failed to turn up for training on Christmas Day of 1970 and McGuinness also found himself in a real dilemma when he caught Best with a girl in his room a couple of hours before an FA Cup match. His behaviour was splitting the dressing room.

During his ban, United played five games, of which three were won and two drawn. It appeared he wasn't indispensable, which accounts for him training harder during his suspension than at any other stage of his career. 'He really flogged himself,' commented one of the Old Trafford coaches at the time. Best admitted he was worried: 'It wasn't so much the letters telling me that United were playing better without me, but the worry that I might have lost my scoring touch.'

That aspect of his play was perhaps a needless concern as Northampton Town were to discover when they were beaten 8-2 in an FA Cup fifth-round tie, with Best leading the scoring charge, bagging a remarkable six of the goals. Kim Book, brother of Manchester City captain Tony, was the Northampton goalkeeper and he described the experience: 'We hadn't an earthly chance against United with Best in that form. Not even the Berlin Wall could have stopped him. The man was brilliant, fantastic, and fabulous. I was depressed to be on the receiving end of an eight-goal walloping, but I would sooner Best be responsible than anyone else. We never knew where he was. The space he found was amazing. He always seemed to be in the right place at the right moment. It was uncanny.

'It got to the stage where I thought he was going to score every time he had the ball. It was very unnerving. He is so fast, so cool, so devastating. Every time the ball went to him, I thought to myself: "Hell, here comes another", and six times I was right.'

Best had once again shown that he still had a lot to offer but the goals still wouldn't come with his old abandon, as he scored only three times in the remaining 17 games to the end of the season. He was embarrassed in the FA Cup semi-final replay defeat against Leeds United at Villa Park where he had his wings clipped by Paul Reaney. He broke through on his own, only to tread on the ball and fall flat on his face. He lay there in the mud and then, sitting on the team coach after the match, he lifted his crest-fallen face from his cards and there, as the Leeds bus slowly cruised past, was the grinning face of Reaney, his ever-present shadow.

It wasn't a bed of roses either for Denis Law, who was on the bench for the two replays, and it seemed rather an indignity to see him coming on as a substitute after a career of such great triumphs. It was further indication that the trinity was starting to break up, though there was a bigger shock in store for him at the end of the season when he was transfer-listed.

In the meantime, United finished a modest eighth in the league with Best scoring in the final game to bring his league total to 15, a personal decline but nevertheless he was the club's top scorer again. In those terms he was doing more than his fair share, but increasingly the player had the feeling that the club was going nowhere and that he was being asked to carry his fading team-mates on his shoulders.

McGuinness's reign as manager lasted 18 months, a short-lived dream that prompted Brian Clough to describe him as a sacrificial lamb. It was an appointment made with the best of intentions, but also it was something of a poisoned chalice expecting such a young and inexperienced manager to sort out the ageing 1968 glory team, not least the trinity. The irony was that in his short time at the helm, his teams twice finished eighth in the First Division and reached three cup semi-finals. Not exactly a story of failure. It was a stressful time all round, and McGuinness certainly felt it. His hair turned white and eventually fell out as he licked his wounds abroad as manager of Aris Salonika in Greece. Even so, his love for Manchester United is still there working in corporate hospitality at Old Trafford and serving as the chairman of the Association of Former Manchester United Players.

Next up after McGuinness was the experienced Frank O'Farrell, who had been successful with Leicester City, leading them to the Second Division Championship. O'Farrell was certainly aware of the problems at United, the legacy of the trinity in particular creating an enormously difficult situation. They were admired and revered so that they couldn't just be unceremoniously dumped on one side. Yet their powers were waning and change was needed. O'Farrell needed time to phase them out gently, but time was something he didn't have, and though he made a good start he found the old pros, and George Best, in particular, increasingly difficult to manage. As David Sadler, his house-mate when the pair of them first landed in Manchester, puts it: 'By the early 1970s under Frank O'Farrell, George was carrying the team, all the way to top of the league for a while. With the team falling apart, he became the team, and it must have been frustrating for him. Much is written about the waste of George not playing on until he was thirty-six, but I never think about that. I just think of the brilliant work that he did, what he gave to United and the game.

'It is easy to analyse his career from this distance, but back then it wasn't. He became the first pop-star footballer, and nobody could have known how to react to all that that entailed. Even Matt Busby, with all his wisdom and understanding of people, could only relate George to situations he had dealt with earlier. But here was someone totally different.

'The triumph at Wembley in 1968 was the culmination of Manchester United's European crusade, but also it was the end of something, certainly for Matt, who had never been really fit after Munich.

'But George was only twenty-two and understandably he felt it should have signalled the lift-off to even greater achievements. Even Matt, for once in his life, had not looked beyond his current team. Pre-Munich he was building all the time for the future; after Munich he was rebuilding out of pure necessity, with no thought of what should follow in the 1970s and 1980s, and the club suffered for that.

'Other top players might have gained consolation from international football, but George knew he was unlikely to feature in any World Cup finals, and I believe that became a major factor in the frustration which contributed to his subsequent problems.'

The year 1972 started badly for Best and United when in January he walked out of the club and missed a week's training. United ordered him to move back into digs with Mrs Fullaway instead of living on his own – except for girlfriends – in the house he had had built for himself in Cheshire's leafy Bramhall. That didn't work, and at the end of the season he skipped United's trip to Israel and turned up instead on the Costa del Sol, from where, with the help of an avid media, he held press conferences claiming he was drinking a bottle of vodka a day. 'Mentally I am a bloody wreck, and I'm finished with football,' he declared.

He changed his mind, came back and was given two weeks' suspension by his club who also told him to go and live with Pat Crerand and his family in an effort to get some order back into his life. That didn't last very long. 'I think my kids drove him mad,' says Crerand.

Just before Christmas 1972, United sacked O'Farrell and announced that Best was up for transfer and would not play for Manchester United again. The letter to him crossed with one from Best announcing his retirement which read: 'I have decided not to play football again, and this time no one will change my mind. I would like to wish the club the best of luck for the remainder of the season and for the future. Because even though I personally have tarnished the club's name in recent times, to me and thousands of others, Manchester United still means something special.' It was a sad way to end, though Best being Best, he became the comeback kid, with still one last return to Old Trafford on the cards.

The following season, with the ebullient Tommy Docherty now in charge, Best asked for one more chance, and was given it because the Doc realised that once he had actually got George out on to the training pitch or in a game, he was no problem. George still had his love for football; it was the bits in between that had become difficult for him. His return was brief, with Best making 12 appearances and scoring twice. His last competitive game for United was when he turned out at Loftus Road against Queens Park Rangers in January 1974. United were beaten 3-0 by the First Division newcomers. Best's magic days looked well behind him with Stan Bowles eclipsing him as an individual star who scored twice. Then Best was gone again, this time to become the wandering star while picking up lucrative fees playing for clubs like Hibs, Dunstable, Stockport County, Fulham, Bournemouth and Cork Celtic before enjoying a new lease of life in America, where he found the slower paced game much more to his liking. In fact, he put together a much more substantial career in America than given credit for, playing for Los Angeles Aztecs, Fort Lauderdale and San Jose Earthquakes, making over 150 appearances and scoring more than 50 goals in four seasons. Not bad for a player in his thirties and supposedly washed-up!

City's Mike Summerbee, a close friend of Best's, recalls his problems towards the end of his playing career: 'I remember being at a club sitting with businessman Selwyn Demmy when this girl came dancing by. She decided to sit down and landed up next to me, and that was how I came to meet the girl who became my wife. Funny really, because if she had sat next to George, she might have become his wife and that might have stopped him going off the rails. He needed someone like Tina, because he became very lonely and his fame thrust him into something he found difficult to handle.

'I tried to help him when he hit problems, but by that time I was married and settled while George found it difficult to work out who was genuine and who wasn't. Ironically, not everyone was good for him, but he was good for them.'

Best himself put a lot of the blame for his problems on the 1968 European Cup triumph and said: 'It was as if everyone thought that winning the European Cup was the ultimate achievement. They were happy to relax and rest on their laurels. But to me, with a whole career ahead of me, it looked as if the future contained nothing but grafting about in the middle of the table, losing as many games as we won.'

That's only half the story though, and as we know more clearly now, the demon drink was also taking its grip. His team-mates were divided in their views. One team-mate who only caught the tail-end of his career at Old Trafford said: 'George thought he was the James Bond of soccer. He had everything he wanted and he pleased himself. He had money, girls and tremendous publicity. He lived from day to day, and right to the end he got away with it when he missed training or ran away. So he didn't care. People made excuses for him; he didn't even have to bother to make them for himself. People talk about pressures and depression. It was rubbish. He just didn't have any responsibilities, nothing to worry about at all. All kinds of people covered up for him, even the press, and he was lucky to get away with it for so long.'

A harsh judgement maybe, but most of his peers were simply still lost in admiration for his talent. As Harry Gregg puts it: 'From the first time I met him in '62 until I left in '67, he was always a pleasant, well-mannered young man. Whatever his problems were off the field, on it the little fella, as Matt Busby and I called him, could be sublime. When George was on song, he was blessed with greatness. He was ice cold, and seemingly free from nerves, even on the big occasions. He had no fear, he could tackle as well as take people on, he was good in the air and there was a devilment about his play when required. Above all, he was supremely confident. George produced some stunning performances.'

The formidable Bill Foulkes also felt more charitable and told me: 'Looking back, I feel guilty. George was a youngster when he came into a great side, and I don't think we senior players took enough interest in him. Older players influenced me a great deal when I was young, but we failed to influence George Best. We all went our separate ways, and I wish now we had involved him more away from the ground.'

Denis Law says he loved playing with Best and that without doubt he was the most gifted player he played with or against. 'He had buckets of talent and – it may surprise some to hear this – he was also one of the best, most dedicated trainers I came across. Although he looked to be all skin and bone, he was built like a whippet.'

Alex Stepney believes it was his great fitness that enabled Best to carry on playing to such a high standard, even after he had launched himself down the slippery slope of late nights and drinking too much. And Nobby Stiles says: 'George was a skinny kid when he arrived at Old Trafford and he never got to have much flesh on him. The strength sprang from deep inside him. He was a phenomenal trainer, and that was true whatever the situation. He could arrive unshaven and smelling of booze, but he was still brilliant when the work started. He was a lovely lad too, there was no edge to him.'

Best had his problems towards the end of his career, but it seems everyone he crossed paths with found him a lovely guy. Journalist Joe Lovejoy, for instance, who wrote an authorised biography of Best describes him like this: 'George is a lovely man, his kindness, generosity and loyalty explaining the willingness of those who know him to make allowances for the wretched illness that is his alcoholism. As a player, he remains second to none in the British pantheon, with only Pele and Maradona to have rivalled him on the world stage.'

The late Malcolm Brodie of the *Belfast Telegraph* also thought highly of the human side of George Best. 'George may have flaws in his complex character, but his devotion to his family, generosity and kindness for his fellow man cannot be disputed. A woman had sent me a letter stating her son was seriously ill, and requested I get George's autograph. Normally, I discard these kinds of request, otherwise you would be plagued by pleas from countless others, but this seemed a special case. I showed the letter to George in the Irish dressing room before kick-off; he read it, didn't sign an autograph, but quietly said: "Call for me at my home around 2pm tomorrow and we'll visit the hospital."

'George kept the appointment and when I duly collected him, he had a brown paper parcel under his arm. The youngster's eyes popped out of his head as his idol walked into the ward of the Royal Belfast Hospital for Sick Children and presented him with the shirt he had worn twenty-four hours earlier. Today, that little boy is headmaster of a school in a Belfast suburb and the jersey has pride of place in his study.'

My epitaph for George came when I wrote a farewell tribute to him in the *Manchester Evening News* and said: 'Slack Alice has got her man early! That was the general reaction when the Irishman turned his back on serious football with Manchester United at the age of twenty-seven to open a night club he cheekily called Slack Alice.

'But in my view, George more than paid his dues to football and by that stage of his life, he was entitled to walk away at any time of his choosing.

'Those who bemoan his relatively early departure have got to remember that he started playing First Division and international football at the age of seventeen, which meant he had ten years of non-stop action into which he packed four hundred and seventy appearances and one hundred and seventy nine goals. He might have finished at Old Trafford as something of a wandering star, but he was hardly a passing stranger. He had a career of substance and of course marvellous achievement. What's more, for most of the decade he played, he hardly missed a game. In fact, in a run of six seasons he made either forty, forty-one or a full-house forty-two league appearances, hardly the record of some fly-by-night.

'He also won thirty-two caps for Northern Ireland without ever being in an Irish team good enough to put him on the big stage of a World Cup, a regret for football lovers as well as for the man himself.'

Despite missing out on the big international competitions, Best still managed to produce some magic moments playing for Northern Ireland. Nobby Stiles was certainly impressed by his club-mate when he played for England against the Irish at Wembley, as he describes in his book, *After the Ball*. Stiles found himself tracking George as he chased after a long ball. He guessed that Best intended to take the ball round Gordon Banks so he launched into a typical Stiles tackle that took man and ball ... except it didn't and Stiles was left on his backside watching Best slide the ball past the goalkeeper. Says Stiles: 'As I got to my feet, I thought: "What a player." Afterwards I shook his hand and said: "Well done, George – only you could have done that." I'll never forget that goal. There he was, with the world falling in on his head, drinking, losing touch with what had made his name, but still able to produce something that made the little hairs on the back of your neck stand up.' That was George, simply the Best, the man who despite the trials and tribulations put a smile on the face of football.

So with Denis Law leaving United in 1973 to play for Manchester City again, then Best sadly departing Old Trafford in early 1974 before his time, Bobby Charlton was left to represent the trinity on his own ... though even he was beginning to feel time was about to be called.

13

Bobby's Legacy

Bobby Charlton's retirement as a player was achieved with a grace and dignity that reflected his play. On giving Tommy Docherty due notice that he planned to quit the game at the end of the 1972-73 season, in which United finished 19th in the league, he said: 'I have had a wonderful life in the greatest game in the world, and I always said that only I would know when I would want to retire. That time has come, and I'll leave the game with some marvellous memories.'

In all, Charlton played First Division football for 17 seasons to total 604 appearances, plus two as a substitute (a club record that stood until the durable Ryan Giggs moved past him in season 2010-11). Charlton scored a record 199 league goals, an achievement that still stands, though United have hopes that Wayne Rooney will overtake him before his scoring days are over. Adding in FA Cup ties, League Cup games and European matches,

Charlton made an incredible 752 appearances for Manchester United for a total of 247 goals.

On the international front, spanning 12 seasons, he held the England appearance record with 106 caps until Bobby Moore went two better. He still holds the England scoring record with 49 goals, one more than Gary Lineker, and five more than Jimmy Greaves.

After his World Cup victory with England in 1966, he was voted Footballer of the Year by the English writers, quickly followed by the European Footballer of the Year award ahead of Eusebio and Franz Beckenbauer, as well as a presentation from the referees as a Model Player. Along the way, he has been presented with both the OBE and made a CBE before being knighted in the Queen's birthday honours of 1994, ten years after being made a director of Manchester United, the club he continues to serve and support.

In March 2009 came the conferment of the Honorary Freedom of Manchester in a ceremony at the Town Hall led by the Lord Mayor, Councillor Mavis Smitheman. The resolution said: 'Sir Bobby Charlton's name is not only synonymous with football and Manchester United, but also with the highest traditions of professional sportsmanship. A long and distinguished career in club and international football justifiably earned him a worldwide reputation, but beyond his playing career he has continued to be a sterling ambassador for Manchester and for sport both at home and abroad, and a truly inspirational figure and role model for many aspiring young sportsmen and women.'

Uplifting words and well deserved, but for United fans the real image is reflected in something I wrote a year or two ago when I said: 'Bobby Charlton running in full stride, cheeks puffed out with the effort, and unleashing one of his thunderous shots, was one of the most stunning sights in English football. When he was in full flow for goal, there was a grace and beauty about him, a balletic quality, which singled him out as one of the most distinctive players in the history of English football. What also made him special was that he didn't just play the game well; he played the game. He had a sporting spirit which saw him commit only one disciplinary offence in the whole of his career, and that a booking for failing to retreat at a free-kick which was subsequently wiped off his record by the Football Association as a mistake. He was an idol without feet of clay, a sportsman supreme whose behaviour was exemplary both on and off the field.'

The following year Charlton joined an elite group of European personalities chosen for not only their professional excellence but their human qualities. The UEFA President's award, introduced by Michel Platini, was given to Alfredo di Stefano and then to Sir Bobby with the tribute that he was 'a shining example of gentlemanly behaviour, great resilience and true courage who is the ultimate ambassador for the game he has graced as a player and every day since he hung up his boots.'

Charlton admits that he has been fortunate with injuries and says: 'I never had anything serious. I still have all my cartilages and I didn't know what a hamstring injury was. Perhaps it was just luck, though I always had a bit of beef on me and it was often the thin ones with no protection that got hurt. David Beckham is, I would say, well put together, and he doesn't miss many games either. I never even wore pads, which you didn't have to in my day.

'The longest I was out with injury was two or three weeks, except for a hernia, but that wasn't a football injury, I did that playing golf! I remember reporting back for pre-season training and telling Ted Dalton, our physio, that I had this lump. He examined me and said, that's you out for three months, you need a hernia operation. It had been a baking hot summer and the courses were rock hard. I had caught the golf bug and I think I had just played too much. I don't think the boss was too pleased with me!'

Now in his seventies, Bobby is still very fit and he played his last game of football to mark his 60th birthday. He accepted an invitation that was made somewhat in jest by the local lads to play in a match between a Salford Select XI and Moss Side Amateur reserves, but he made it a condition that he should be allowed to play the full 90 minutes without being substituted. He only made two substitute appearances in his professional career and playing a bit part was not his idea of a football match, even at near pensionable age. 'It was my birthday present to myself,' he told me, and one suspects it was his favourite gift.

There is, of course, much more to Sir Bobby Charlton than simply his playing ability. As Sir Matt Busby once put it to me: 'The name of Bobby Charlton will stand forever. Time will add to his stature rather than diminish it. He arrived at Old Trafford a shy, perhaps slightly bewildered boy of fifteen. The shy boy has blossomed now into a man with a great sense of assurance, confidence and responsibility. His heart and mind have been forever at Old Trafford, wrapped up in the interests of Manchester United. We trod the same road for a great part of our careers, aiming for the same achievements and sharing the disappointments and tragedy of Munich as well as the triumphs.

'One of the delightful aspects of his character is that he has retained a tremendous enthusiasm. As a player, losing always meant something to him, as well as winning. It made him a better professional.

'His shyness never showed on the field of play. I remember the goals he scored when he was only eighteen. I have vividly implanted on my mind the sight of him volleying David Pegg's centre home in the FA Cup semi-final against Birmingham at

Hillsborough in the year before Munich. It was a tremendously hit shot and he repeated it in his first international playing for England against Scotland at Hampden Park.

'I can't begin to list all the other wonderful goals he has scored or detail his proud international career, except to say what a marvellous contribution he made in the World Cup of 1966 with his so valuable goals. Could I also ever forget his header in the European Cup final in 1968, a goal that set us on the path towards the victory that had been our aim for so long?

'He has broken all records and won everything possible there is to win. Yet he has remained completely unspoilt, still prepared to do more than his fair share for Manchester United.'

Tributes are legion, like this from his old England manager, Sir Alf Ramsey: 'Probably the best known footballer in the world, he has been a wonderful ambassador for England, not only as a footballer, but also in the way in which he has upheld the prestige of his country in every possible sense.'

Opponents admired him just as warmly, like his old foe from Benfica and Portugal, Eusebio, who, despite defeat, said after the European Cup final: 'My good friend Bobby Charlton even scored with his head following a corner from George Best. As a sportsman, I congratulated him because he had never scored in that way in a big game. He is a great man, a great footballer and a great friend. In the world of football, friendship is very important even though we defend different clubs and countries. He is a true gentleman and my friendship with Bobby Charlton is very strong.'

Sir Bobby's fondness for football is just as strong as when he was younger, as I realised when I interviewed him a few years ago for an article in a Carling Cup final programme when Manchester United beat Wigan 4-0. His thoughts on the state of the game came bubbling out as keenly as ever, as he said: 'So much about football is better today: the pitches, the ball, security for the players, medical support, nutrition, specialised training. Nothing is missed if they think it will improve the players or the team. We were very basic in my day, though don't run away with the idea that we wouldn't be able to play in today's game. With all the advantages available now, we would simply be better players,' he said.

'Big money doesn't help make better players; in fact, I believe a hungry sportsman is likely to be more dangerous than a comfortable one, and is perhaps willing to go that little bit further. So it becomes more important than ever to get players with the right character who want to play, because it is a love of playing and winning that drives you on.

'I think more football clubs should take former players on to their boards. I think we can be a bridge between the playing staff and the directors. I can't teach Alex Ferguson anything about managing, none of us can, but occasionally he comes for a chat. I might tell him something. It's probably in one ear and out the other, but he is very gracious about it. He expects my support and I am happy to give it.'

And that's Sir Bobby Charlton, as keen as ever about the game, proud of his achievements and as enthusiastic about Manchester United as he was all those years ago when he was first spotted ghosting through the Northumberland mist.

Charlton tended to be something of a loner as a young footballer, with a small circle of close friends. At the outset of his career, he was looked upon by many of my newspaper colleagues as being moody and difficult; perhaps to some he came over as big-headed after his early rise to fame. But as they all had to agree eventually, it was a modesty and shyness that had made him difficult to interview and roll out appropriate quotes for public consumption. As he matured he became much more socially aware. For instance, he responded readily around the time of the 1966 World Cup to become the president of Boys' Club Week in Manchester. This was a fund raising effort that saw him touring boys' clubs in the city, speaking to hundreds of people and personally autographing more than 700 pictures of the United team to those who raised more than £1.

For the dozen who earned most, he arranged a lunch, a tour of Old Trafford and tickets for a match. As Jim Buckley, organiser of the Federation of Boys' Clubs and chairman of the World Cup committee in Manchester told me at the time: 'No one could have entered more into the spirit of club week than Bobby Charlton. He helped us enormously to reach our record £5,000.'

By then he was that rare person: a star without temperament, one of football's gentlemen and an example you could hold up to the closest scrutiny for any starry-eyed youngster. As a player, he broke into the first team on the back of his thunderous goals but by the mid-Sixties he was much more the complete footballer and still arguably the most graceful performer in the game. After his switch back into midfield, he used to remind me of Di Stefano. The rhythm of his movement and passing was beautiful to watch, and along with Law and Best, the trinity were the biggest box-office draw in the business. Charlton's knack was to bring great personal qualities to the team while retaining the essence of a team player.

At one point, after his World Cup success with England, Bobby Charlton stood side by side with Her Majesty the Queen, US President Lyndon B Johnson, United Nations Secretary General U Thant and Prince Philip, Duke of Edinburgh after being nominated for a place in the top 20 of the most admired people in the country in a national teenage poll. You got a flavour of the fans' regard for Charlton in a letter to the *Manchester Evening News* prize postbag which had asked readers to vote for sport's greatest gentleman. The winning correspondence read: 'The essential feature of Charlton's integrity is its preservation throughout football's most violent years. Historians may well depict the last decade or so [the 1980s] as the era which first felt the impact of big money pressures, the explosiveness of European competitions and the rise in hooliganism on our terraces and sadly sometimes on the field too. No former player had this combination to contend with and no present player approaches the respect Bobby commands from his fellow players or the affection from his fans. Few would have blamed him if the shock of Munich, which transformed him overnight from a club juvenile to an elder, had unsettled his innate sportsmanship. Since those dark days we have had a display of behaviour and performance for which the only word is incomparable.'

Bobby was 11 when he first thought about Manchester United. It was 1948 and the day United played Blackpool in the Cup final at Wembley. In the morning, he had played for East Northumberland Boys and he'd had a goal disallowed. For schoolboys, they used to lower the crossbar by putting an extra piece of wood across and the referee said his shot had gone through the gap. It was a long time ago but Bobby recalls: 'I thought the goal was good and I remember being torn between listening to the Cup final and thinking about that disallowed goal!'

The first time he saw United was over the fence. Charlton described to me: 'It was the day in 1953 that United signed Tommy Taylor from Barnsley. I had played in an England Schoolboys trial at Maine Road and our bus took us past Warwick Road [Old Trafford]. In those days you could see over the wall and that was my first glimpse of the club that would become my life.'

He says his headmaster at his first school was football daft and he even stopped him going to the rugby school. 'We hadn't much cash so our strip used to be white shirts so that we could find our own. One of the teachers made us a set of shorts out of blackout curtains. The headmaster was so pleased that he ordered a set of red shirts and on the day they arrived he sent for me and made me dress up. I was wearing a pair of my dad's sawn-off long pants but was proud wearing one of the new shirts and carrying a black pit helmet under my arm to look like the ball. Then he told me to run into the classroom singing the introductory tune that used to start *Sports Parade* in those days. I was captain because my Uncle Tommy used to blow the ball up for us. I used to take one home on Friday night and bring it back the next day for the match.'

Charlton went on: 'I enjoyed my early years at Old Trafford, especially when I reached the side that played in the Manchester Amateur League. We were all about eighteen but it was an open-age competition so we were playing against men. They often arrived in boiler suits and sometimes we kicked off at tea time after they had finished work. The first game I was reserve, which meant I had to be the linesman. I remember my flag shooting up and down every time these big men shouted offside.'

Charlton's football life journey embraced honours galore for both club and country until his final game at Old Trafford against Sheffield United on 28 April 1973. That end of the season had amounted to a farewell tour with opposition teams keen to pay tribute to a man who had graced their profession. The news of him going was announced in a press conference with the 35-year-old Charlton saying in typically modest fashion: 'I always thought press conferences were for prime ministers and other such people, certainly not professional footballers, but I've been under so much pressure that I thought it would be the easiest thing to do if I told you, the press, altogether.'

But that wasn't his last appearance in a red shirt. That came rather appropriately in Verona, Shakespeare's city of gentlemen. United were playing in an Anglo–Italian Cup competition; Newcastle United won the tournament with Fiorentina runners-up, but at least Sir Bobby was able to finish as he had begun against Charlton Athletic in 1956, scoring two goals. It made him wonder whether he had made the right decision to retire, but that feeling was banished when his team-mates gave him a standing ovation after presenting him with a clock they had clubbed together to buy. The ornate timepiece depicts the four seasons and is still displayed on the mantelpiece in his home, and I suspect it takes pride of place among his memories.

After calling it a day, Charlton had to plan the next stage of his life. I don't think he had seriously got down to the business of acquiring coaching qualifications but that was short-circuited when he was invited to become the manager of Preston North End. The bonus for him was when he realised after training with his players that he could still play, and after discussions with Nobby Stiles, his friend who had become his coach at Preston, he re-registered as a player. He played 38 times in league and cup for Preston and scored eight goals. There was life in the old dog yet. Long term though, Charlton as a manager was not proving successful and after a dispute with his board over the buying and selling of players, he resigned. His life now took a new direction with a directorship in a travel company before returning to what lay closest to his heart, an involvement with football. He launched and ran the Bobby Charlton Soccer and Sports Academy for boys and generally became involved in Manchester United again, not least becoming a director. He travelled widely on United's behalf as an ambassador, a role that has since been extended to include trinity man Denis Law and several other distinguished former players. Today Sir Bobby Charlton can be seen watching his beloved team from the Old Trafford directors' box, the emotions of the game still flickering across his face, intent as always.

Each of the trinity made distinctive contributions to Manchester United. Sir Bobby Charlton, first in and last out, has emerged the leader of the big three, with an involvement that is still ongoing and likely to continue so until he can no longer reach his theatre of dreams.

The United trinity are an important strand in the history of Manchester United. It's important to do justice to three remarkable footballers and rich characters, all different but united in the common cause of Manchester United and close to the hearts of all the club's supporters. But critical though history is, football speeds along at a bewildering pace, with so many aspects of the game unrecognisable these days, compared to when Charlton, Law and Best graced Old Trafford.

Each generation seizes on new heroes, and though the old-timers will insist the current crop aren't as good as the great players of their own youth, the fact is that a great club like United will always produce top performers.

A roll call of players who have worn the red shirt will soon make clear that the stardust has been sprinkled liberally on any number of outstanding individuals, which set me thinking about who could become the next United trinity. You will no doubt have your own ideas but I would like to tell you who in my view are the next great trinity – those who could one day be cast themselves in bronze and stand in sculpted glory on a plinth outside Old Trafford.

14

The Next Trinity

It's 50 years since the trinity lit up the theatre of dreams, and since then there have been any number of great players who have worn the famous red shirt, especially in the modern era of Sir Alex Ferguson, but is there a trio worthy of being measured alongside Charlton, Law and Best?

Although time has yet to add lustre to their reputations, we already know that Ryan Giggs, Paul Scholes and David Beckham are special players, who we can recognise for their immense contributions to their football club and for the thrilling entertainment they have provided for the fans.

Significantly, it was one of the old trinity brigade who introduced David Beckham to Old Trafford. Young Beckham was an enthusiastic pupil at one of the schoolboy coaching camps that Bobby Charlton used to run, and he stood out as a youngster of great potential. When Beckham won a skills award as the best player of his intake, Charlton realised it was time to alert United with a recommendation that saw Sir Alex and his scouts pay immediate attention. Not that it was difficult to interest Beckham in joining United. He had long been a Red, and one day, after playing for his local junior team, Ridgeway Rovers, he was greeted by the news he had been longing for. Mum Sandra was at the game and remembers: 'I stood waiting outside the changing rooms. He was always the last out and when he finally emerged I just said to him: "It was a good job you had a good game."

'"Why was that," he asked. I replied that the Manchester United scout had been at the match and that he was coming round to the house later. He jumped up in the air and cried because he had always been worried that United wouldn't find him in London.'

Of course, the local London clubs had also been aware of Beckham's potential and he had been invited for trials at Third Division Leyton Orient. Then, slightly against his inclinations, he signed forms for the school of excellence at Spurs. It was a move which delighted his granddad, a Tottenham supporter, but David and his dad, Ted, knew it was designed only so that he could get better coaching and make progress. His heart still lay with Manchester United and after a number of invitations north during the Easter and summer school holidays, he signed schoolboy forms for Manchester United on his 14th birthday. Manager Sir Alex Ferguson was aware that it would be a big step to bring a young boy from 200 miles away to live in digs in Manchester, so he always made a point of keeping in touch with him. Every time United played in the London area, the Beckham family would be invited to the game.

As former United captain Steve Bruce recalls: 'This weedy, spiky-haired kid always seemed to be hanging about. Every time we went to London, he was there ... One day in the dressing room at the League Cup final at Wembley, he was picking up the boots and putting them into the skip just to be involved. We knew at the time, from the treatment he was getting, that he must be a bit special.'

Rival clubs, especially Tottenham, didn't like it when Beckham walked out on them to play for Manchester United, but the player never had any doubts. George Best, when he was young, ran away back to Belfast because he was homesick and Sir Matt Busby had to persuade him to return, but Beckham always felt Manchester was his second home. 'The first time I came to Manchester, I just knew it was the place for me. I just felt right. The fact that the manager treated me like one of his own sons made it easier.'

At the height of those happy early days, Beckham told me: 'What I know is that I love it up in Manchester. I don't expect I'll ever lose my London cockney accent, and I don't want to, but joining Manchester United was the best move I could have made.'

When it came time to leave school at 16, United offered him a six-year deal, two years on the club's youth training scheme, two years as an apprentice and then a minimum two years as a professional. His father, Ted, said: 'When David heard the offer, he jumped ten feet in the air and started screaming: "That's what I've always wanted!!"'

Although the England Schoolboys selectors had decided he was too small and slender to play at international level, he soon won a place in the United side which won the FA Youth Cup in 1992, with starlets like Ryan Giggs, Gary Neville, Paul Scholes and Nicky Butt who went on to win the unique treble and play for England, or in the case of Giggs, for Wales.

Beckham made his first-team debut as a substitute at Brighton in the League Cup at the start of season 1992-93, but he had to wait two more years before getting another chance. The manager still thought the slim-line Beckham needed toughening up and so he was farmed out on loan to Preston North End, a move that worried the player. 'When players went on loan, I thought it was because their clubs didn't rate them. The manager said it would do me good though, and in fact I loved it there. The players were brilliant with me and though they obviously reckoned I was cocky and overconfident at first, they soon treated me like one of them.' Season 1994-95 saw him make seven first-team appearances for United, plus three as a substitute, though he did score his first goal, netting in a 4-0 win at home against Galatasaray in the Champions League. The following season saw him getting into full stride. He came on as a substitute for Phil Neville in the opening game and scored in a 3-1 defeat against Aston Villa at Old Trafford.

Alan Hansen famously said on television that 'you don't win anything with kids' but Beckham stayed in the side along with the other youngsters. United won their next five matches and then came with a rush at the end of the season to pip Kevin Keegan's Newcastle for the 1996 championship. Beckham made 26 league appearances and found the net seven times. He also scored the winner against Chelsea at Villa Park to put his team through to the final of the FA Cup at Wembley against Liverpool. Eric Cantona scored the only goal to give Beckham a league and FA Cup double in what was really his first season as a regular.

Goals were becoming Beckham's speciality as he demonstrated on the opening day of the following season, 1996-97, at Selhurst Park when he spotted Wimbledon goalkeeper Neil Sullivan off his line. He let fly from just inside his own half to score a 60-yard wonder goal that became one of the defining moments of his career. Photographers and David Beckham go together like salt and pepper, and happily the BBC's *Match of the Day* cameras were there to record the first of many super goals. Said Beckham: 'I honestly meant to do it. I saw the goalkeeper off his line and so I just had a go. To be fair, I struck it well and a curve towards the end got the keeper. He told me at the end of the game that he thought it was a great goal. The ball seemed to be in the air for ages and then the place just erupted. It changed my football life.'

Free-kicks, hit with pace and remarkable swerve, became his signature, and in those days Alex Ferguson felt free to pay handsome tribute to his prodigy: 'David is Britain's finest striker of a football, not because of God-given talent, but because he practises with a relentless application the majority of less gifted players would not contemplate.'

Beckham picked up his second championship medal and also marked that season by winning his first England cap, playing against Moldova in September 1996. Then, in the summer of 1998 and the World Cup in France, great things were expected of England under Glenn Hoddle, but the tournament turned out to be a disaster for England and for Beckham in particular. When he made his retaliatory and petulant flick at Argentina's Diego Simeone to find himself dismissed – and England, down to ten men, knocked out of the tournament on penalties – even Hoddle seemed ready to seize on Beckham's departure as a convenient excuse for England's downfall. Most fair-minded people accepted that England failed for far more serious reasons, but I'm sure that is not how it must have felt at the time standing in Beckham's boots. On his return home, he was vilified mercilessly, especially at West Ham on the first away league trip of the new season, where they were burning his effigy. He says now: 'Some people seemed to think it a real crime, but I never saw it that way. I have got to be honest and say that I never even felt guilty, because everyone makes mistakes in football, and what I did was hardly outrageous. Let's face it, I had never been sent off before. I'm not a violent person, but the United supporters certainly helped me.

'I noticed the clapping in the first game I played back at Old Trafford when I walked to the corner flag near the visiting fans who were all jeering. I couldn't help but be aware of it because of all the stick I had been taking, and it was very moving. It was kind of like a standing ovation and I couldn't help smiling. It meant a lot to me after everything that had happened, and the way the United supporters stuck with me was unbelievable. During and after the World Cup there was a lot of criticism and all kinds of things were going on, but as soon as I got back to Old Trafford I realised there were still people who liked and loved me.

'It had crossed my mind that going abroad might be one way of getting some peace, but I soon realised that I didn't want to be anywhere but Old Trafford. Alex Ferguson was very supportive. He phoned me the day after it happened and he also rang my mum and dad, which was brilliant because they were not used to twenty or thirty film crews outside their house waiting for me to arrive home from France.'

So with the help of manager and fans, Beckham held his nerve as United steadily mounted their bid to win the treble of league, FA Cup and Champions League. He continued to play an important role, mostly as a wide-right player with a licence to roam, and always honing his ability to whip in crosses which proved a nightmare for opposing defences.

His crossing excellence was never more in evidence than in the first leg of the key Champions League quarter-final against Inter

Milan in March 1999. Twice he dipped in searing centres for Dwight Yorke to score with headers in a 2-0 win, before helping the team to play comfortably for a 1-1 draw in the San Siro to go through to the semi-finals against Juventus. Beckham's crossing was again instrumental in undermining the Italians, as United drew 1-1 in the first leg at Old Trafford before reaching the final with a superb 3-2 fighting victory in Turin. In between those two European ties, he put in a super-strike against Arsenal to set United up for a 2-1 replay victory that took the Reds into the final of the FA Cup.

Then began an electric 11 days of trophy hunting, with Beckham taking his game to an even higher plane with decisive moments which saw Alex Ferguson's team clinch the unique treble. First up for grabs was the league title, with a showdown against Spurs at Old Trafford. David Ginola, the Tottenham winger who had been voted Player of the Year by both the PFA and the football writers, was lined up against them, but Beckham made it clear who was the real player of the year. Les Ferdinand had put the visitors ahead with an early goal, but Beckham put United back into the game with a powerful shot just before half-time, and with the help of a goal from substitute Andy Cole the championship came to Old Trafford.

The following weekend it was the FA Cup at stake, with Newcastle the opposition at Wembley in the final and United seemingly in early trouble when Gary Speed put Roy Keane out of the game with a damaged ankle. Teddy Sheringham took his place but the key move was switching Beckham into Keane's role in central midfield. The way Beckham ran midfield had echoes of the original trinity and the way Bobby Charlton had orchestrated the team 50 years before. The manner in which Beckham swung the ball out to the wide men with his wonderful passing immediately conjured up for me the vision that Charlton used to display from midfield. Both men played with their heads up. Beckham teamed up with Paul Scholes in the middle of the park to run the game and underline his growing confidence, as well as his transformation from villain at the start of the season to hero. He never stopped running, passing and prompting as he revelled in his midfield role, and even after Speed had caught him in the face with his boot, he kept his temper and composure.

It was his 58th game of the season and he had manager Alex Ferguson purring after the 2-0 victory had clinched the Double: 'I have rested most of the players at some stage of the season, but not David Beckham. I have played him throughout it all, but then I know his nature. I know he has the best stamina of any player at the club. He has had fantastic energy since being a young boy, and despite everything he has been through, I have never doubted him.

'After Roy Keane's injury, Beckham moved into the central role alongside Paul Scholes and the pair of them responded magnificently. I thought Beckham was brilliant, tremendous ... He's a great player but he also has an incredible appetite for the game, and when you have ability harnessed to work rate you can hardly ask for anything more.'

Beckham's display at Wembley softened the blow of being without the suspended Keane and Scholes for the European final against Bayern Munich in Barcelona. Ferguson summed up the mood when he said: 'People are saying that to go to the Nou Camp without Roy Keane will be an uphill task. Yes, we will be without Paul Scholes as well, but David Beckham is just dying to show what he can do.'

The suspensions prompted Ferguson to keep Beckham in the middle and after going behind to an early goal from Bayern, it looked as if it might have been the wrong selection. There was nothing lacking in Beckham's individual performance though, and it all came right in the end, thanks to that glorious last-ditch revival in injury time that typically had Beckham showing the way. Playing with a frenzied urgency, yet ice-cool when it came to the delivery of two superbly hit corner kicks, Beckham's first cross was steered in by Teddy Sheringham for an equaliser, and then he delivered a second corner for Ole Solskjaer's winner.

Beckham had lifted United to European glory and a fabulous treble and told me: 'I will never forget the last few minutes. Time was up, and of course Bayern Munich were in front. I looked round and saw that the Cup was on its way down, ready for presentation, with the Bayern colours draped on it. A couple of minutes later, I had my hands on it and it was ours. When I was a boy, I used to watch on television and see people picking up the European Cup. I used to think it was big, but not as big as it actually is, or as brilliant.'

Beckham's delight took me back to the trinity and the emotional celebrations when Charlton and company lifted the trophy in 1968. Both campaigns had had their thrills and spills; different eras but a similar commitment and joyful conclusion based on adventurous football. Rather surprisingly, Charlton's thoughts as he watched the final in Barcelona were all in the present. His own European Cup triumph all those years ago remained, for him, in the past. 'I didn't think at all about '68 when I was in Barcelona for the final against Bayern Munich in May 1999. All I remember thinking was how hard it is to win this competition. It takes two years, because firstly you have to qualify by winning your domestic league, or you did before the competition became the Champions League with qualification extended.

'I didn't think about our success in '68 at all during the match itself, because this is a new era, new players, new techniques, a new way of playing, it's completely different now. It probably slipped through my mind that I wished I was out there playing, but those days had gone for me, and the thought didn't last long.

'Everything was so exciting that there didn't seem time to think back thirty years. Everyone had been talking about the treble, but in December I hadn't given it a thought because there was such a long way to go. As the season progressed, I said to myself we are still in everything, going well in the FA Cup, doing well in the Premiership and progressing in Europe. But after those big FA Cup ties against Liverpool, Chelsea and Arsenal, along with even harder matches in Europe against Inter Milan and Juventus, I thought maybe things would suddenly catch up with us.

'But then we beat Tottenham for the league title, and I never doubted once we had reached the Cup final that we would beat Newcastle. The really tough one was Bayern Munich in the Champions League final. They had hardly lost a match in their own league, but during the day of the final in Barcelona, I thought, I'm not going to say this to anyone, but I feel comfortable and that we were good enough not to be humiliated, or anything like that.

'Then, when we got to two minutes from the end and Bayern were winning, I thought I had better start thinking of something to say so that at least we could be good losers. I knew I would have to speak to Franz Beckenbauer and I was ready to say, "Well done Franz, you have had a fantastic season." I had it all planned as Lennart Johansson, President of UEFA, came past me on his way down to be ready to present the Cup to Bayern. He shrugged as if to say, bad luck Bobby.

'Then Teddy Sheringham scored an equaliser to send the president all the way back up the stairs to his seat because we had a lifeline of extra-time. By the time he reached where I was sitting, we had scored the winner. He had missed both goals and had to go back down again, only this time in readiness for the presentation to us.

'When Ole Solskjaer scored the winner, for me the world stood still. I froze as he stuck out his foot and the ball went into the top of the net. After that, I honestly couldn't tell you what I did. It was just the most incredible feeling. All United people had been in despair and suddenly we had won.

'It's difficult to compare my feelings in 1968, because in Barcelona I was just happy. At Wembley all those years before when the final whistle went, I was just drained, so exhausted, mentally as well as physically.

'I was so proud in the Nou Camp. Their moment had come. I knew they were resilient, but to be honest I had given up, and I did them an injustice. I don't know whether the treble will ever be done again, but I do know it can never be done so dramatically.'

David Beckham's final game for United was against Everton at Goodison Park on 11 May 2003. He left with a flourish by scoring from a free-kick in a 2-1 win. All told, he had played 265 league games for United and scored 62 goals, sharing in the club's most successful ever era. Although his departure seemed to drag on for ages, he had not been able to say farewell to the fans, but this was put right when he returned to Old Trafford for UEFA's exhibition match against a European team staged to mark United's half-century of participation in European competition. Injury prevented him from captaining the European side but he went out on to the pitch at half-time to tell the 73,000 crowd: 'I have waited four years for this. The one thing I have looked forward to since I left is going back to say goodbye to the fans, because I never really had the chance to do that. I always feel that Old Trafford is my home, my rightful home. I'm obviously from London but I spent so many years there and it's my club. It's the club I have always supported and the club I will always support. It's the best stadium in the world for me. The Bernabeu is incredible, but United is the club where I feel I grew up.'

David Beckham left United to join Real Madrid in 2003 but at his peak in the Nineties became the most talked about footballer in the world, and I am sure in his heart the club still holds a very special place, as became clear when he followed Sir Alex into retirement in May 2013. He stepped down at the age of 38 after becoming a global icon, with commercial interests said to amount to a fortune worth more than £165 million. He won 19 major trophies, which included league titles in four different countries, he played for six clubs, and is the only England player to score at three World Cup tournaments.

I first met Ryan Giggs as a bright-eyed youngster leading the charge of the FA Youth Cup winning team of 1992, and I have watched him become a footballing senior citizen with more honours than any other Manchester United player in the club's history. It's a remarkable story that saw him complete his 900th first-team game in February 2013. He has now made over 150 appearances more than Sir Bobby Charlton, which in itself is incredible. The 22 years he has spent at Old Trafford has seen him win 13 championships, four FA Cup winners' medals, two Champions League trophies, and at the time of writing he is still going strong.

Giggs also has his links with the original trinity – hailed as the new George Best as he burst on to the scene with his prodigious skills, the first member of the talented FA Youth Cup winning team to break into the senior side. It was the manner of the boy as much as his great talent that first caught my attention. It's the eyes which strike you, dark and unwavering, they gaze unflinchingly straight at you, suggesting an honesty that has seen him through some testing times to become one of the most respected players in the game. As Sir Alex Ferguson once put it to me: 'Ryan Giggs has led his life well, both on and off the field, and it cannot always have been easy for him in his younger days when, with his outstanding and exciting ability, allied to his good looks, he was forced to walk the celebrity road.

'I tried to protect him from the glare of publicity at first, because he was so young when he first came into prominence. But he was also clever enough to shun most of the hype himself, a wise decision which I think suited his personality and allowed him to develop his game to the point where he could perform successfully against the best in the world. He is a calm person with a natural composure, which balanced with his passion to play, gives him an ideal temperament capable of handling the pressure of playing at the highest of levels. When he became our longest serving player he had won everything, yet his enthusiasm and ambition are undiminished.

'I use him as a role model for young players coming into the club. I am proud to think I may have helped in his development. In fact, any father would be proud to have a son like Ryan Giggs. He has been one of the game's best players for over a decade, with an exceptional level of consistency and skill. Nobody could underestimate for one minute Ryan's contribution to our successes. He has been central to everything we have achieved and hopefully he will continue to help the club to stay at the top. To say he is a great professional would be grossly understating the way he conducts his life and career. He has always done things in an impeccable manner and I cannot remember him causing me a single moment's anxiety.

'Watching Ryan blaze down the wing with opposition players trailing in his wake is one of the finest sights in football. Is it any wonder that he has always been considered one of Old Trafford's favourite sons? He is without doubt one of Manchester United's all-time greats.'

The sight of Giggs flying through the opposition inevitably awakes memories for me, at least of the way George Best could devastate the opposition with his piercing runs. Off the field they had little in common, but in terms of football brilliance the trinity lived on when the ball lay at the feet of Ryan Giggs.

Team-mate Gary Neville is another admirer and says: 'The sharpness of his movement is something you cannot appreciate unless you have played against him. I know how good he is, because I had to play against him in training every week. If he runs at you and takes you on, you cannot get near him. To me, he is the best left-winger in the world. Giggsy has just got everything. He is brave, he is elusive, he is quick and he works hard. He has got a different level of stamina, like David Beckham, from everyone else at the club. I was the type of person who always liked to be at the front in training runs, just for my self-confidence, but if Giggsy decides he wants to go full out, he just breezes past you. It is almost like he is taking the mickey.'

Although Giggs is essentially Mr Nice Guy, to get to the top in football and, what's more, stay there for such a long time, requires a hard core of steel and determination, qualities he showed from quite an early age. If only George Best had shown the same dedication for football towards the end of his career, we might have enjoyed the Irishman's talents for a lot longer. Giggs somehow had an in-built determination. For instance, he is the son of Danny Wilson, a top-class rugby league player, but when his parents' marriage broke up Ryan was strong-minded enough to change his surname to that of his mother, Lynne Giggs. It was as Ryan Wilson that he first appeared in schoolboy teams, only becoming Giggs after signing for United. It was his father's transfer from Cardiff to Swinton Rugby League Club that brought young Giggs, aged seven years old, to Manchester. He was very much a Welshman and spoke with a Welsh accent until he managed to get rid of it to avoid the inevitable teasing. It seemed his transition from Welsh to Englishman was complete when he was picked for England Schoolboys and made captain.

But Giggs insists: 'I am a Welshman, and proud of it, but when I was quite young my family moved to the Manchester area and so naturally I went to school there. Playing for my school, Moorside, qualified me to play for the area teams and then on to the international side. It's all quite logical really. If you play for an English school, it's a natural step to go on to play for the country of that school. It was only later that I elected to play for Wales as the country of my birth. Before that, I was proud to captain the England Schoolboys team. I played nine times in all. We won seven of them and just lost to Germany and Scotland.'

Giggs, alas, never got the opportunity to perform on a big international stage, because of course Wales rarely qualified for the senior competitions. It was something that George Best would have understood after failing to make the World Cup finals or European Championships with Northern Ireland.

Giggs signed for United in February 1988, thanks to the alertness of Harold Wood, a United steward who manned the dressing rooms at The Cliff training ground. Explains Giggs: 'Out of school I played for a local junior team called Deans in a Sunday league and Harold Wood must have been impressed because he told Sir Alex Ferguson there was a boy he should have a look at playing near where he lived. The manager set the scouting wheels in motion and they invited me to join them. I was in fact going for coaching at that time to Manchester City, but that was because our manager at Deans was a City scout and he had three or four of us on City's books. I didn't have to think twice though when the United invitation came, because I had always been a United fan. It was a dream!'

It wasn't long before the players were aware of the new arrival, as Giggs recalls: 'One of my first training sessions with the senior squad brought me up against Viv Anderson. I was about fourteen or fifteen at the time and it was a practice match against the first team. I was on the left wing and Viv was marking me. I think he thought he was in for an easy morning and he said he hoped I'd had a good breakfast. I got the impression that that was going to be the only good thing likely to happen for me that morning. Anyway, after I had skipped past him a few times, I wouldn't say he lost his temper, but it looked to me like he was beginning to!' Shades of George Best here and the way he had tormented Harry Gregg by sending him diving the wrong way when the Northern Ireland goalkeeper had joined some of the United youngsters in a scratch practice game.

Giggs made his first-team debut as a substitute against Everton, but two months later on 4 May 1991, just before the end of the season, he made a full debut against Manchester City, and marked it by scoring the only goal of the game in a 1-0 win. He says: 'I couldn't forget that goal because although it is down in the record books as mine, I have to admit that I didn't actually score it! It was an own-goal by Colin Hendry, the Manchester City centre-half. I made a run across him and I think it put him off . . . He said he certainly didn't want the goal and I could have it. So it went down as my goal.'

In the course of his long career, Giggs has a huge catalogue of special goals, most of which he emphatically scored himself, like the quickest United goal ever when he scored against Southampton after 15 seconds in November 1995 on the way to a 4-1 win. But the goal no United fan will ever forget was the mesmerising winner to beat Arsenal in the FA Cup semi-final replay at Villa Park in April 1999. I asked Giggs to talk me through it: 'I shall never forget it myself either, because it was such a big match and the one people still talk about. I started on the bench but came on after an hour. The game went into extra-time and I scored in the one hundred and ninth minute. I didn't appreciate until I watched it on television exactly what I had done. I thought I was about thirty yards out and I couldn't believe I had run so far with the ball and beaten so many players. It all went so quickly when I was out there and didn't seem so extraordinary. I have got to be honest though, and say that when I watched it later on television, I was quite impressed!' United fans certainly won't forget the way Giggs pounced on an error by Patrick Vieira to start heading for the Arsenal goal. He left Vieira and Lee Dixon behind before cutting past Martin Keown and beating Dixon again as the full-back tried to cut him off. He then finished with an unstoppable drive to beat David Seaman, whipped off his shirt and celebrated by whirling it round over his head. Sir Alex Ferguson said: 'Our players and fans will be talking about it for years.'

Comparisons with Best from the original trinity are compelling. Just as Giggs sliced open the Arsenal team, so Best had Benfica on the rack when he scored in Lisbon to become 'El Beatle'.

Giggs was still only 17 and pretty naïve back in 1991, as he revealed when he nutmegged Nottingham Forest's Roy Keane. It wasn't long before Keane had his revenge to send the youngster flying, as Giggs recalls: 'It was the first time I had come across Keano. As I lay on the ground, he looked down at me and said something to the effect: "Get up, you soft git." I tell him now that I sat on the floor thinking, "Who is this muppet?"'

Giggs was the first of the youngsters from the revitalised youth set-up to break into the first team. Soon, he would be followed by Gary Neville, David Beckham, Nicky Butt, Paul Scholes and Ben Thornley who in the meantime were on their way to winning the 1992 FA Youth Cup. Giggs was the captain of the youth team but his first-team duties prevented him playing in many games. He was, though, recalled for the two legs of the final against Crystal Palace, as youth team manager Eric Harrison fondly remembers: 'Winning the Youth Cup was one of the greatest moments of my time in football. It gave me terrific pride and satisfaction to watch that marvellous group of youngsters become the first side to win the trophy for United in twenty-eight years. And they did it in the kind of style befitting a team wearing the famous red shirts.

'Nobody epitomised that side more than Ryan Giggs, who was not only the captain but also one of the guiding lights in a team that had few flaws. He was absolutely brilliant in every youth match he played, and it was fitting that it should be he who picked up the trophy at the end of the two-legged final against Crystal Palace. He wasn't on his own in that team, but he was the first to step forward into senior football. He has since become one of the world's great players. He could find a place in any team in the world. A great player and a lovely lad, he hasn't changed as a person since he walked through the doors at Old Trafford. He was a natural from the word go, and in little or no time everyone at The Cliff training ground was raving about him developing into a world-class player.

'Ryan had the lot and he was so abundantly talented that it would have been a major mystery if he hadn't made it to the top.

It's true to say that there have been players who looked certainties to become great stars but somehow failed to reach their potential and fell by the wayside. Nobody expected that to happen to Ryan, who not only possessed all the required ingredients, but also was totally dedicated and single minded in his approach to everything he did.'

Inevitably, Giggs found himself being described as 'the new George Best', something he found slightly embarrassing but says: 'I think I was only about fifteen when the first headline appeared ... but it never bothered me. I just took it as a compliment. I had never seen him play of course, but my mum and grandparents had and they told me plenty about him. I never let it get to me, though, and simply took it that I was heading in the right direction. I met him quite a few times later and he was always really nice with me.'

I can well understand the comparison. Giggs and Best had a lot in common, not least the ability to run at speed with the ball still under control. If there was a difference between their styles, Giggs was more reliant on pace as opposed to Best's superb balance that saw the ball seemingly fastened to his bootlaces. Giggs was perhaps marginally the better team man, with his crossing from wide positions, while Best was more reliant on expressing himself with his mastery of the ball. He was willing to pass but more often he chose to go it alone. Happily for the team, what at first appeared to be selfishness could produce match-winning moments.

Of course, Giggs always had the advantage of Sir Alex Ferguson as his manager, a man who has never had any problem frightening away the media but who was always helped by the fact that Giggs never went out of his way to court publicity anyway, as he explained: 'When I first arrived on the first-team scene, it coincided with a massive explosion in football with the launch of the Premiership, the impact of Sky Television and the introduction of the Champions League. The game expanded enormously and the players came under the spotlight. I came at the right time for marketing, but I was young and I think I was really helped by the manager sheltering me and limiting what I did with the media. I also felt that at twenty-two, people could easily get sick of seeing me and I didn't want that to happen because I was aiming for another ten years at least. So I stepped back a bit. The incredible fascination of the media with David Beckham also helped me to lead a quieter life, which suited me.

'Sir Alex brought me to Manchester United and steered me right the way through. He especially helped me in my younger days, involving me in training with the senior squad at just the right time, playing me in the first team at the right time, and just as important, resting me at the right time. I had implicit trust in him. Who wouldn't, as one of his players, after leading us to such sustained success?'

For all his natural tendency for a quiet life, there still came a defining moment that determined that he wouldn't be going down the celebrity path blazed by his team-mate, David Beckham. 'The high profile relationship I had with Dani Behr, the TV presenter, was the turning point for me,' Giggs explained. 'Before I knew it, we were being photographed outside my house and cameramen followed us everywhere. It was very uncomfortable. At that point, I decided the celebrity lifestyle wasn't for me. Around that time, I felt my commercial work was also affecting my work. I thought, "No, football is my bread and butter. It has to, and always will, come first."'

If only George Best had had a similar priority, we might have been spared his tragic end. Such was their contrasting personalities however, there was no way Best would have followed the Giggs route. The Irishman loved his football, but he loved other aspects of life too.

Once he had broken into the first team, Giggs didn't have to wait long for his first piece of silverware. After finishing runners-up to Leeds in 1992, the following season saw United win the Premiership by ten points from Aston Villa and bring the trophy back to Old Trafford for the first time in 26 years. Giggs's contribution was considerable, missing only one league game and scoring nine goals.

Ryan Giggs was in on the ground floor of United's most successful era. The following year brought a league and FA Cup double, and the trophies continued to come until his personal honours board listed 26 and he had become one of only four players to win three sets of league and FA Cup doubles. The pinnacle, of course, was winning the unique treble in 1999, with Giggs heavily involved in all three competitions. Alex Ferguson juggled his squad to try and keep everybody fresh for fighting on three fronts, with Giggs making 25 appearances in the Premiership, six in the FA Cup and nine in Europe that season.

The challenge of Europe looms large in his life and Giggs has a vivid recollection of the dramatic Champions League final against Bayern Munich, at least the closing stages. 'I remember it for the last two or three minutes. The previous ninety are not worth recalling because, frankly, it was a bit of a boring game. Once Bayern had scored, I think they settled for winning one-nil with the only chance of increasing their score the occasional break-away. At the same time, we were under-performing so it was hardly memorable until injury time when Teddy Sheringham and Ole Solskjaer each scored to win us the match. One minute we were thinking we were out of it, and then suddenly we had won it.

I remember the final for our refusal to accept defeat and then the almighty explosion to snatch victory.

'I like the European atmosphere. The matches are presented in a way that spells out the difference between domestic fixtures and Champions League. I think all the players enjoy the build-up and spectacle. It reminds you of the millions watching around the world, the distinctive music, the Fair Play shaking of hands with your opponents. It adds to the excitement for both the players and the people watching in the stadium and on television.'

On the international stage, Giggs had a long 16-year career, having made his debut for Wales in October 1991 at 17 years and 321 days, the youngest ever Welsh international. Giggs saw a stack of players come and go for Wales without unfortunately ever playing in a team capable of reaching the finals of the European Championships or World Cup. He missed a number of games through injury, and at one point was being criticised in Wales for pulling out of games. Nevertheless, he still won 64 caps before announcing his retirement from international football with the European Championship qualifier against the Czech Republic in Cardiff on 2 June 2007 his final appearance. It was hardly the record of someone who didn't care for his country, though that last match did rather reflect the path his international career had taken. Giggs played well, indeed the whole team played well, but they were forced to settle for a goalless draw that looked likely to repeat a familiar story – failing to qualify for the European Championship finals, to leave the World Cup quarter-final under Jimmy Murphy in Sweden way back in 1958 as the last time they figured in the finals of a major tournament. Wales's loss was undoubtedly United's gain.

Ryan Giggs will always have time for people, though, as you can perhaps judge from his testimonial match against Celtic in 2001 when he led the teams out with his young sister Bethany by his side. He explained to me: 'I have always been close to Bethany and I thought it would be nice for her. Players who get testimonials are usually older than me and they can involve their children. I hadn't any children then but I did have a nice sister. I have a brother as well, Rhodri, but he is a bit older and I don't think he would have appreciated me leading him out by the hand! The whole night bowled me over. I was stunned by the massive crowd, and though it's usually the money people think about when a testimonial is mentioned, it's the appreciation of the fans that gets to you. I couldn't believe how good it was.'

There was further appreciation for Giggs in the Queen's birthday honours of June 2007, when he was awarded the OBE for his services to sport. It was nothing less than he deserved, because this man not only plays football rather well, he plays life rather well, too.

If Ryan Giggs is a modest and publicity-shy character, the really quiet man of the modern trinity – the player who is the antithesis of the David Beckham celebrity circus – is Paul Scholes, the professionals' pro.

When I wrote the book *A Perfect 10*, my choice for my favourite top ten United players of all-time read: Duncan Edwards, Sir Bobby Charlton, Nobby Stiles, George Best, Denis Law, Bryan Robson, Eric Cantona, Ryan Giggs, David Beckham and Cristiano Ronaldo. You will see that there is no Paul Scholes in that list, and one day at the Carrington training ground I was challenged on this by Rio Ferdinand who said he was surprised to see no mention of his old team-mate. I replied that I had regretted leaving him out, but that it hadn't been easy to include everybody of merit. I challenged Ferdinand by asking him who I could have left out to make way for Scholes. He replied 'David Beckham', to which I said: 'But I've written more about the colourful Beckham than any other player, so I simply had to have him in my line-up'. To which my critic said: 'So this is a celebrity team then, not necessarily a football line-up.'

Ouch! I took his point. Paul Scholes is such a quiet guy that it's easy to overlook him. I am not making that mistake this time. He is definitely in my present-day trinity. In my reporting days at the *Manchester Evening News,* I used to call him the Artful Dodger, because nobody at Manchester United was more elusive than the ginger-haired midfield man. It was a nickname that fitted, because not only was he hard to pin down on the pitch, he was even harder to find off it! He was a bundle of action on the field, but once the game was over he disappeared like a flash, heading back home to his house in Cheshire and his family. He hated interviews, didn't have an agent and wasn't interested in boosting his income with promotional and commercial work. In fact, when the club's own television station finally persuaded him to appear in front of their cameras, they opened a bottle of champagne to celebrate the occasion!

The strange thing is that once you started chatting to him, he talked easily and helpfully with a ready, bubbly laugh, though he still insisted that he would much prefer to lead a quiet life away from television lights and reporters' notebooks. However, it became increasingly difficult for the local lad from nearby Salford to dodge the limelight as his fame as a footballer grew and he became more and more an important player for, not just Manchester United, but England. For instance, he certainly could not do much about the media interest which fell in on him like an avalanche when he scored a hat-trick for England against Poland at Wembley soon after Kevin Keegan had taken over from Glenn Hoddle as manager.

Keegan, naturally enough, became a firm favourite of the little guy and said: 'He's a fantastic player and because he plays with so many big names at Manchester United he is very under-rated. Watching him in training, you can see how much he loves his football, and you should watch him in our shooting sessions. He certainly keeps the goalkeepers busy. He is a phenomenal trainer, a player who constantly impresses, and he can also play anywhere.' It was soon apparent when Sven-Goran Eriksson took over from Keegan as England manager that he held the United midfielder in similarly high regard and he quickly made him an integral part of his team.

Scholes still strove, though, to keep as low a profile as possible. 'I just don't enjoy interviews. They embarrass me. I suppose I get nervous. I hate talking about myself. I always run out of the back door at our training ground to avoid the press. I leave the interviewing to the other players,' he explained. 'I like a quiet life. I don't drive a Ferrari, it's not my style ... I don't have an agent and I don't want one. I don't want to go in front of cameras and all that stuff.'

Sir Alex Ferguson says simply: 'Paul Scholes is a lot of people's favourite footballer, and understandably so when you study the superb passing and wonderful vision he brings to his game in the middle of the park. I rate him one of the best finishers at the club and he always scores a good total of goals for a midfield player. He is rightly recognised by England as a reliable and first-rate performer.'

'Priceless' was the word picked out to describe him by the *Manchester Evening News* midway through season 2003-04 after a string of peerless performances which left team-mate Gary Neville saying: 'I wouldn't swap Paul Scholes for anybody. He is quite simply the most complete footballer I have ever played with. He is the best. He can do everything on a football pitch, absolutely everything. He can run, pass, dribble, shoot and he has that eye for goal. It's a knack and he's brilliant at it.'

After retiring from the England scene to prolong his club career, Scholes announced his retirement from United at the end of the season in May 2011, leaving on a high after helping the Reds win their 19th league championship. He also joined the select band of United players who have scored 150 goals in all competitions. Although scoring was always an important feature of his game, it was his passing and vision that were truly remarkable, and Sir Alex had no hesitation inviting him to join his junior coaching staff with special instructions to the youngsters to study how he passed the ball, the range, the accuracy, the pace, the weight and the tactical insight.

But then he changed his mind and returned to the fray for the 2011-12 season, though his appearances were restricted by injury, until he decided to follow in the footsteps of his manager and mentor and quit at the same time to take up his coaching duties.

Scholes played more than 700 games for United to rank third behind Bobby Charlton, Bill Foulkes and Ryan Giggs in terms of appearances for the club. He made his full debut in season 1994-95 and as a midfielder he invariably got more than his fair share of goals. His best scoring season saw him hit 20 in all competitions in season 2002-03, but he really came into his own in the treble-winning season of 1998-99. He played well in all three competitions, scoring one of United's two goals against Newcastle in the final of the FA Cup, and enjoyed a key strike for an away goal against Inter Milan in the quarter-final of the Champions League.

But Europe that year was a bitter-sweet experience for him because in the next round, the semi-final, he came on as a substitute to pick up a yellow card that meant suspension, along with Roy Keane, from the final against Bayern Munich. Yellow cards were always a worry for Scholes, with his tackling quite out of character for such a cultured player. Fans at times laughed at his attempts to win the ball, often swinging his leg and completely missing but with the intent so obvious that the referee would book him. It always seemed to me to be the classic 'little guy' determined not to be pushed around by bigger people. Indeed, Scholes once said in a radio interview that if someone caught him early in a game, it was always in the back of his mind that he needed to get them back. He added that the bookings he received towards the end of his career were influenced by his reputation.

The fact remains, though, that over his career Scholes received 99 yellow and four red cards. He was booked 32 times in the Champions League, more than any other player in the competition. Of course, Scholes played a lot more games than most, but even so Arsene Wenger found himself at one point suggesting that there was 'a little bit of a darker side' to him.

My view is that Denis Law from the trinity made Scholes look like a choir boy, and I prefer to dwell on his touch, his passing, his vision and his calmness under pressure. As Socrates, the star of the Eighties' Brazil side, once put it: 'Paul Scholes is good enough to play for Brazil. I love to watch Scholes, to see him pass, the boy with the red hair and the red shirt.'

So there you have my modern trinity; too recent perhaps to put alongside the mighty Charlton, Law and Best, but I am sure there are thousands of present-day followers for whom Giggs, Beckham and Scholes represent their dreams and football desires. Who knows, perhaps one day in the future there will be a bronze statue outside Old Trafford extolling their mighty deeds of '99 as winners of league, FA Cup and the European Cup.

The unique treble is, and will remain I'm sure, an unsurpassed achievement that not even the Charlton, Law and Best threesome got near – but having said that, none of my present-day trinity have been crowned European Footballer of the Year. It's practically impossible to compare different eras, with so many variables like the quality of their team-mates around them. I do know, though, from my point of view that it has been a privilege and a huge pleasure to have watched and known from a front-line seat all the generations who have played in the theatre of dreams over the last 50 years.

Some people, admittedly mostly Manchester United fans, tell me I have had the best job in the country. And I suppose if you are a Red, the prospect of travelling with United to every match all over the world, and talking to the players on an almost daily basis, must seem a pretty enviable way of making a living. My length of service with the *Manchester Evening News* would certainly suggest that I found it pretty agreeable, too, an assignment which I reckon involved me reporting on more than 2,000 United matches and writing some several million words about them.

Although it's now 18 years since I retired from the *Manchester Evening News*, I still haven't been able to walk away, and until he retired I helped Sir Alex write his programme notes and have completed a number of projects for United such as scripting the history of the club for the museum when it was first set up, and also providing the script for the historical display panels that line the Munich tunnel.

I contribute to MUTV and for six years edited *Legends*, a magazine for the club's former players. It means I still got to talk to the United greats, even if a major topic of conversation had become discussions about their hip and knee replacements!

A guy asked me recently, maybe noting my absence from the

Evening News: 'Didn't you use to be David Meek?' Well, I suppose I did, but I like to feel I have never in fact been away. Once involved with Manchester United, it's difficult to part company, as my predecessors also discovered.

The earliest histories of the club refer to HP Renshaw as the *Evening News* reporter in 1890 when United were known as Newton Heath and he had 36 years in the job. Club and newspaper were very close in those days. In fact, shortly after moving to a new ground at Bank Street, Clayton, the club was so short of money that the wooden shed at the ground that housed the *Evening News* telephone was declared to be the club's registered office. Tom Jackson followed Harry Renshaw and despite being away in the army during the war, he wrote about United for 26 years until he became one of the eight journalists who lost their lives in the Munich air crash. The present United correspondent for the *Evening News* is Stuart Mathieson, my successor, and he looks like another stayer with 18 years already under his belt. So it's certainly a job that grows on you.

I have enjoyed walking down memory lane with Charlton, Law and Best and then coming bang up to date with my impressions of the latter-day trinity of Giggs, Scholes and Beckham. The beauty of Manchester United is that I find the heroes of today are not all that much different from the stars of yesteryear in terms of their ability, ambition and service to this awesome institution.

The latter-day trinity is made up of peerless players, though I can't but feel that Charlton, Law and Best deserve to be up on their pedestal because they represent a singular chapter of Manchester United's history born out of the tragedy of Munich and then just ten years later conquering Europe. The nine-foot bronze statue was unveiled on 28 May 2008 by chief executive David Gill who conceived the idea as United cast around for some way of marking the passing of George Best, and rightly came to the conclusion that he shouldn't be separated from his trinity partners.

Back in 2000, the Football Writers' Association had completed their own trinity of tributes to the big three by awarding Best a gala evening, following similar celebrations with Sir Bobby Charlton in 1989 and Denis Law in 1994. I was delighted to be asked to make the lead tribute, reflecting my admiration, but it was chairman Paul McCarthy who best summed up the night when he said: 'Anybody who loves football, loves George Best. He could turn a game in a split-second with a combination of peerless talent, exquisite skill, strength, bravery and courage. George played in an era where superstars had but a fraction of the protection the current crop receive from referees but he never hid, was never afraid to dazzle even in the face of brutality. I bow to the fact that Bobby Moore, Sir Bobby Charlton, Tom Finney and Sir Stanley Matthews can all lay claim to the title of Footballer of the Millennium, but for me Georgie Best Superstar is the man!'

Less than five years later, in November 2005, the world reverberated in shock at the announcement of Best's death, at the age of 59, in London's Cromwell Hospital after an eight-week battle against multiple organ failure. An estimated 100,000 people lined the streets of Belfast for the funeral cortege, with Denis Law among the former United team-mates carrying the Irishman's coffin to the steps of Stormont. In a moving tribute, Bobby Charlton said: 'Football has lost one of its greats, and I have lost a dear friend. He was a marvellous person.' Just over 40 years had passed since they made their first appearance together for United, and the real-life trinity were suddenly no longer.

Time moves on, and time heals, but the memory of the United trinity remains, with Bobby Charlton and Denis Law still gracing the hallowed halls of Old Trafford. Now, alongside the departed

George Best, their tribute in bronze faces Old Trafford outside the East Stand, not far from the statue of their one-time master and mentor.

'It's fantastic that we are facing Sir Matt Busby,' says Denis Law.

The United Trinity –
The Complete Record

BOBBY CHARLTON

Born: Ashington, Northumberland, 11 October 1937

Nationality: England (106 caps, 49 goals, 1958–70; World Cup winner 1966)

United debut: 6 October 1956, v Charlton Athletic (H), Division One, 4–2 (2 goals)

United farewell: 28 April 1973, v Chelsea (A), Division One, 0-1

Team honours won: League 3 (1956–57, 1964–65, 1966–67), FA Cup 1 (1963), European Cup (1968), Charity Shield 2 (1965, 1967 – both shared)

Personal honours: European Footballer of the Year 1966, FWA Footballer of the Year 1966; OBE 1969, CBE 1974, knighthood 1994

Season-by-season record

Season	League		FA Cup		League Cup		Europe		Other	
	Apps	Goals	Apps	Goals	Apps	Goals	Apps	Goals	Apps	Goals
1956–57	14	10	2	1	–	–	1	1	–	0
1957–58	21	8	7	5	–	–	2	3	–	0
1958–59	38	29	1	0	–	–	–	–	–	–
1959–60	37	18	3	3	–	–	–	–	–	–
1960–61	39	21	3	0	0	0	–	–	–	–
1961–62	37	8	6	2	–	–	–	–	–	–
1962–63	28	7	6	2	–	–	–	–	–	–
1963–64	40	9	7	2	–	–	6	4	1	0
1964–65	41	10	7	0	–	–	11	8	–	–
1965–66	38	16	7	0	–	–	8	2	1	0
1966–67	42	12	2	0	0	0	–	–	–	–
1967–68	41	15	2	1	–	–	9	2	1	2
1968–69	32	5	6	0	–	–	8	2	2	0
1969–70	40	12	9	1	8	1	–	–	–	–
1970–71	42	5	2	0	6	3	–	–	–	–
1971–72	40	8	7	2	6	2	–	–	–	–
1972–73	44(2)	6	1	0	4	1	–	–	–	–
Total	604(2)	199	78	19	24	7	45	22	5	2

DENIS LAW

Born: Aberdeen, 24 February 1940

Nationality: Scotland (55 caps, 30 goals, 1958–74)

United debut: 18 August 1962, v West Bromwich Albion (H), Division One, 2–2 (1 goal)

United farewell: 7 April 1973, v Norwich City (H), Division One, 1–0

Team honours won: League 2 (1964–65, 1966–67), FA Cup (1963), Charity Shield 2 (1965, 1967 – both shared)

Personal honours: European Footballer of the Year 1964

Season-by-season record

Season	League Apps	League Goals	FA Cup Apps	FA Cup Goals	League Cup Apps	League Cup Goals	Europe Apps	Europe Goals	Other Apps	Other Goals
1962–63	38	23	6	6	–	–	–	–	–	–
1963–64	30	30	6	10	–	–	5	6	1	0
1964–65	36	28	6	3	–	–	10	8	–	–
1965–66	33	15	7	6	–	–	8	3	1	1
1966–67	36	23	2	2	0	0	–	–	–	–
1967–68	23	7	1	0	–	–	3	2	1	0
1968–69	30	14	6	7	–	–	7	9	2	0
1969–70	10(1)	2	0(2)	0	3	1	–	–	–	–
1970–71	28	15	2	0	4	1	–	–	–	–
1971–72	32(1)	13	7	0	2	0	–	–	–	–
1972–73	9(2)	1	1	0	2	1	–	–	–	–
Total	305(4)	171	44(2)	34	11	3	33	28	5	1

GEORGE BEST

Born: Belfast, 22 May 1946

Died: London, 25 November 2005

Nationality: Northern Ireland (37 caps, 9 goals, 1964–77)

United debut: 14 September 1963, v West Bromwich Albion (H), Division One, 1–0

United farewell: 1 January 1974, v Queens Park Rangers (A), Division One, 0–3

Team honours won: League 2 (1964–65, 1966–67), European Cup (1968), Charity Shield 2 (1965, 1967 – both shared)

Personal honours: European Footballer of the Year 1968, FWA Footballer of the Year 1968

Season-by-season record

Season	League Apps	League Goals	FA Cup Apps	FA Cup Goals	League Cup Apps	League Cup Goals	Europe Apps	Europe Goals	Other Apps	Other Goals
1963–64	17	4	7	2	–	–	2	0	0	0
1964–65	41	10	7	2	–	–	11	2	–	–
1965–66	31	9	5	3	–	–	6	4	1	1
1966–67	42	10	2	–	1	0	–	–	–	–
1967–68	41	28	2	1	–	–	9	3	1	0
1968–69	41	19	6	1	–	–	6	2	2	0
1969–70	37	15	8	6	8	2	–	–	–	–
1970–71	40	18	2	1	6	2	–	–	–	–
1971–72	40	18	7	5	6	3	–	–	–	–
1972–73	19	4	0	0	4	2	–	–	–	–
1973–74	12	2	0	0	0	0	–	–	–	–
Total	**361**	**137**	**46**	**21**	**25**	**9**	**34**	**11**	**4**	**1**

Complete Match-By-Match Record

Key: Name in **bold** = scored one goal; name in **bold underlined** = scored two goals; name in ***bold italics underlined*** = scored three goals.

Competitions: CS = Charity Shield; Div 1 = Division One; EC = European Cup; ECWC = European Cup-Winners Cup; FAC = FA Cup; ICC = Inter-Continental Cup; ICFC = Inter-Cities Fairs Cup; LC = League Cup

Date	Opponent	Comp	Venue	Score			
1963–64							
18 January	West Brom A	Div 1	A	4–1	**Best**	**Charlton**	**Law**
25 January	Bristol R	FAC	H	4–1	Best	Charlton	***Law***
1 February	Arsenal	Div 1	H	3–1	Best	Charlton	**Law**
8 February	Leicester C	Div 1	A	2–3	Best	Charlton	**Law**
15 February	Barnsley	FAC	A	4–0	**Best**	Charlton	**Law**
19 February	Bolton W	Div 1	H	5–0	**Best**	**Charlton**	Law
22 February	Blackburn R	Div 1	A	3–1	Best	Charlton	**Law**

Complete Match-By-Match Record

Date	Opponent	Comp	Venue	Score			
26 February	Sp Lisbon	ECWC	H	4–1	Best	**Charlton**	_Law_
29 February	Sunderland	FAC	H	3–3	**Best**	**Charlton**	Law
4 March	Sunderland	FAC	A	2–2	Best	**Charlton**	Law
9 March	Sunderland	FAC	N	5–1	Best	Charlton	_Law_
14 March	West Ham U	FAC	N	1–3	Best	Charlton	Law
18 March	Sp Lisbon	ECWC	A	0–5	Best	Charlton	Law
21 March	Tottenham H	Div 1	A	3–2	Best	**Charlton**	Law
23 March	Chelsea	Div 1	H	1–1	Best	Charlton	Law
27 March	Fulham	Div 1	A	2–2	Best	Charlton	Law
4 April	Liverpool	Div 1	A	0–3	Best	Charlton	Law
6 April	Aston Villa	Div 1	H	1–0	Best	Charlton	Law
13 April	Sheffield U	Div 1	H	2–1	Best	Charlton	Law
25 April	Nottingham F	Div 1	H	3–1	Best	Charlton	_Law_

1964–65

Date	Opponent	Comp	Venue	Score			
22 August	West Brom A	Div 1	H	2–2	Best	**Charlton**	Law
24 August	West Ham U	Div 1	A	1–3	Best	Charlton	Law
29 August	Leicester C	Div 1	A	2–2	Best	Charlton	Law
2 September	West Ham U	Div 1	H	3–1	**Best**	Charlton	Law
5 September	Fulham	Div 1	A	1–2	Best	Charlton	Law
8 September	Everton	Div 1	A	3–3	Best	Charlton	Law
16 September	Everton	Div 1	H	2–1	**Best**	Charlton	Law
26 September	Tottenham H	Div 1	H	4–1	Best	Charlton	_Law_
30 September	Chelsea	Div 1	A	2–0	**Best**	Charlton	Law
3 October	Burnley	Div 1	A	0–0	Best	Charlton	Law
10 October	Sunderland	Div 1	H	1–0	Best	Charlton	Law

THE UNITED TRINITY

Date	Opponent	Comp	Venue	Score			
17 October	Wolves	Div 1	A	4–2	Best	Charlton	**Law**
27 October	Djurgardens	ICFC	H	6–1	**Best**	**Charlton**	*Law*
31 October	Liverpool	Div 1	A	2–0	Best	Charlton	Law
7 November	Sheffield W	Div 1	H	1–0	Best	Charlton	Law
11 November	B Dortmund	ICFC	A	6–1	**Best**	*Charlton*	Law
21 November	Blackburn R	Div 1	H	3–0	**Best**	Charlton	Law
28 November	Arsenal	Div 1	A	3–2	Best	Charlton	**Law**
2 December	B Dortmund	ICFC	H	4–0	Best	**Charlton**	Law
5 December	Leeds U	Div 1	H	0–1	Best	Charlton	Law
12 December	West Brom A	Div 1	A	1–1	Best	Charlton	**Law**
16 January	Nottingham F	Div 1	A	2–2	Best	Charlton	**Law**
20 January	Everton	ICFC	H	1–1	Best	Charlton	Law
23 January	Stoke City	Div 1	H	1–1	Best	Charlton	**Law**
30 January	Stoke City	FAC	A	0–0	Best	Charlton	Law
3 February	Stoke City	FAC	H	1–0	Best	Charlton	Law
6 February	Tottenham H	Div 1	A	0–1	Best	Charlton	Law
9 February	Everton	ICFC	A	2–1	Best	Charlton	Law
13 February	Burnley	Div 1	H	3–2	**Best**	**Charlton**	Law
20 February	Burnley	FAC	H	2–1	Best	Charlton	**Law**
24 February	Sunderland	Div 1	A	0–1	Best	Charlton	Law
27 February	Wolves	Div 1	H	3–0	Best	**Charlton**	Law
10 March	Wolves	FAC	A	5–3	**Best**	Charlton	**Law**
13 March	Chelsea	Div 1	H	4–0	**Best**	Charlton	Law
15 March	Fulham	Div 1	H	4–1	Best	Charlton	Law
20 March	Sheffield W	Div 1	A	0–1	Best	Charlton	Law
22 March	Blackpool	Div 1	H	2–0	Best	Charlton	**Law**

Complete Match-By-Match Record

Date	Opponent	Comp	Venue	Score			
27 March	Leeds U	FAC	H	0–0	Best	Charlton	Law
31 March	Leeds U	FAC	A	0–1	Best	Charlton	Law
3 April	Blackburn R	Div 1	A	5–0	Best	*Charlton*	Law
17 April	Leeds U	Div 1	A	1–0	Best	Charlton	Law
19 April	Birmingham C	Div 1	A	4–2	**Best**	**Charlton**	Law
24 April	Liverpool	Div 1	H	3–0	Best	Charlton	**Law**
26 April	Arsenal	Div 1	H	3–1	**Best**	Charlton	**Law**
28 April	Aston Villa	Div 1	A	1–2	Best	**Charlton**	Law
12 May	Strasbourg	ICFC	A	5–0	Best	**Charlton**	**Law**
19 May	Strasbourg	ICFC	H	0–0	Best	Charlton	Law
31 May	Ferencvaros	ICFC	H	3–2	Best	Charlton	**Law**
6 June	Ferencvaros	ICFC	A	0–1	Best	Charlton	Law
16 June	Ferencvaros	ICFC	A	1–2	Best	Charlton	Law

1965–66

Date	Opponent	Comp	Venue	Score			
14 August	Liverpool	CS	H	2–2	**Best**	Charlton	Law
28 August	Northampton T	Div 1	A	1–1	Best	Charlton	Law
1 September	Nottingham F	Div 1	H	0–0	Best	Charlton	Law
4 September	Stoke City	Div 1	H	1–1	Best	Charlton	Law
8 September	Newcastle U	Div 1	A	2–1	Best	Charlton	**Law**
11 September	Burnley	Div 1	A	0–3	Best	Charlton	Law
15 September	Newcastle U	Div 1	H	1–1	Best	Charlton	Law
6 October	HJK Helsinki	EC	H	6–0	**Best**	**Charlton**	Law
9 October	Liverpool	Div 1	H	2–0	**Best**	Charlton	**Law**
16 October	Tottenham H	Div 1	A	1–5	Best	**Charlton**	Law
6 November	Blackburn R	Div 1	H	2–2	Best	**Charlton**	**Law**

THE UNITED TRINITY

Date	Opponent	Comp	Venue	Score			
13 November	Leicester C	Div 1	A	5–0	**Best**	**Charlton**	Law
17 November	ASK Vorwaerts	EC	A	2–0	Best	Charlton	**Law**
20 November	Sheffield U	Div 1	H	3–1	**<u>Best</u>**	Charlton	**Law**
1 December	ASK Vorwaerts	EC	H	3–1	Best	Charlton	Law
4 December	West Ham U	Div 1	H	0–0	Best	Charlton	Law
11 December	Sunderland	Div 1	A	3–2	**<u>Best</u>**	Charlton	Law
15 December	Everton	Div 1	H	3–0	**Best**	**Charlton**	Law
18 December	Tottenham H	Div 1	H	5–1	Best	**Charlton**	**<u>Law</u>**
27 December	West Brom A	Div 1	H	1–1	Best	Charlton	**Law**
1 January	Liverpool	Div 1	A	1–2	Best	Charlton	**Law**
8 January	Sunderland	Div 1	H	1–1	**Best**	Charlton	Law
12 January	Leeds U	Div 1	A	1–1	Best	Charlton	Law
15 January	Fulham	Div 1	A	1–0	Best	**Charlton**	Law
22 January	Derby Co	FAC	A	5–2	**<u>Best</u>**	Charlton	**<u>Law</u>**
29 January	Sheffield W	Div 1	A	0–0	Best	Charlton	Law
2 February	Benfica	EC	H	3–2	Best	Charlton	**Law**
5 February	Northampton T	Div 1	H	6–2	Best	***<u>Charlton</u>***	**<u>Law</u>**
12 February	Rotherham U	FAC	H	0–0	Best	Charlton	Law
15 February	Rotherham U	FAC	A	1–0	Best	Charlton	Law
26 February	Burnley	Div 1	H	4–2	Best	**Charlton**	Law
5 March	Wolves	FAC	A	4–2	**Best**	Charlton	**<u>Law</u>**
9 March	Benfica	EC	A	5–1	**<u>Best</u>**	**Charlton**	Law
12 March	Chelsea	Div 1	A	0–2	Best	Charlton	Law
19 March	Arsenal	Div 1	H	2–1	Best	Charlton	**Law**
26 March	Preston NE	FAC	A	1–1	Best	Charlton	Law
13 April	P Belgrade	EC	A	0–2	Best	Charlton	Law

256

Complete Match-By-Match Record

Date	Opponent	Comp	Venue	Score			
1966–67							
20 August	West Brom A	Div 1	H	5–3	**Best**	Charlton	<u>**Law**</u>
23 August	Everton	Div 1	A	2–1	Best	Charlton	<u>**Law**</u>
27 August	Leeds U	Div 1	A	1–3	**Best**	Charlton	Law
31 August	Everton	Div 1	H	3–0	Best	Charlton	**Law**
3 September	Newcastle U	Div 1	H	3–2	Best	Charlton	**Law**
7 September	Stoke City	Div 1	A	0–3	Best	Charlton	Law
10 September	Tottenham H	Div 1	A	1–2	Best	Charlton	**Law**
17 September	Manchester C	Div 1	H	1–0	Best	Charlton	**Law**
24 September	Burnley	Div 1	H	4–1	Best	Charlton	**Law**
8 October	Blackpool	Div 1	A	2–1	Best	Charlton	<u>**Law**</u>
15 October	Chelsea	Div 1	H	1–1	Best	Charlton	**Law**
29 October	Arsenal	Div 1	H	1–0	Best	Charlton	Law
12 November	Sheffield W	Div 1	H	2–0	Best	**Charlton**	Law
19 November	Southampton	Div 1	A	2–1	Best	<u>**Charlton**</u>	Law
26 November	Sunderland	Div 1	H	5–0	Best	Charlton	**Law**
30 November	Leicester C	Div 1	A	2–1	**Best**	Charlton	**Law**
3 December	Aston Villa	Div 1	A	1–2	Best	Charlton	Law
17 December	West Brom A	Div 1	A	4–3	Best	Charlton	**Law**
26 December	Sheffield U	Div 1	A	1–2	Best	Charlton	Law
27 December	Sheffield U	Div 1	H	2–0	Best	Charlton	Law
31 December	Leeds U	Div 1	H	0–0	Best	Charlton	Law
28 January	Stoke City	FAC	H	2–0	Best	Charlton	**Law**
4 February	Burnley	Div 1	A	1–1	Best	Charlton	Law
11 February	Nottingham F	Div 1	H	1–0	Best	Charlton	**Law**
18 February	Norwich C	FAC	H	1–2	Best	Charlton	**Law**

THE UNITED TRINITY

Date	Opponent	Comp	Venue	Score			
25 February	Blackpool	Div 1	H	4–0	Best	**Charlton**	Law
3 March	Arsenal	Div 1	A	1–1	Best	Charlton	Law
11 March	Newcastle U	Div 1	A	0–0	Best	Charlton	Law
18 March	Leicester C	Div 1	H	5–2	Best	**Charlton**	**Law**
25 March	Liverpool	Div 1	A	0–0	Best	Charlton	Law
27 March	Fulham	Div 1	A	2–2	**Best**	Charlton	Law
28 March	Fulham	Div 1	H	2–1	Best	Charlton	Law
1 April	West Ham U	Div 1	H	3–0	**Best**	**Charlton**	**Law**
10 April	Sheffield W	Div 1	A	2–2	Best	**Charlton**	Law
18 April	Southampton	Div 1	H	3–0	Best	**Charlton**	**Law**
22 April	Sunderland	Div 1	A	0–0	Best	Charlton	Law
29 April	Aston Villa	Div 1	H	3–1	**Best**	Charlton	**Law**
6 May	West Ham U	Div 1	A	6–1	**Best**	**Charlton**	**Law**

1967–68

Date	Opponent	Comp	Venue	Score			
12 August	Tottenham H	CS	H	3–3	Best	**Charlton**	Law
19 August	Everton	Div 1	A	1–3	Best	**Charlton**	Law
26 August	Leicester C	Div 1	H	1–1	Best	Charlton	Law
16 September	Sheffield W	Div 1	A	1–1	**Best**	Charlton	Law
20 September	Hibernians	EC	H	4–0	Best	Charlton	**Law**
23 September	Tottenham H	Div 1	H	3–1	**Best**	Charlton	**Law**
27 September	Hibernians	EC	A	0–0	Best	Charlton	Law
30 September	Manchester C	Div 1	A	2–1	Best	**Charlton**	Law
7 October	Arsenal	Div 1	H	1–0	Best	Charlton	Law
14 October	Sheffield U	Div 1	A	3–0	Best	Charlton	**Law**
25 October	Coventry C	Div 1	H	4–0	**Best**	**Charlton**	Law

Complete Match-By-Match Record

Date	Opponent	Comp	Venue	Score			
28 October	Nottingham F	Div 1	A	1–3	**Best**	Charlton	Law
16 December	Everton	Div 1	H	3–1	Best	Charlton	**Law**
23 December	Leicester C	Div 1	A	2–2	Best	**Charlton**	Law
26 December	Wolves	Div 1	H	4–0	<u>**Best**</u>	**Charlton**	Law
30 December	Wolves	Div 1	A	3–2	Best	**Charlton**	Law
6 January	West Ham U	Div 1	H	3–1	**Best**	**Charlton**	Law
20 January	Sheffield W	Div 1	H	4–2	<u>**Best**</u>	**Charlton**	Law
27 January	Tottenham H	FAC	H	2–2	**Best**	**Charlton**	Law
17 February	Burnley	Div 1	A	1–2	**Best**	Charlton	Law
27 March	Manchester C	Div 1	H	1–3	**Best**	Charlton	Law
12 April	Fulham	Div 1	A	4–0	<u>**Best**</u>	Charlton	**Law**
15 April	Fulham	Div 1	H	3–0	**Best**	**Charlton**	Law
20 April	Sheffield U	Div 1	H	1–0	Best	Charlton	**Law**
24 April	Real Madrid	EC	H	1–0	**Best**	Charlton	Law
27 April	West Brom A	Div 1	A	3–6	Best	Charlton	**Law**

1968–69

Date	Opponent	Comp	Venue	Score			
10 August	Everton	Div 1	H	2–1	**Best**	**Charlton**	Law
14 August	West Brom A	Div 1	A	1–3	**Best**	**Charlton**	Law
28 August	Tottenham H	Div 1	H	3–1	**Best**	Charlton	Law
31 August	Sheffield W	Div 1	A	4–5	**Best**	**Charlton**	<u>**Law**</u>
7 September	West Ham U	Div 1	H	1–1	Best	Charlton	**Law**
14 September	Burnley	Div 1	A	0–1	Best	Charlton	Law
18 September	Waterford	EC	A	3–1	Best	Charlton	<u>*Law*</u>
21 September	Newcastle U	Div 1	H	3–1	<u>**Best**</u>	Charlton	**Law**
25 September	Estudiantes	ICC	A	0–1	Best	Charlton	Law

THE UNITED TRINITY

Date	Opponent	Comp	Venue	Score			
2 October	Waterford	EC	H	7–1	Best	**Charlton**	*Law (4)*
5 October	Arsenal	Div 1	H	0–0	Best	Charlton	Law
9 October	Tottenham H	Div 1	A	2–2	Best	Charlton	**Law**
16 October	Estudiantes	ICC	H	1–1	Best	Charlton	Law
26 October	Queens Park R	Div 1	A	3–2	**Best**	Charlton	**Law**
2 November	Leeds U	Div 1	H	0–0	Best	Charlton	Law
16 November	Ipswich T	Div 1	H	0–0	Best	Charlton	Law
30 November	Wolves	Div 1	H	2–0	**Best**	Charlton	**Law**
7 December	Leicester C	Div 1	A	1–2	Best	Charlton	**Law**
14 December	Liverpool	Div 1	H	1–0	Best	Charlton	**Law**
21 December	Southampton	Div 1	A	0–2	Best	Charlton	Law
26 December	Arsenal	Div 1	A	0–3	Best	Charlton	Law
4 January	Exeter City	FAC	A	3–1	Best	Charlton	Law
11 January	Leeds United	Div 1	A	1–2	Best	**Charlton**	Law
18 January	Sunderland	Div 1	H	4–1	**Best**	Charlton	*Law*
25 January	Watford	FAC	H	1–1	Best	Charlton	**Law**
1 February	Ipswich T	Div 1	A	0–1	Best	Charlton	Law
3 February	Watford	FAC	A	2–0	Best	Charlton	**Law**
8 February	Birmingham C	FAC	A	2–2	**Best**	Charlton	**Law**
24 February	Birmingham C	FAC	H	6–2	Best	Charlton	*Law*
26 February	Rapid Vienna	EC	H	3–0	**Best**	Charlton	Law
1 March	Everton	FAC	H	0–1	Best	Charlton	Law
12 April	Newcastle U	Div 1	A	0–2	Best	Charlton	Law
23 April	AC Milan	EC	A	0–2	Best	Charlton	Law
15 May	AC Milan	EC	H	1–0	Best	**Charlton**	Law
17 May	Leicester C	Div 1	H	3–2	**Best**	Charlton	**Law**

Complete Match-By-Match Record

Date	Opponent	Comp	Venue	Score			

1969–70

Date	Opponent	Comp	Venue	Score			
9 August	Crystal Palace	Div 1	A	2–2	Best	**Charlton**	Law
13 August	Everton	Div 1	H	0–2	Best	Charlton	Law
16 August	Southampton	Div 1	H	1–4	Best	Charlton	Law
23 August	Wolves	Div 1	A	0–0	Best	Charlton	Law
1 November	Stoke City	Div 1	H	1–1	Best	**Charlton**	Law
8 November	Coventry C	Div 1	A	2–1	Best	Charlton	**Law**
12 November	Derby Co	LC	A	0–0	Best	Charlton	Law
15 November	Manchester C	Div 1	A	0–4	Best	Charlton	Law
19 November	Derby Co	LC	H	1–0	Best	Charlton	Law
17 December	Manchester C	LC	H	2–2	Best	Charlton	**Law**
17 March	Burnley	Div 1	H	3–3	**Best**	Charlton	**Law**
21 March	Chelsea	Div 1	A	1–2	Best	Charlton	Law

Denis Law came on as a substitute in three games where Best and Charlton were also playing: v Leeds U, FA Cup (A), 0–0; v Leeds U, FA Cup (N), 0–1; v Manchester City, Div 1 (H), 1–2

1970–71

Date	Opponent	Comp	Venue	Score			
22 August	Arsenal	Div 1	A	0–4	Best	Charlton	Law
25 August	Burnley	Div 1	A	2–0	Best	Charlton	**Law**
29 August	West Ham U	Div 1	H	1–1	Best	Charlton	Law
2 September	Everton	Div 1	H	2–0	**Best**	**Charlton**	Law
5 September	Liverpool	Div 1	A	1–1	Best	Charlton	Law
9 September	Aldershot	LC	A	3–1	**Best**	Charlton	**Law**
12 September	Coventry C	Div 1	H	2–0	**Best**	**Charlton**	Law
19 September	Ipswich T	Div 1	A	0–4	Best	Charlton	Law
24 October	West Brom A	Div 1	H	2–1	Best	Charlton	**Law**

THE UNITED TRINITY

Date	Opponent	Comp	Venue	Score			
28 October	Chelsea	LC	H	2–1	**Best**	**Charlton**	Law
7 November	Stoke City	Div 1	H	2–2	Best	Charlton	**Law**
14 November	Nottingham F	Div 1	A	2–1	Best	Charlton	Law
18 November	Crystal Palace	LC	H	4–2	Best	**Charlton**	Law
21 November	Southampton	Div 1	A	0–1	Best	Charlton	Law
28 November	Huddersfield T	Div 1	H	1–1	**Best**	Charlton	Law
5 December	Tottenham H	Div 1	A	2–2	**Best**	Charlton	**Law**
12 December	Manchester C	Div 1	H	1–4	Best	Charlton	Law
23 December	Aston Villa	LC	A	1–2	Best	Charlton	Law
26 December	Derby Co	Div 1	A	4–4	**Best**	Charlton	**Law**
2 January	Middlesbrough	FAC	H	0–0	Best	Charlton	Law
5 January	Middlesbrough	FAC	A	1–2	**Best**	Charlton	Law
30 January	Huddersfield T	Div 1	A	2–1	Best	Charlton	**Law**
13 March	Nottingham F	Div 1	H	2–0	**Best**	Charlton	**Law**
20 March	Stoke City	Div 1	A	2–1	**Best**	Charlton	Law
3 April	West Ham U	Div 1	A	1–2	**Best**	Charlton	Law
10 April	Derby Co	Div 1	H	1–2	Best	Charlton	**Law**
12 April	Wolves	Div 1	H	1–0	Best	Charlton	Law
17 April	Crystal Palace	Div 1	A	5–3	**Best**	Charlton	*Law*
19 April	Liverpool	Div 1	H	0–2	Best	Charlton	Law
24 April	Ipswich T	Div 1	H	3–2	**Best**	**Charlton**	Law
1 May	Blackpool	Div 1	A	1–1	Best	Charlton	**Law**
5 May	Manchester C	Div 1	A	4–3	**Best**	**Charlton**	**Law**

Complete Match-By-Match Record

Date	Opponent	Comp	Venue	Score			
1971–72							
14 August	Derby Co	Div 1	A	2–2	Best	Charlton	**Law**
18 August	Chelsea	Div 1	A	3–2	Best	**Charlton**	Law
20 August	Arsenal	Div 1	H	3–1	Best	**Charlton**	Law
28 August	Wolves	Div 1	A	1–1	**Best**	Charlton	Law
31 August	Everton	Div 1	A	0–1	Best	Charlton	Law
4 September	Ipswich T	Div 1	H	1–0	**Best**	Charlton	Law
11 September	Crystal Palace	Div 1	A	3–1	Best	Charlton	**Law**
18 September	West Ham U	Div 1	H	4–2	_Best_	**Charlton**	Law
25 September	Liverpool	Div 1	A	2–2	Best	**Charlton**	**Law**
9 October	Huddersfield T	Div 1	A	3–0	**Best**	**Charlton**	**Law**
16 October	Derby Co	Div 1	H	1–0	**Best**	Charlton	Law
18 October	Burnley	LC	A	1–0	Best	**Charlton**	Law
23 October	Newcastle U	Div 1	A	1–0	**Best**	Charlton	Law
27 October	Stoke City	Div 1	H	1–1	Best	Charlton	Law
30 October	Leeds U	Div 1	H	0–1	Best	Charlton	Law
13 November	Tottenham H	Div 1	H	3–1	Best	Charlton	**Law**
20 November	Leicester C	Div 1	H	3–2	Best	Charlton	**Law**
4 December	Nottingham F	Div 1	H	3–2	Best	Charlton	**Law**
11 December	Stoke City	Div 1	A	1–1	Best	Charlton	**Law**
18 December	Ipswich T	Div 1	A	0–0	Best	Charlton	Law
27 December	Coventry C	Div 1	H	2–2	Best	Charlton	Law
1 January	West Ham U	Div 1	A	0–3	Best	Charlton	Law
15 January	Southampton	FAC	A	1–1	Best	**Charlton**	Law
19 January	Southampton	FAC	H	4–1	**Best**	Charlton	Law
22 January	Chelsea	Div 1	H	0–1	Best	Charlton	Law

THE UNITED TRINITY

Date	Opponent	Comp	Venue	Score			
29 January	West Brom A	Div 1	A	1–2	Best	Charlton	Law
5 February	Preston NE	FAC	A	2–0	Best	Charlton	Law
12 February	Newcastle U	Div 1	H	0–2	Best	Charlton	Law
26 February	Middlesbrough	FAC	H	0–0	Best	Charlton	Law
29 February	Middlesbrough	FAC	A	3–0	**Best**	**Charlton**	Law
4 March	Tottenham H	Div 1	A	0–2	Best	Charlton	Law
18 March	Stoke City	FAC	H	1–1	**Best**	Charlton	Law
22 March	Stoke City	FAC	A	1–2	**Best**	Charlton	Law
25 March	Crystal Palace	Div 1	H	4–0	Best	**Charlton**	**Law**
1 April	Coventry C	Div 1	A	3–2	**Best**	**Charlton**	Law
3 April	Liverpool	Div 1	H	0–3	Best	Charlton	Law
29 April	Stoke City	Div 1	H	3–0	**Best**	**Charlton**	Law

Denis Law came on as a substitute in one game where Best and Charlton were also playing: v Manchester City, Div 1 (H), 1–3

1972–73

Date	Opponent	Comp	Venue	Score			
12 August	Ipswich T	Div 1	H	1–2	Best	Charlton	**Law**
2 September	West Ham U	Div 1	A	2–2	**Best**	Charlton	Law
6 September	Oxford U	LC	A	2–2	**Best**	**Charlton**	**Law**
9 September	Coventry C	Div 1	H	0–1	Best	Charlton	Law
12 September	Oxford U	LC	H	3–1	<u>Best</u>	Charlton	Law
28 October	Tottenham H	Div 1	H	1–4	Best	**Charlton**	Law

Season-By-Season Summary

1963–64

Matches played together: 20   W12 D4 L4   Percentage won: 60%

Matches without all the trinity: 36   W18 D6 L12   Percentage won: 50%

Goals scored by trinity: Law 26, Charlton 6, Best 5

Percentage of goals by trinity: 71%

Average goals per game by trinity: 1.85

1964–65

Matches played together: 50   W29 D11 L10   Percentage won: 58%

Matches without all the trinity: 10   W7 D3 L0   Percentage won: 70%

Goals scored by the trinity: Law 35, Charlton 17, Best 12

Percentage of goals by the trinity: 60%

Average goals per game by the trinity: 1.28

THE UNITED TRINITY

1965–66

Matches played together: 37   W19 D13 L5   Percentage won: 51%

Matches without all the trinity: 21   W10 D5 L6   Percentage won: 48%

Goals scored by the trinity: Law 17, Best 16, Charlton 12

Percentage of goals by the trinity: 58%

Average goals per game by the trinity: 1.22

1966–67

Matches played together: 38   W23 D9 L6   Percentage won: 61%

Matches without all the trinity: 7   W2 D3 L2   Percentage won: 29%

Goals scored by the trinity: Law 25, Charlton 11, Best 7

Percentage of goals by the trinity: 54%

Average goals per game by the trinity: 1.13

1967–68

Matches played together: 26   W15 D6 L5   Percentage won: 58%

Matches without all the trinity: 28   W14 D7 L7   Percentage won: 50%

Goals scored by the trinity: Best 17, Charlton 13, Law 10

Percentage of goals by the trinity: 68%

Average goals per game by the trinity: 1.54

1968–69

Matches played together: 35   W15 D8 L12   Percentage won: 43%

Matches without all the trinity: 23   W8 D8 L7   Percentage won: 35%

Goals scored by the trinity: Law 27, Best 12, Charlton 6

Percentage of goals by the trinity: 75%

Average goals per game by the trinity: 1.29

Season-By-Season Summary

1969–70

Matches played together: 12   W2 D6 L4   Percentage won: 17%

Matches without all the trinity: 47   W21 D17 L9   Percentage won: 45%

Goals scored by the trinity: Law 3, Charlton 2, Best 1

Percentage of goals by the trinity: 46%

Average goals per game by the trinity: 0.50

1970–71

Matches played together: 32   W15 D8 L9   Percentage won: 47%

Matches without all the trinity: 18   W5 D5 L8   Percentage won: 28%

Goals scored by the trinity: Best 17, Law 16, Charlton 6

Percentage of goals by the trinity: 71%

Average goals per game by the trinity: 1.22

1971–72

Matches played together: 37   W18 D10 L9   Percentage won: 49%

Matches without all the trinity: 18   W6 D6 L6   Percentage won: 33%

Goals scored by the trinity: Best 15, Law 12, Charlton 11

Percentage of goals by the trinity: 62%

Average goals per game by the trinity: 1.03

1972–73

Matches played together: 6   W1 D2 L3   Percentage won: 17%

Matches without all the trinity: 41   W12 D13 L16   Percentage won: 29%

Goals scored by the trinity: Best 3, Charlton 2, Law 2

Percentage of goals by the trinity: 78%

Average goals per game by the trinity: 1.17

THE UNITED TRINITY

Overall

Matches played together: 293   W149 D77 L67 Percentage won: 51%

Matches without all the trinity: 249 W103 D73 L73 Percentage won: 41%

Goals scored by the trinity: Law 173, Best 105, Charlton 86

Percentage of goals by the trinity: 64%

Average goals per game by the trinity: 1.24

Most consecutive games scoring: 19 (31 goals) – v Sheffield U (14/10/67) to v West Brom A (14/8/68)

Most consecutive games without scoring: 5 – v Chelsea (22/1/72) to v Middlesbrough (26/2/72)

Number of times all three of the trinity scored in a game: 8

Acknowledgements

I am indebted to Ian Marshall of Simon and Schuster for the idea of *The United Trinity* and giving me the opportunity to write it. I am also grateful for the help of Tom Whiting who provided a structure to the project with his imaginative editing after my initial rush to get so many wonderful memories into a book. I extend my greatest appreciation, though, to Sir Bobby Charlton, Denis Law and George Best whose football brought such joy and entertainment to followers of Manchester United, not least to the author. My thanks certainly go to the many people who readily dug deep into their memory banks to help me paint a fuller picture of three great European Footballers of the Year who lit up the Sixties as football took off on a flight of fancy that is still soaring.

Index

271

Index